HOWAR

Howard Jacobson [...] six works of non-fiction. He won the Bollinger Everyman Wodehouse Prize in 2000 for *The Mighty Walzer* and then again in 2013 for *Zoo Time*. In 2010 he won the Booker Prize for *The Finkler Question*; he was also shortlisted for the prize in 2014 for *J*.

ALSO BY HOWARD JACOBSON

FICTION

Coming From Behind

Peeping Tom

Redback

The Very Model of a Man

No More Mr Nice Guy

The Mighty Walzer

Who's Sorry Now?

The Making of Henry

Kalooki Nights

The Act of Love

The Finkler Question

Zoo Time

J: A Novel

Shylock is My Name

Pussy

Live a Little

NON-FICTION

Shakespeare's Magnanimity (with Wilbur Sanders)

In the Land of Oz

Roots Schmoots

Seriously Funny: An Argument for Comedy

Whatever It Is I Don't Like It

The Dog's Last Walk

The Swag Man (Kindle Single)

When will Jews be forgiven the Holocaust? (Kindle Single)

HOWARD JACOBSON

Mother's Boy

VINTAGE

1 3 5 7 9 10 8 6 4 2

Vintage is part of the Penguin Random House group of companies
whose addresses can be found at global.penguinrandomhouse.com

Penguin
Random House
UK

First published in Vintage in 2023
First published in hardback by Jonathan Cape in 2022

Copyright © Howard Jacobson 2022

Howard Jacobson has asserted their right to be identified as the
author of this Work in accordance with the Copyright,
Designs and Patents Act 1988

Photograph credits, p. 178:
F. R. Leavis: Keystone Press/Alamy Photo
Allen Afterman: The Sheep Meadow Press

penguin.co.uk/vintage

Printed and bound in Great Britain by Clays Ltd, Elcograf S.p.A.

The authorised representative in the EEA is Penguin Random House Ireland,
Morrison Chambers, 32 Nassau Street, Dublin D02 YH68

A CIP catalogue record for this book is
available from the British Library

ISBN 9781529115673

Penguin Random House is committed to a sustainable future
for our business, our readers and our planet. This book is made
from Forest Stewardship Council® certified paper.

To Jakey and Neetie

My life has been full of terrible misfortunes, most of which never happened.

— *Michel de Montaigne*

My mother died today. It is 3 May 2020. She is ninety-seven years old. I have had premonitions of her dying for the last seventy of those years, on occasions hearing her calling my name in the night. But last night she was silent and today she crept under the radar of my forebodings.

Many are succumbing to Covid-19 but my mother hasn't died of any virus. Two days ago, she complained of a bad pain in her head and fell almost immediately into unconsciousness. My sister, who lives with her, and her daughter, who lives round the corner, were quickly by her bedside. My brother and I are locked down in Portishead and London respectively and have been unable to get to Manchester to see her. Quietly and unobtrusively, she drifts out of this world altogether. This was always her chosen way of going, without fuss or notice. I don't know whether she'd have wanted us to be with her – given her bodily compunctions, probably not – but she would definitely not have wanted us to take any risks getting there.

I am upset that the pain she complained of was in her head.

She feared for her head. I too, when I was small, feared for her head. As a young woman she suffered migraines so badly that when she went to bed with her hands over her eyes I was afraid she would not survive the night. Ours was a mental relationship. It was our heads that joined us. I dread dying with a pain in mine.

We'd spoken on the phone a few days before she died and, but for my having to repeat everything I said twice – three times if it was a joke – we'd had a good conversation. At the beginning of the year, when the virus was first mentioned, she had expressed surprise I was taking elaborate precautions. 'Oh, Howard, you aren't worrying about *that*, are you?' As though she hadn't schooled me to prepare for eventualities undreamed of either by the wildest dystopians or the most minute obsessives.

The day I left home to go to university she'd reminded me to take enough toilet paper.

'What, for three years?'

'Until you settle in.'

'I think Cambridge will have toilet paper,' I said. But I took a roll just in case.

Yet now that we really did have to contend with a calamity equal to her anxieties, she had turned perversely carefree. 'Oh, Howard ...' It was like having Mr Micawber for a mother. One minute sunk in the deepest gloom, facing imminent catastrophe, the next sitting up on the back of a coach, cheerfully eating chestnuts out of a paper bag. Had she not been ninety-seven and bedridden I might have imagined her doing cartwheels.

By the time of our final conversation, however, she had rethought and was back to her old apocalyptic self. 'I've worked out what this virus is up to,' she told me. 'It won't be happy until it's taken everyone and everything.' After which, she moved on seamlessly to cheese. I'd been sending her gifts of mature Cheddar cheese because we all like mature Cheddar cheese in our family, ideally grilled on toast, and because she can't eat chocolates and doesn't much care for flowers. This Cheddar grills especially well. 'But I don't want you to send me more,' she insisted. 'It must be costing you a fortune.'

I told her I could afford it. Her reasoning wasn't always easy to follow but I thought I could see what led her to ask next how my book was going.

'OK.'

'What is it again?'

'A memoir.'

'What's it about?'

'Me, Ma, what do you think?'

She sounded concerned. 'Is that a good idea?'

'Probably not.'

'What *about* you?'

Was she worrying I'd write about my failed marriages? The bad job I'd made of being a father? The friends I'd let down? My gift for unhappiness? Her?

'About how I became a writer.'

'You were always a writer.'

'I know, but I was forty before I wrote anything.'

'You couldn't have been!'

'Well, I was.'

'I don't believe that.'

'Well, it's true.'

'So what was stopping you?'

'That's one of the questions I'm asking in my memoir. But the short answer is being Jewish.'

'Being Jewish! Oh, you aren't going to be horrible, are you?'

'I hope not. After all, if it was being Jewish that held me back it was being Jewish that got me going.'

I have said her reasoning took unexpected turns, but what she said next soared into the realms of the fantastical. She told me she loved me.

I'm ashamed to say I roared with laughter. 'Ma,' I said, 'that's not the kind of thing we say to each other.'

And it wasn't. Love talk was not us.

'Well, I do love you,' she said.

I should have known then that she was dying. I'd laughed but I was overwhelmed by feelings I didn't recognise. 'I'm glad,' I said ... then plunged into the deep, dark chambers of the hitherto unexpressed, '... because I love you.'

There. Said it. She nearly a hundred, I in my seventies, and we'd finally said that we loved each other.

It astonishes me.

What – that we'd said it, or that it had taken so long?

Both.

Since I began writing these reminiscences while she was still alive, I will keep her as though alive throughout them. Tense doesn't matter that much when you're remembering, anyway. Things that didn't happen could have happened or could happen yet. You can be too fussy about the actualities. Best to throw open the windows and let the winds of peradventure blow through as they will.

1

INFANT SORROW

I am born. It is August 1942. My father steps out of his barracks in North Wales, puts out his hand and feels no rain, looks
up and sees no bombs, hopes the quiet sky augurs well for my
mother who is due to give birth to me any minute, indeed
might already have done so, and hops onto a train. Men didn't
feel it necessary to witness the miracle of creation first-hand
in those days; it was enough to be in the vicinity. I think he
will be pleased to discover I am a boy. Many years later he buys
me boxing gloves and he may already be imagining going a
few rounds with me as he settles back in the compartment and
goes to sleep. For an active man he sleeps a lot. I will inherit
this gene from him. Alas, not the boxing gene as well. It's a bit
early to be confessing I was a disappointment to him. But I
can't introduce him without also introducing the remorse in
which I clothe every memory and thought of him. 'I'm sorry,
Dad, I wasn't the boy you'd have picked had you been offered
an assortment.'

My mother must have been pleased to see him. I'd given
her a rough few hours and there were spiders on the coverlet.

We were in rural Cheshire, because bombs had been falling on Manchester. Not much my father could have done about the bombs but he was just the man to sort the spiders. I see him coming into the ward carrying a bunch of flowers in one of those claw-hammer hands of his. He'd clipped his moustache and was wearing his red regimental beret at a jaunty angle. He was a handsome devil. I must have been pleased to see him too. 'So that's Daddy,' I'd have thought. 'Not bad.'

It was family mythology that the strange position I'd adopted in the womb accounted for why I could never do a backflip or a somersault; why I was always travel-sick – I even had chains on my tricycle – and still cannot ride backwards in a taxi or a bus; and why I was – and remain – unable to hang from a wall bar, climb a lamp post, draw a map, run a marathon, wrap a parcel, or clean up after a dog.

Over time I grew to favour another explanation, also to do with the womb but harder to substantiate: that I'd been born a Jew.

Wear your sweater inside out in Lithuania and they say you're 'going Jew'.

It isn't hard to see what they're getting at. The Jew is oriented differently. All thumbs, at sixes and sevens, the wrong way round. A malfunction of nature.

'Rubbish!' my mother says. 'Your father was very practical.'

She's right. I must be careful not to see every Jew in my image or allow 'Jewish' to become a synonym for physical incompetence. 'My hands are so clumsy that I cannot even write so as to read it myself,' Montaigne wrote, and he wasn't Jewish. Nor, by his own admission, could he ever 'carry a hawk and fly her, nor hunt the dogs, nor speak to a horse'. Whereas my father was variously an upholsterer, a tailor, a manufacturer of coffee tables, a magician, a taxi driver, a balloonist – by which I mean that he twisted balloons into the shapes of animals, not that he was an aeronaut – and while I doubt he fared any better talking to horses than Michel Eyquem de Montaigne, he did once astonish into silence a horse bearing the weight of Sir Oswald Ernald Mosley, leader of the British Union of Fascists, in circumstances I will relate in their proper place. Suffice it to say here that Mosley saw a short muscular Jew approaching in a fury, ducked low like the cowardly black-guard he was, and allowed his horse to take the blow intended for him.

It's just a thought: but could my father's multi-competence – he fixed cars, too, rewired houses, replumbed bathrooms, tiled roofs, repaired washing machines, knocked through hatches between the kitchen and the living room in every house we ever lived in – explain why my hands are good for nothing? Because – except for typing, and for that I use only my left forefinger – they weren't ever needed.

How much more than a forefinger does a writer need?

Well, there is something more. Maladjustment. It's my theory that only the unhappy, the uncomfortable, the gauche, the badly put together, aspire to make art. Why would you seek to reshape the world unless you were ill at ease in it? And I came out of the womb in every sense the wrong way round. Which includes being Jewish.

'Oh, shut up!'

My mother expostulating. It is no exaggeration to say she will never merely remark when she can expostulate. Ours is and always has been an expostulatory family. Maybe we all came out of the womb with something to complain about.

We often squabbled about how far back a child's memories could go. 'I wonder if you have something to hide,' I used to say to her. 'Why else are you so unwilling to believe me when I tell you I remember everything? Spiders crawling across your belly. Bombs falling. The sound of fighting from across the Channel. The suffering of the Jewish people.'

She had the decency to laugh – a lovely, warm, melodious laugh as though the joke had caught her unawares. My father would love that laugh all his life, and because it had a special timbre when I was its cause – sounds vain, but it isn't – he encouraged me to coax it out of her. *Tell your mother what you just told me. Tell her about the pig.* (I'll come to the pig.) When I was going well I could get the tears to stream down her face from behind her glasses. My father watched, enthralled. Then he joined in, and his laugh too would have a special timbre. It was as though I acted as their go-between.

What made her think I was joking on this occasion, though, I'm not sure.

'Why else,' I'd go on, 'have I always had such a long face? I came into the world a Jew at a bad time to be a Jew.'

'You came into the world in a very nice nursing home in Cheshire. There were no bombs falling on Prestbury. You were miles from the Channel. Most of the time you were fast asleep. You weighed in at over ten pounds, you were the colour of apricots and you had a round face.'

In this context, let it be noted, she didn't mention the spiders. In later years, when she began to worry about my temperament, she would theorise that it was the spiders that had made me gloomy. I liked the image. Before I had language I had a spider walking over my brain.

There must be cultures where to say a spider has been walking over your brain denotes initiation into the madness of art. My own culture has a less fanciful, more brutal idea of what comprises initiation. It makes every boy child an amputee. Or at least a part-amputee. What precisely that initiates you into only time will tell.

*And he that is eight days old shall be
circumcised among you, every man
child in your generations . . .*

Opponents of circumcision point to the barbarism of the
rite – the wounding, the defacement, the antiquity, the brutal perversity of removing what God, in His infinite wisdom,
gave, and now, in His infinite whimsicality, insists that we
remove. What they forget to mention – though it would
serve their cause as well as all their other objections – is the
ignominy of having your private parts on full show to the
family.

My dear, protective mother, who would not have anyone
harm a hair on my head, is getting ready to shout 'rubbish'
again. She believes eight days after birth is too soon to know
the meaning of ignominy.

And what about pain, Ma?

But I'm faking this. I have no desire to reproach her for
what she permitted to be done, for what – let's be honest –
she wouldn't have known how to prevent, short of fighting
with my father – who was a stickler for tradition – and alien-
ating the entire community. Nor do I resent the procedure.
Aesthetically I give it my blessing. But a psychologist specialising in the subject once told me that the hyper-close
mother–son relationship commemorated in Jewish jokes and
folklore dates from the guilt engendered in the maternal
bosom on the Eighth Day. Some mothers are said to lose the
ability to breastfeed thereafter, thus extending into evermore
the chain of remorse and tireless expiation.

Since my mother and I are at this stage of my life inter-
changeable I'll say it for her – *Rubbish.*

For I never went without milk. The Yiddish word *ongeshtopt,*

9

meaning stuffed to bursting, perfectly describes my infancy. I was so *ongeshtopt* with milk I could barely stay awake. But then again, explain why photographs of me in my pram, or rattling the bars of my cot when I *am* awake, show a baby misfit.

This is how, despite my mother's scepticism, I remember myself: a failed baby, metaphysically at sea, but above all miserable in my body, demeaned by all the appurtenances of baby-being and perambulation, not wanting to be lifted, not wanting to be put down, resenting being pushed, resisting being rocked, uncomfortable in the sort of clothes that people who have forgotten what it's like to be a baby choose for them. A romper suit is not any baby's outfit of choice. But because I wore a serious expression I looked over and above incongruous in mine. It bound me like a giant bandage – though swaddling was supposed to have gone out of fashion – and gave others access to God knows what or why via a couple of metal crotch studs that made lying on my front an agony and lying in every other position degrading. Any garment less suitable for romping in than a romper suit is hard to imagine. Not that romping was in my nature. Sedentary sullenness was in my nature. It was a pity that no one thought to find or design me a sulking suit, a Hamlet Babygro – as inky as the cloak the Prince wore to let his mother know he knew her name was frailty – with matching bib.

It cut deeper than fashion. It wasn't just the way my mother garbed and bound me I found humiliating. Naked, I felt no better. I rebelled against my own integument – the creamy plumpness, the roundness, the dimples, the rashers of blubber behind the knees. Look up at any rococo ceiling and you'll see babies not only revelling in their greasy fatness but contorting their bodies so that every crease and collop is visible below. Do I envy them their indecorous abandon? Perhaps I do. But like most acts of envy it's in vain. The wherewithal to frolic is not given to everyone and the wherewithal to frolic like a putto was certainly never given to a Jew. Gaze up at the next rococo ceiling you find yourself under. How many of those cherubs look as though they're called Menachem or Pinchas?

Allow me to be indecorous. I didn't much care for being 'changed' either. Not 'changed' for another baby – that might not have been so bad – I mean 'changed' in the hygienic sense.

It's all shame at this period in an infant's life. One indignity succeeding another. Some don't mind. Some do. Those that do, turn to art as a way of transcending belittling circumstance. Make another, bigger world and you've found another, bigger role for yourself in it. I can't remember when I first knew I wanted to write but I can remember *why* I wanted to write. If I got in first with criticism of myself, I could win ascendancy over shame. If I laughed at myself I forestalled those who would laugh at me.

So it was that I knew preternaturally early that I had to be a writer. Of such sour, ungrateful, unlikeable little fellows as I was – I am afraid to say – are writers made. It can come as a terrible shock to readers who love books to discover that there is a lot less to love about those who write them. The best way to look at it is this: just as God fashioned man out of dust, so, out of charmless material, is the magic that is art conjured.

I was my mother's first child. She was still a teenager when I was born and her younger sister was probably only just out of single figures. My grandmother, too, was young and yet to be a grandmother to anyone else. You could say I was a learning experience for them all. They practised on me, anyway. Though I like remembering, there is much I'd prefer to forget, and it's part of my needing to forget this that I don't want to be precise about how inexpert any of them were, or how proficient any of them became. But I think it's fair to say that

The author in the arms of his mother

theirs was a laboratory for mothers and I the biological specimen.

'*Rubbish!*' I can hear all three of them saying it – my trio of weaving goddesses, my Fates, my Andrews Sisters. '*Rubbish!*' '*Rubbish!*' '*Rubbish!*'

This rubbishing betrays my maternal origins. I was well into middle age before I discovered that my mother's grandparents on both sides came from Lithuania. 'Russia' was the universal answer to all our questions about the past. Where did we come from? There, out there. Where was there? They seemed to be pointing in the direction of Sale and Altrincham. Hale Barns. Wilmslow. Well-to-do Jewish South Manchester, and we knew damn well we hadn't come from there. Keep on asking and they tell you somewhere in the vicinity of Russia. It didn't matter where exactly. Just the word 'Russia' was enough to conjure a malodorous village of superstitious, Jew-hating pig-farmers high in the Ural Mountains. Novoropissik I called it and haven't been back. 'Think about something else,' my parents advised. 'We're English now. Be grateful and do your homework.' But the clues were always there to see. Jew to Jew, Lithuanians are the great disparagers. When the Jewish revivalist movement known as Hasidism spread from the Ukraine in the eighteenth century, its chief enemies were the Lithuanian Mitnagdim, or 'opponents'. Jewishness for Mitnagdim was austere, rational, intellectual – a religion of the mind. 'Rubbish,' they said when the Hasidim came cartwheeling out of the east, pantheistic, populist, charismatic, resembling so many Karamazovs with flying fringes.

Ironically, that was exactly the part of the world my father's family came cartwheeling out of, though no one could have been less of a Hasid than he was. To the music of religion he was tone deaf. But he had the big Russian soul thing – by which I mean he could dance the kazatsky like a Cossack, and did so at many a family simcha (a simcha being a celebration at which your Russian father, if you are lucky enough to have one, dances the kazatsky like a Cossack) – looked capable of wrestling a bear, and rubbished nothing. Life was to be relished not denigrated. So, like Schleswig-Holstein, I was born into the middle of a schism, though the parties to the Schleswig-Holstein dispute knew why they were fighting whereas, when it came to me, my parents were not aware they had competing claims. But they felt life differently and so entertained different ambitions for me.

Am I saying they unconsciously wrestled for my soul?

If I answer yes, I intend no reproval. I consider myself lucky to have been tugged this way and that – now my mother's quiet, agonisingly shy, sorrowing, studious, disapproving boy, later, as my father's influence grew, a yay-saying entertainer

13

and show-off in his likeness. For a writer, at least, it's a blessing to be your parents' battleground and eventually to be at war with yourself.

My mother was nothing if not critical and inevitably made a critic of me. My father, without ever reading a novel, made me a novelist because he was himself a novel.

Max and Anita. Jakey, she called him. Neetie, he called her. It was my impression that for all their common Eastern European origins they were – and I now think they remained – foreign to each other. Was it my role to act as their interpreter? Was that why I had to write: to explain them to themselves?

It hardly needs to be said that the battle they fought for my soul, whatever its objective, bore no theological aspect. My father didn't care that I was being led along a path that would inevitably end in rationalism. All he feared was that I was becoming a mother's boy, an auntie's boy, a grandma's boy. The word he used was 'spoilt', but the word he thought was 'feminised'.

If the same thought crossed my mind, I sent it packing. There was too much pleasure to be had, once I accepted that shame was to be my lot, in being fussed over. I wonder now at their conscientiousness when it came to 'attending' to me 'personally'. Were they too interested? Did they, when the occasion merited it, stand in a circle and clap my efforts? But that's a question for today; at the time no such compunctions interfered with the sick pleasure I took in being the centre of their attentions.

Given the need to be applauded that has marked my life as a writer, and before that as a husband, and before that as a little boy with a big vocabulary, I must assume my taste for plaudits originated in theirs.

It gets worse. Take it as read that it will always get worse, that one embarrassment will always spawn a hundred more ...

Abashed by the conventional terminology for the intimacies of the bathroom, my mother came up with a euphemism for a chamber pot that I have never encountered since. As I never saw it written down, I can't spell it. Myer is the nearest I can get. Later I discovered it was an abbreviation of Jeremiah, itself a play on jerrycan, so I suppose it should be spelt Miah, but that conjures up a vision of maidenly Judaean loveliness entirely inappropriate to a myer's function.

What does the choice of Jeremiah as a name for a chamber pot say about my mother's attitude to the workings of nature? Was it from her I inherited a distaste for the body and its productions that has never left me? I could ask her, but that would be to broach a subject we have managed to avoid for as long as we have known each other. I take comfort from the fact that there was wit, not to say scholarship, in her lighting on Jeremiah. That most lachrymose of Old Testament prophets to be the patron saint of chamber pots! If it was intended as a joke it was a good one. And it remains a good joke however it was intended and however much it still horrifies me.

What more aptly doleful setting was there for the jeremiads I would go on delivering all my life?

A question I don't want to ask, and certainly don't want answered: were the three Fates, who attended lovingly to my every function, still present and appreciative, still marvelling, when I reached the age of ascending that little throne of lamentations all on my own?

And that, I solemnly promise, as I pass out of this humiliating period of my life, is the last indecorousness you will hear from me.

2

A NOODGE TOO FAR

From the more mortifying of the forgoing reminiscences my father is blessedly absent. I belonged to women. The man of the family was away. At war. One of us, at least, was a warrior.

In my mind's eye is a photograph of him in uniform, manly and yet just the slightest bit shy, now positioned on the mantelpiece, now on my mother's bedside table, now on the television, as though she moved it like a chess piece to follow him around the country from barracks to barracks. But there was no television yet, so my mind's eye can't be trusted.

He was a warrior but not exactly at war. He was stationed with his parachute regiment, sometimes in Wales, sometimes near Salisbury Plain, but hadn't yet jumped out of a plane and probably never would. They'd made him the regimental tailor for no other reason than that he wasn't fit enough to parachute over enemy territory and was a Jew. They also serve who only sit and sew.

Just to be clear – it wasn't because he was a Jew that they wouldn't let him jump. Quotas were common in those days: only so many Jews at this or that school or university; only so many Jews in the BBC; no Jews at all at the golf club. As recently as the 1960s, for example, Westminster School was finding ways to limit the admission of Jews, one of them being to insist that entrants 'profess the Christian faith'. But in the 1930s and 40s as many Jews who wanted to throw themselves out of an aeroplane could. Only bad health kept my father from strapping on a parachute.

When, more than fifty years later, he lay dying in hospital, he charged me with clearing the more sentimental of his friends from the ward. He would grit his teeth. 'Get 'em out of here!'

My father inspired long-lasting loyalties. He was a nice man. Strong in his beneficence. Vivid in his kindness. He did things for people. Practical things like going out in the snow to start their cars or mend a puncture, fixing their plumbing (he was a great neighbour to have when your pipes burst), replacing fuses, helping them get over grievous loss, sometimes consol-ing their wives – but I wouldn't want to make too much of that. Everything he did fell into the category of favour. Nobody ever paid him. By us, his wife and children, he was considered altogether too soft a touch. Yet here he was, with just a few days to live, wanting none of the people he'd gone out of his way to help anywhere near him. It was their emo-tionalism he couldn't bear. It was as though their sobbing stole the silence necessary for resolve. He was preparing himself for something bigger than gratitude ... or love.

One of the most persistent of these friends was Gerd, a man he'd known since primary school, a one-time mini-cab proprietor with a red face, wet mouth and blazing personality, a soppy melodramatist who fell in and out of love, made and lost fortunes of his own, spent time in prison for losing other people's, and was said to have driven a getaway vehicle for a notorious Manchester gang. The reason he didn't spend time in prison for that, my father used to joke, was that the gang hadn't got away. Gerd was a terrible driver. He was also what my father called a noodge. A pestiferous person.

He sat on the bed, sobbing into his moustache, holding and stroking my father's hand, telling him he loved him.

'Do me a favour, Gerd,' my father said. 'Go home and kiss your wife.'

'My wife's dead,' Gerd said.

My father didn't have the strength to enquire when or how but he managed a 'Sorry to hear that', and returned his friend's squeeze.

'Dead to me,' Gerd went on.

My father had forgotten what had happened. Gerd and his wife Greta had split up when she discovered he was seeing another woman. Nothing unusual about that except that the other woman he was seeing had been lying in a comatose state in a Manchester hospital for the whole time he'd been seeing her. According to reports, he visited her every day and held her unresponsive hand. 'My husband's left me for a vegetable,' Greta went about saying. Though some admired Gerd's unrequited devotion, Greta enjoyed the lion's share of sympathy. Even the men who as a rule forgave one another everything thought she had a point.

Today Gerd was redder-faced than usual. He had a wild tale to tell me. 'This you won't have heard from your father,' he said.

My father ground his teeth and made a fist with the hand Gerd wasn't slobbering over.

'You gai schloffen,' Gerd said. Sleep.

'I'll be schloffing soon enough,' my father said. 'Now I want some quiet.'

Seeing his eyes close, Gerd leaned foward and gently kissed his brow. He beckoned me to bring my chair closer to his. 'I want you to hear this.'

Even when my father wasn't dying Gerd's words came out as bubbles. Now he dribbled like a spaniel.

'I don't know what he's told you, but you know your old man was a para.'

I did. But a flightless para who had the time, while the war was raging, to make me a soldier suit, the exact replica of his, in which I'd march up and down the living-room floor singing army songs and saluting, and a yellow sports coupé pedal car which I drove around the living room and tried to run down my grandmother. You could say I had a more dangerous war than he did. 'Wrong!' according to Gerd. 'Obviously he hasn't told you about the Battle of Arnhem.'

I knew about Arnhem. In September 1944, several battalions of the Parachute Regiment dropped behind enemy lines just outside Arnhem in Holland with the intention of securing the road bridge over the Neder Rijn. Ill-equipped for an artillery battle, the paratroopers lost a thousand men. Six thousand more were captured. So yes, I answered Gerd, while my father slept, I knew all about Arnhem. And I knew my father was never there. Gerd took my hand. His eyes were wild.

'Don't you think he would have gone had they let him?'

'I'm sure he would have.'

'Well, he did. He went.'

'To Arnhem? How did he get there? By bus?'

'He parachuted in.'

'He wasn't allowed. He told me that a hundred times.'

'That was to stop your mother worrying.'

'She wouldn't worry if he told her now.'

'You know your father – he doesn't boast about his exploits.'

'What exploits? He was a tailor.'

In his excitement, Gerd produced so much saliva he could barely speak. His eyes boiled. He seemed to be listening out for gunfire. 'You remember the film *A Bridge Too Far*? That's his story. They wanted him to play himself but he refused. So they got Sean Connery.'

'Do me a favour, Gerd . . .'

'It's all there in the film. He rescued two wounded soldiers from the bridge. Carried them away from the German guns on his back, one at a time. Saved the first, then went back for the second. That's your father for you.'

Now my *eyes* had begun to boil. 'Gerd, Gerd, talk sense. Where did you get this rubbish?'

He was sobbing, his face sodden, his whole frame shaking. 'I was one of them,' he said. 'I was one of the wounded paras.' He opened his shirt. There was a neat hole in his shoulder. 'And but for him . . .'

His shaking woke my father who managed to sit up in bed. He pulled at my sleeve. 'Get the noodge out of here,' he begged me. 'Whatever he's telling you, take no notice.'

The trouble was, I wanted to believe it.

When he returned from whatever he'd been doing in the war my father set up a small upholstery business. My mother's brother, Uncle Monty, now in his nineties and possessed of remarkable powers of recall, reminded me recently that it was called Howard's Upholstery. It was as a blow to the heart. How could I have forgotten that? Sometimes, to forget an honour or a compliment is to prove oneself unworthy of it. Now I'm wondering what else besides making me a car and a soldier's uniform my father did for me that I've forgotten.

I've decided his workshop must have been somewhere in Hightown or Cheetham Hill, those suburbs just to the north of central Manchester where most of the poorish Jewish families of Polish, Ukranian and Lithuanian extraction lived. The further into Hightown you went, the more like Eastern Europe it felt; the further into Cheetham Hill you ventured, the more the foothills of rural Britain beckoned. Two hundred more miles and you'd be in Scotland. The great trek of the self-improved to the lanes and golf courses of Prestwich and Whitefield had not yet begun for the poorest of us, but when it did, Cheetham Hill Road was the route you took to get there. Though both my parents were born in Manchester, I can't use the word 'trek' without envisaging them trudging from Novoropissik to get here. It must have been easier for my father to make it from Eastern Russia, I often thought, than for my mother to get out of the Baltic, but I only thought that because my father's family felt less remote – in geography and in time – than my mother's. There was a boldness about him, at any rate, that made him irritated by the relative timidity of the Lithuanians he'd married into. I exclude my mother, whose cleverness he revered, though it would remain the fight of his life to get her into glamorous dresses and out of the house. Sometimes, when she tried on a number she felt no longer suited or fitted her, he'd take a tape measure and a piece of upholsterer's chalk and kneel at her feet like Christian Dior, letting out a seam here, tucking up a hem there, even going to the lengths, when necessary, of sewing her into it. Perhaps because it felt like an appeal to his husbandly protection, he treated her reserve with gentleness. But the social diffidence of those close to her angered him. Her fatalistic mother. Her shrinking sister. Her shamefaced, sheepish, scaredy-cat son.

I saw little more of my father in the immediate aftermath of the war than I'd seen of him during it. Once in a while he worked in the house, filling a cushion or re-covering a chair, but all I remember of those occasions is the smell of kapok and the sight of him with a mouthful of tacks. I marvelled that they didn't make his tongue bleed. 'Here, try,' he'd say, knowing that my mother would play merry hell with him for even making a joke of it. Otherwise he'd come home tired, ask what was for tea, and fall asleep without touching it.

As for the kitchen hatch to which I've already alluded, neither the first nor any of the succeeding ones was ever finished. He'd knock a hole through the wall to the living room, tidy up the brickwork, and then leave it as a place to store letters and magazines. My mother, who had never wanted or seen the point of a hatch, enquired occasionally as to its progress. But mainly she let the subject alone. It was his *mishegas*. Husbands had worse obsessions.

He comes back into my life when I'm six or seven and giving trouble. I have a brother now and a sister is on the way. I haven't made a good job of no longer being the 'cynosure of all eyes'. That's a phrase I will pick up years later from *Jane Eyre* but it's hard to believe I didn't already have it in its negative form in my armoury of dissatisfactions. I was still fussed over but not as much and not exclusively. And I wasn't called 'beautiful'. Articulate yes – the miserable employ a wider vocabulary than the happy because they have more to express – beautiful no. Beauty was what my brother had. I saw it with my own eyes the day I beheld him for the first time. Having gone down with measles or chickenpox I was removed from my mother's company – let's call this The First Exile – in the last weeks of what I didn't know was her pregnancy. In 1940s Hightown there was no introducing children to the siblings growing inside their mothers' bellies. We didn't talk to them or feel them kick or buy them presents in advance of their arrival. One day you didn't have a brother or a sister, the next day you did. So why I'd been removed from my own house and given a little bed in my grandmother's nine doors away I had no idea. And then I did.

The morning was bright after a rainy night when I was walked back home, made to stand outside in the muddy street, and told to look up at the window where my mother, flushed and radiant in a loose, pink-ribboned dressing gown, was holding aloft that which – I was not yet able to bring myself to give it human form and say 'he who' – finally explained everything. I say 'holding aloft' as though he were a trophy. That's how I tell it today for laughs. 'The first sight I have of my brother is my mother raising him above her head like the FA Cup. And there's my father in the background, spraying kosher wine as though it were champagne, chewing tacks and doing a Mexican wave for one.' Anachronisms apart, the longer I allow a picture to form, the less like a cup for raising and the more like a lover for embracing he appears. There is a word 'embosoming'. I wouldn't have known it then but I knew what it denoted. A younger brother will reach out and take a lot of what belongs to you, but of all thefts the maternal bosom is the first and worst. He came into the world, on his own account, having been the right way up for nine months, with golden curls. My mother enfolded him, cradled him, embosomed him, as though she had never taken anything as precious to her chest before. The very opposite to a failed baby. An accomplished baby. A perfected baby. A prize baby.

I turned, almost at once, into a naughty child. How far this naughtiness and the reasons for it were detected I have no idea. Everyone was too busy looking at *him* to notice that I'd started to tear pages out of my mother's books and scrawl all over them with crayons; that I was pulling wallpaper off the walls, that I was gouging eyes out of the soft toys I'd never wanted but certainly didn't want to see passed on to him; that I was getting ready to gouge his eyes out if I could only grab a minute with him alone. It was when such an opportunity did present itself and I was able to sneak in Chinese burns to both his wrists that my father stepped in.

He was not of a generation of men who put their mind to parenting. I doubt the verb 'to parent' even existed then. But he had strong views on what a son should and shouldn't be. And what they boiled down to was that a son shouldn't be a *kunilemelly*, my father's own demeaning pronunciation of Kuni Lemel, a character in an early-twentieth-century Yiddish operetta. In the original operetta Kuni Lemel was a bumpkin; in the operetta of my father's family a *kunilemelly* was a hyper-sensitive, easily wounded, forever embarrassed, ungrateful, enfeebled and unmanly boy. Me.

I had been well on the way to being a *kunilemelly* in my father's eyes, even before the abrupt intercession of a baby brother. As witness his anger when he caught my mother standing me in an enamel bowl, rolling up my trousers and washing my legs – a sacred if pagan anointment at which I fancy (perhaps erroneously) that my grandmother and auntie were often present. 'Can't he wash his own legs at his age? What's wrong with a bit of dirt, anyway? What are you trying to do – scrub the boy away?'

Was that his concern – that they were taking the boy out of me? Or did he fear for what was happening to the man in himself. Thinking about it later, when reading about the wives of miners washing their husbands' backs in *Sons and Lovers*, I wondered if jealousy played a part. From *Sons and Lovers* to *Oedipus Rex* was a small step in the history of sons usurping fathers. Why wasn't my mother washing *his* legs?

Which means – if there is anything in the Oedipus idea – that he felt the very pangs I did when my brother stepped into the enamel bowl and the priestesses charged with purifying my body turned their attention to purifying his.

Hating in others what you hate in yourself accounts for half the violence in the world, so why shouldn't it account for some of the violence in our house?

It would go some way to explaining, anyway, why the dog's dinner I made of being an older brother angered my father to the degree it did. He began to find excuses to pick on me, knock my hands away from my face – 'Stop playing with yourself' (do you *hear* that?) – complain about the noise I made, complain about the noise I didn't make, send me to bed early. Later on, when he was working too hard and I could hear his heart beating in his chest, he would take me to my room and punish my latest transgression with his belt. Not so hard that I bled or howled – my room was not suddenly transformed from a library of little boy's books and Meccano parts to a Sadeian torture chamber – but hard enough. And whatever the actual pain, to be bent over the bed and strapped would have been sufficient humiliation had he only waved the belt in the air above me. Sometimes he let me choose which end I wanted, as though any boy in his right mind would choose the buckle. Time has taught me to be fair to him: he was still a young man and hadn't got rid of as much of his surplus youthful energy shooting at Germans as other men had. Nor was he the only father doing this in Hightown and Cheetham Hill in 1950. Things were different then. Maybe society is harsher after a war. Or maybe the idea of the stern Victorian father had some way to go yet before it died. And one doesn't even need to invoke literal fatherhood. The teachers at the grammar school I was to go to would be even freer with the cane or the slipper. One teacher even named the slipper he beat us with. Percy. As in 'Percy wants a word with you'. In mid-century Britain, quasi-sadists walked the streets at night and in the day taught French and Latin to quaking grammar school boys. But I raged against my father's strappings in my soul, whether or not every boy in the country was bending over a bed at the same time I was. Those were the years when I made a promise to myself to be avenged on him. 'You will die,' I vowed. 'Not only for your savagery, but for your insensitivity to the feelings of a child, you will die. At my hands you will die. And your death will be slow and agonising.' (As, indeed, God forgive me, it turned out to be.)

★

He grew into a lovable man and would show great tenderness to me when we both were older. It was he who drove me to Piccadilly on the morning I left to start my first term at Cambridge. 'So what will you be doing there?' he asked, no doubt praying I wouldn't answer. I told him I'd be studying English Literature. 'All those books will come in handy after all,' he said. *All those books* had caused a few arguments in the past. From about my thirteenth year I had started to frequent a second-hand bookstall on Shudehill in Manchester from which I'd bring home what would eventually turn into a sub-stantial library of dirty books – that's dirty in appearance, not content. 'Have you read the last lot you bought?' my father would enquire when he caught me sneaking up the stairs with a complete set of the novels of Edward Bulwer Lytton, bought for about a shilling a volume. 'That's not how it works,' I'd said. 'These are for reading later, or for research.' I thought him a philistine. Today, inspecting the Edward Bulwer Lytton on my bookshelves, all unread, I'm beginning to think he had a point.

He found me a seat on the train, took my luggage and put it on the rack above my head. There was no hugging. He shook my hand. 'Don't forget to write to your mother,' he said.

I was surprised to find myself tearful. Ridiculous: I was only going to Cambridge, for God's sake. True, in those days you had to change trains at least five times to get from Manchester to anywhere south-east of Peterborough, and to get to Cambridge was particularly vexatious and necessitated chang-ing at March twice, but I could still be back home in a day if I needed to be.

Suddenly he clapped his hand over my eyes. Was this to stop me crying? It seemed an extreme measure. 'Get off the train,' he ordered.

'Now?'

'Now.'

I could see enough through his fingers to make out that the person he'd seated me opposite – a rather pale and silent railway employee who I thought would make the perfect travelling companion – was dead.

Everything then happened quickly. He had me and my luggage on the platform. He emptied the compartment. He called the guard. He conferred with other passengers. He spoke to the police. He checked the time of my next train. Perhaps I only imagined that he offered to drive it.

My first day as a man and my father had appropriated it.

Motives matter. I didn't doubt he'd taken complete control because he thought I wouldn't have been able to.

I intrigued him more as I aged than I had as a child. He had more time for me, more time for all of us. In the history of relations between a father and his son there are likely to be many epochs. These were clearly marked in my father's case – the absence, the indifference, the terror, the mellowing, the reconciliation. The terror didn't last long with me, partly because its focus changed and my sister became its object. But this belongs to another time. To return to strict chronology, I don't believe the scourgings had started in the period of which I speak. I was surely too small to withstand a strapping campaign in the early aftermath of my brother's appearance on my stage, and besides, my father himself wasn't yet in the doldrums. I still, however, resented being told off and dispatched to my room for nothing more serious than going around with a long face, refusing to eat at the same table as my brother, and giving Chinese burns to both his wrists.

Eventually I decided enough was enough, packed a bag, and ran away from home.

I must have been six.

3

FLIGHT

I have a photograph of my mother's mother on my bookcase. I called her Andy – babyspeak for grandma – and loved her with a brooding grandson's desperation. I can turn from my computer screen and see her. She is flanked by her cousins, both of whom are better dressed than she is. They have the fur of dead animals on their shoulders and are carrying handbags which might well have been expensive at the time. They are wearing gloves and have their hands clasped confidently in front of them, as though preparing to be introduced to the Lord Mayor. My grandmother's coat is open and inexpensive. She isn't wearing gloves. Her handbag, which is more of a shopper, is made of tapestry and looks as though it's come from a bring-and-buy sale. The seller must have been amazed when somebody bought it. Not impossibly she had other, smarter handbags in her cupboards. After she died, the clothes her daughters had given her over the years were found in her wardrobe, still in their boxes or the tissue paper in which the shop assistants had carefully folded them. Items of bed and table linen the same, in some cases with the price tags still on.

I, too, with the help of my mother, had bought her a silk blouse for her birthday and presented it to her like a little lover. She had held it to her chest and then put it away along with all her other gifts. What was she keeping them for? Some other time. Some other time when? When she was more deserving, when she could do them more justice, when the Messiah came – who knew? The Almighty was a name often on her lips. Maybe the Almighty would show Himself in her bedroom one morning and tell her it was time to unwrap a new dress. *Now, Bessie! The time is now. Let's start with the silk one with the scarlet flowers. Show me. Yes. How lovely you look in that. Give me a twirl. How perfectly it fits you. Don't put it away, wear it. And the new shoes. No, not tomorrow. Today.*

As the hearse containing my grandmother's wasted remains pulled away from our house, her daughters ran after it, clawing at the doors, wailing. I had seen hearses leaving from our street

My grandmother 'Andy' flanked by her cousins Sophie and Annie

before. People died more often fifty years ago. Or they died more visibly. But I'd never seen such public despair or heard more terrible cries. I was, I think, twenty at the time. Too old, and you would have thought too heartbroken, to be self-conscious. But the Jew-thing had me by the throat: were people looking, were they judging us, did they find our show of grief primitive? (Yes, yes, I know: every time I wondered what *they* thought, I was betraying what *I* thought. In all likelihood our Gentile neighbours were too distressed by what they saw to have an opinion about who we were and where we'd come from. It was I who found the show of grief primitive.)

This isn't to say I wasn't devastated for my mother. One shouldn't see a parent mourn. I drove to the funeral with my father and my mother's brother Monty who was in a bad way too. In accordance with tradition, only the men went to the cemetery. Was the idea that men coped better with the brute finality of death? A mistaken assumption in my case. But at least I shed fewer tears in their company than I would had I been among the women. I made up for it later, when we discovered the drawers and drawers of folded clothes. There are wasted lives and there are waiting lives. The waiting life is crueller. At least a wasted life has seen action. A waiting life is all suspense. My grandmother can't be very old in this photograph. She was only in her early sixties when she died, though she looked ninety. But you can see she's tired and unhappy. Her two cousins appear to have worries of their own, but they occupy their positions in the photograph with a certainty my grandmother doesn't. I am half inclined to wonder whether she even knows where she is – not only which city but which country. But that's a cruel thought to entertain. I scan the photograph to see if there's any trace of a smile on her face, and just possibly I see one, but it's only a trace. And kindness?

I'm not sure. All I'm sure of is that she looks far away from anywhere.

But I never felt far away from her. It was to her house, anyway, that I fled to seek sanctuary from my father's baffled anger.

She was alarmed to see me on her doorstep. My parents would be worried sick, she said. 'They won't care,' I told her. 'It's over between us.'

I loved being in my grandmother's house so long as my grandfather was out. He was ill-tempered, unfriendly, and often drunk, though I found it hard at the time to distinguish between the effects of alcohol and his natural abhorrent self. He had been dashing when he was young and wanted to be thought dashing again, but you need to leave the house for that. This he did often enough. He worked in a raincoat factory in the day and behind a bar at night. Many a Jewish man his age worked in a raincoat factory but few pulled pints in a pub. To a tiresome degree, Jews embrace sobriety. Or at least to a tiresome degree they are critical of anyone who doesn't. I don't know how many exhibitions documenting Jewish life in nineteenth-century Russia or Poland I've seen that show photographs of peasants swigging vodka side by side with Jews studying the Talmud. After a while you come away liking the vodka-swiggers more.

The last of my mothers-in-law – Dena of blessed memory – exchanged dark glances with her daughter the first time we were introduced at a restaurant in Swiss Cottage because I ordered a glass of a wine that was new to me and allowed the waiter to let me smell the cork. That cork had more alcohol on it than my mother-in-law-to-be had seen consumed in the whole of her life. I knew what her dark glances denoted. *Give him up. He is an orgiast who'll make every day a living hell for you and bring ruin on your name.* My mother-in-law didn't live to see that happen, but for as long as she was alive I had only to consult a wine list in the company of her and her daughter to observe that neither had given up on the suspicion that it one day might.

My grandfather was out of step with his community. And yet he could pass for a moderately religious Jew. He davened, that's to say prayed in Hebrew, fluently and led the Pesach, that's to say the Passover, service without cuts or breaks for gossip. Without joy, either, but that's another matter.

Did he roll home roaring drunk? Did he raise his hand to his family? If he did I didn't see it. His felonies were background music to my growing up. What I did see with my own eyes was that he was charmless, surly and objectionable. But then I took objection easily in those days.

His parents, whom we knew, generically, as Bobby and Zaide – all great-grandparents were known as Bobby and Zaide – lived, like all great-grandparents who had not made any money, in Hightown, a kind of staging post between the Pale of Settlement and Cheetham Hill. Imagine Bialystok on Irwell. And Tevye the dairyman delivering the milk by horse. Zaide sat waistcoated in his chair when we visited, his hands on his knees, as though waiting to be consulted on matters bearing on the future of the Tsar. Yet on the wall behind was a photograph of him in First World War British Army gaiters and my grandfather alongside him. The photograph fascinated me. How handsome my grandfather had once been. How proud they both were to be in uniform.

I didn't realise at the time that I would recall this image whenever Jewish loyalty to Britain was questioned. But that's the way family memory works. It sustains you in the face of calumny. No, we are not traitors to this country just because there is another place whose well-being happens to concern us. You will not impugn our honour and our sacrifices in order to satisfy a crude ideology itself cooked up in hearts more

My grandfather and great-grandfather in battledress

alien than ours ever were. Hanging on a wall which in so many ways called up faraway associations, the photograph spoke eloquently to me of the complex nature of loyalty. Were I to number the objects that helped make a Jew of me, this would feature more prominently than the tefillin my grandmother bought me for my bar mitzvah, or the menorahs I and my first wife received as wedding gifts.

Bobby spoke only Yiddish to me and was said to speak no other language to anyone else though she'd lived in Manchester for more than sixty years. Over the ticking of the clock and the chatter of uncles, aunts and cousins, she was hard to hear. Her conversation was like a sort of gargling, incomprehensible to me though I took her meaning to be benign as she ended every sentence with a pinch of my cheeks and the gift of a small coin that might have been a kopeck. Given the size of her family – my grandfather was one of about a dozen children – it amazed and impressed me that she even knew who I was. Maybe she didn't. But when I picture her now I see a kind of dynastic warmth far back in her cataracted eyes. Whoever I was to her, I was part of the tribe. For all that, I was always glad to leave her house. After the cheek-pinching and gift-giving I probably turned a small profit, but the foreignness frightened me.

There's some irony in its being this (to me) obscurest and least-loved branch of my family that I came to learn most about. In 1991, while writing *Roots Schmoots*, I visited the small Lithuanian towns in which Bobby and Zaide had grown up and I even drove along the very road they'd travelled by horse and cart to meet and declare their undying love to each other more than a hundred years before. What did I find out? That they'd changed their name from Schwartzbrod to Black. That Zaide had been a glazier and played in a klezmer band, which explained the musicality he bequeathed to some of his children (though not, alas, my grandfather), one of whom became a piano teacher. And that in the year of my birth, long after they'd left, their one-time neighbours cooperated willingly with the Nazis to remove all evidence that they'd ever lived.

After Andy's death, my grandfather fell into a sort of bewilderment and came to live with us. I was away at university at the time and must have had to share my bedroom with him when I came home at the end of term. I say 'must have' because it's hard to credit and I've wiped away the memory in disgust. When I see someone lying in the bed next to mine it's my brother and I'm leaning over him while he sleeps to make sure he's breathing. I feared he wouldn't make it through the night and it would be my fault. For what? Silly question. For having once hoped he wouldn't make it through the night. I had no such concerns about my grandfather and would more likely have suffocated him with a pillow than leaned across to check that he was breathing.

What I recall most about him in that period – other than that the podiatric equivalent of a tree surgeon had to be called in to cut his toenails under an anaesthetic, so long and mildewed had he allowed them to grow – is how defeated he was. *Avanti a lui tremava tutta Hightown*, but he was nothing now other than rattling sputum and geriatric lechery. Under the pretence of not being able to reach something he unaccountably needed, a pepper pot, a newspaper he had no intention of reading, a cube of sugar he was not allowed in his tea, he would feel up any girl my brother or I brought home, or any friend my sister did. The phrase 'Excuse me, love, ta', delivered in a repulsive old man's phlegmy voice, remains a family jest.

Thus, when they no longer have their youth or heroism to recommend them, are our venerable forebears remembered.

Whatever violence he did or didn't wreak on his wife and children I took their side in any estimation of him. Some men, I came to understand early, should never marry or have a family. There are two ways of looking at that: one angrily, from the point of view of the family having to suffer his gracelessness and resentment; the other piteously, from the point of view of the man who made the wrong choice or allowed the wrong choice to be made for him. That there was this second point of view came to me, as on a shaft of illumination from on high, as I was out walking with him through Hightown one afternoon. I had spent very little time with him alone and was frightened. He was, I think, taking me to a children's party at the pub he worked at in the evening. He held my hand. That in itself was a surprise. That he held it companionably, in a gentle and even loving manner, was more of a surprise still. But the illumination of which I speak came as a consequence of the number of people who greeted him as we walked along, who crossed the street to talk to him, who manifestly knew him well and liked him. In conversation with them he became a different person from the one I knew and feared. He was amiable and sunny. He made them laugh. He even introduced me as his grandson with, if I wasn't mistaken, a measure of pride. My first response was the natural one: if you can be so nice to these people, you old fucker, why do you have to be such a shit at home? The phenomenon of the man who was hail-fellow-well-met to everyone except his wife and children was familiar to me from my mother's ruminations on the subject. Maybe men were just like that in those days. Or maybe my mother generalised from her own experience of a husband who was certainly not of that sort, but sometimes seemed to have more time for friends whose cars had broken down on the Derbyshire moors than he had for us. But there was no preventing another thought from forming. What a tragedy it was for this unexpectedly convivial man whose company was clearly highly prized, who loved to be out and about and enjoyed the give and take of lively conversation, to be confined in a dark house he didn't much like with a wife it was possible he no longer loved. We don't believe in caging wild animals. We believe it is their right to roam free according to their natures. The way to look at it, it now seemed to me, was this: if my grandfather let down his family by reserving his most vivacious self for everybody else, he no less betrayed the man he was the moment he turned the key in the door and descended with drooping spirits into the uneventful quiet of home.

I tell this more or less as I felt it at the time. And believe me or believe me not, I swear blind that I could sense the novelist's calling stirring in me. One day I would describe my grandfather not only as he looked to us but as he looked to others and himself. My favourite character in all literature is

Count Stiva Oblonsky in *Anna Karenina*. When I say my favourite character I don't mean I like him. I should say my favourite characterisation. Oblonsky the faithless, feckless husband who makes his wife's life a misery but whose fecklessness insists its own rights as an expression of urgently voluptuous life. The domestic decencies, Tolstoy shows, are not the only measure of what we amount to. However right we are to condemn, we see life only partially when we do. That day out with the promiscuously sociable man who also happened to be my domestically disgruntled grandfather was preparing me for Oblonsky.

I was still relieved he wasn't in when my grandmother opened the door to me.

She had three children. Two daughters — my mother and Joyce — and a son, Monty, who had served in the navy as a sparks in Trincomalee and was still footloose at the time I've been describing. He would become a good friend to me in later years, and remains so still, but at the time it was the women I had fled home to be with.

And here, as I summon up memory of my auntie Joyce (she has been dead many years), guilt musters its forces, and I'm uncertain whether I should honour her with silence — simply walk away from all recollection of her — or spill out everything I have to be ashamed of. Shame — shame again. What I am ashamed of is that as I grew older I rejected her. She showed me up, I thought, by the old-fashionedness of her clothes, the awkward way she carried herself, and her all-round timorousness. By the time I was a teenager she was giving off all those signals of spinsterliness that will make a teenage boy — uncomfortable enough in his own skin — wince. Her back was slightly stooped. There was the odd hair on her chin that a more watchful, beauty-conscious woman would have taken care to remove.

My uncle Monty, my mother, and my auntie Joyce

She wore old lady's stockings. Fearing that other boys my age, seeing us together, would take her for my girlfriend, I was careful to keep a distance between us when we went out.

And yet we had been inseparable when I was a little boy and she was barely out of her teenage years. I didn't love her as I loved my grandmother. That would have been impossible. Fragile as her own hold on the world was, my grandmother enveloped me in the warmth of an infinite protectiveness. She was a burrow of safety. My auntie was too young and too prickly to be that. But she had been there from my earliest years. For good or bad I was the indecorous putto on the ceiling of her maidenly imagination. Unseemly as it is to say it, mine were probably the only undraped privates she had ever seen. We were at a different stage now. I could feel she wanted to play a part in making something of me, and I loved her for that.

Like many women of her class and generation she'd been forced to leave school before she could finish her education. It cost too much to keep a person over fourteen at school. My mother had suffered the same fate, but because she was married and had children it seemed to matter less. My auntie, though, was considered an exceptionally unfortunate case. She was clever enough to have gone on to university. Schooling me not only gave her something to do; it was her way of going on educating herself.

How old I was when she began to take control of my education I can't say for certain, but it makes sense to assume it was about the time my brother was born, for that would have been when my mother, of necessity, had relatively little time for me. Her concern was less for my moral improvement – which department would have fallen to my grandmother to administer – than for my intellectual growth. My love of reading I owe entirely to my mother, so I am talking about cultural matters in a more general way – going to the cinema, listening to music, learning to play whist and snap!, strolling through parks, visiting archaeological sites, acquiring new words, even learning French and shorthand, though I must have been a bit more than four when those lessons began. I think I was a godsend to her, as nieces and nephews often are to uncles and aunties whose own path to procreation and family rearing isn't clear.

I was company for my essentially husbandless grandmother too; she would bundle me into my coat, grasp my hand, and take me, if I was lucky, to the kosher butcher's in Hightown where impossibly complex negotiations about the age and cuts of meat invariably ended in her buying just a chicken. Or, rather, a hen, for a hen made the best of all chicken soups.

I believed I could hear chickens being decapitated in the back room and smell the blood as it spurted from their necks. I even picture the hen's legs still kicking in my grandma's shopping bag as we bring it back to make soup with, but that's probably fancy. Funny – considering how far we'd come from Novoropissik – the part chickens continued to play in my young life.

To the butcher my grandmother spoke a language I'd only heard at Bobby and Zaide's. But at least the butcher understood her. I should say that a small amount of Yiddish passed between my parents too, and between my father and Andy, though it was so expressively delivered, especially by my father who loved its hyperbolic music, that I could read its meaning from the tics and shrugs that accompanied it. (Today, when I am writing and a stray Yiddishism leaps unbidden into my mind, I remember my grandmother and thank her for gifting me such a resource – the wherewithal to express an exuberance or a fatalism, a sense of the terrors or superabundance of life, I can't otherwise find the English for. It's in the same spirit of giving that I pass on my few scraps of this marvellously omnivorous and yet exquisitely subtle tongue to my readers. *Gey gezunterheyt.*)

After the butcher's, the shops we spent most time in were those that sold that soft, seemingly pre-digested baby bread we call challah, bagels, chopped and fried fish balls, herring, liver and tasteless cheese. Baltic food, I suppose it was. The taste for it has not gone away with acculturation. If anything, modern Jews have fetishised it. Even Titanic's, the famous Manchester deli opened by a survivor of the disaster, lasted a hundred years before competition finally caused it to close. But other kosher nosheries still abound. What's changed, at least in the poorer parts of Manchester and London, is the clientele. The atmosphere in such corner shops and delis is not less religious than it was, but more. In the days when Yiddish was the currency, extreme Orthodoxy wasn't. Then, Jewish Manchester bristled with the excitement of an old world adapting to a new, now it's just the opposite. Black hats proliferate the way factory chimneys once did. When I shopped with my grandma we met the eyes of people we thought we knew, even if we didn't. There would be no such recognition now. Our kind of family has gone from here.

Whether my auntie ever went with Andy and me on these expeditions I don't remember. I don't see her there. She was less interested in what might be termed the customs of the hearth, in particular when they wore a religious aspect, and I fancy that part of her plan was to extricate me from all that. She took me to 'town' (our thrilling word for the city centre) where I first saw how many things frightened her – crowds, dogs, babies, bus conductors. Parks the same, with the frightening addition of ducks and birds. I once overheard my father say that she couldn't say boo to a goose. I think he feared that I couldn't say boo to a goose either. He was right to be worried. When we walked by the boating lake in Heaton Park, it was the geese that said boo to us.

Looking back, I realise what a sacrifice of her nervous system she made, venturing out into a world she found dangerous in order to make it feel not so dangerous to me. But all along, I must now accept, her trepidations were preparing me – though it happened slowly and over many years – to cast her off. I was too tremulous on my own behalf to be generous to any weakness of that sort in other people. If babies on a bus frighten you, you want to be in the company of somebody who can stare them boldly in the eye.

As I grew older she spent more time indoors with me, teaching me secretarial skills which she thought would come in handy, though they never did, and French, which gave me a head start at grammar school. When we did go out it was to ruined castles and monasteries. I already had something of a Gothic imagination – a passion for poetic dilapidation, broken arches, stones echoing with the chants of medieval monks – and she encouraged it. What must we have looked like wandering round these unweeded ruins together, peering into oubliettes and negotiating crumbling fortifications, she slightly bent and fearful of every sound and movement, I serious beyond my years, lost in vague fancies, holding on to her hand as though it were she who might save me from mishap, though in truth it was the other way round?

Why do I even ask the question, *what must we have looked like?* Who do I suppose was looking?

I. I was looking.

For my thirteenth birthday she bought me a long-playing record of Laurence Olivier being Hamlet and Henry V. I learned the Agincourt speech off by heart but it was the haunting morbidity of Olivier's Hamlet that really spoke to me. 'How long will a man lie i' the earth ere he rot?' he whispers as though from the chill of his own sepulchre. I never see a contemporary production of *Hamlet* without wishing it were Olivier playing skittles with the bones. 'Mine ache to think on't.'

Mine too. You can get too close to a play. And if those were my fears he gave voice to in the graveyard, then that was my guilt he blustered his way through when he espied the corpse of poor waterlogged Ophelia, denied Christian burial because she died by her own hand, though it was Hamlet's cruelty that sent her mad.

'I loved Ophelia,' he cries, challenging her brother Laertes to prove who loved her more.

'Forty thousand brothers
Could not with all their quantity of love
Make up my sum.'

This might be to put it melodramatically, but I as good as

buried my Ophelia – also without fitting ceremony – when I became a teenage boy who didn't want to be seen holding hands with a spinster. I began to see less and less of her. I never once invited her to visit me at university though she'd done so much, in her own way, to get me there.

She stunned us all in the end. She took dancing lessons in her forties and was so good that she progressed to giving them. And that was how, reader, she came to meet a man who took her out of Cheetham Hill to his lovely half-timbered house in Surrey, where she enjoyed wedded bliss, surrounded by friends who all turned out to be members of the local Liberal Party. The end ...

Not quite. Barely into middle age, she was diagnosed with a cancer that was surely operable, and died of fright.

Sitting in the parlour I could hear my father at the front door, negotiating with my grandmother for my return. I folded myself into a ball of porcupine resistance in anticipation of being bundled out. I took it as a good sign that she hadn't asked him in. But what if he had forced an entry? I listened to the door shut then waited to hear his footsteps. But there was only the slow, weary tread of my beloved grandmother. 'Don't look so relieved,' she said. 'I've only won you a day.'

'One day?'

'Well, tonight, and then tomorrow.'

'And tomorrow night?'

'You go home.'

'This is home.'

'This is your second home.'

I was prepared to settle for that.

I am not able to recall many details of this or the next house my grandmother lived in, though I thought of them both as my second home. I can't see the disposition of the rooms or the furniture. Was there a garden? Was there a cellar? Was there a cat? All I can summon is the atmosphere, the same in both houses, of making do with not very much, armchairs that were comfortable by virtue of being old, and a musty feeling of something ever so slightly devout, not of conviction but of observance, and not very conscientious observance at that, though even that was a great deal more than anything that obtained in my house. I am not saying my grandparents kept a strictly pious house, only that faith had been in their families in the past, so motes of it remained – floaters of faith, echoes of it rather than the practice, the form rather than the function, like newish laces in a dilapidated shoe. I think I see a china rabbi in a display cabinet. I think I see a silver wine goblet for the prophet Elijah to drink from on his passage from house to house at Passover. And maybe the odd *siddur*, or Hebrew prayer book, lying about. What was pleasing to me about these fragments of what-had-once-been I find hard to explain. I shied instinctively from the prayerful. I found synagogues terrifying. But I like a whiff of sanctity, not to say superstition, coming off other people and must have liked it then too.

There's a marvellous passage in Isaac Bashevis Singer's short novel *The Magician of Lublin* where a one-time unbeliever comes upon a barrel filled with pages torn from holy books in the antechamber of a synagogue. 'An exalted scent arose from the tattered leaves,' he writes, 'as if, lying there in the barrel, they had continued being read by themselves.'

So it was with the fragments of Jewishry in my grandparents' house. They worshipped themselves.

I still don't feel right around the Orthodox, but I wouldn't want to live in a world peopled only by rationalists.

Among a thousand other calls on my loyalty and affection,

what must have drawn me to my grandmother's was the Old Religion without, if you like, religion at all, just the sense of being wrapped in a well-worn shawl, crooned over in an ancient tongue, and kept safe from harm.

I loved being with my grandmother not least because, in the most natural way in the world, she took me back to a place I knew nothing about, and that she probably knew next to nothing about herself, but that at some time in the past had been ours. She reconnected me.

4

'MY CUP OF HAPPINESS'

On my thirteenth birthday according to the Jewish calendar –
which, when you do the maths, turns out to be just a few years
after the creation of the world – I am bar mitzvahed. I wear a
new lovat suit for the occasion and over it a prayer shawl that
my grandmother has bought me. Everyone in the family is
very proud of the Bar Mitzvah Boy apart, of course, from the
Bar Mitzvah Boy. I might be misremembering but I have a
horrible feeling that the trousers of my new lovat suit are
short. I squint into the past. Short pants to become a man
in – could my mother really have done that to me?!

I am nervous and uncomfortable. Shuls – synagogues – have
always had this effect on me. Even when I have been there for
someone else's bar mitzvah, concealed at the back where the
chuntering old men who haunt synagogues long after they are
dead can't see me to 'shush' me, I have hated shul. Had my
father been more at home in a synagogue himself, had he
been better able to read Hebrew and known more about what
was happening – when to stand, when to rock backwards and
forwards, when to say 'Amen' while staring forbiddingly at

46

latecomers – a bit of ritual confidence might have rubbed off on me; but all I picked up from him was a diffidence and uncertainty greater than my own. And now here I am, standing on the bimah with a leather box strapped to my forehead, the scroll containing the Word of God open before me, and nowhere to hide. My friends snigger, hoping to make me laugh and spoil my reading. You'd have more success trying to make me scream, boys.

I know the portion of the Law I have to read by heart and indeed only pretend to be reading. I've practised it for so long that more than half a century later I will still be able to recite the opening lines, though without remembering what any of the words mean. Something about Esther, confounder of that anti-Semite Haman. Why Esther when she's the heroine of Purim, a festival that's celebrated in March, and this is September, I don't know. Maybe I have it all wrong. But I will remember until the day I die my Hebrew teacher breathing foulness into my face and saying 'That Esther! She was a peach.' Thereby forever ruining peaches for me, women called Esther, and Hebrew teachers.

He has been coming to the house to teach me for months. Hours before he arrives, my mother lays down sheets of newspaper. This is not because she is obsessively houseproud but because the Hebrew teacher is what, were it not for his sacred function, we wouldn't scruple to call a tramp. He is known to walk around Manchester from the house of one bar mitzvah boy to another, but from the look of his feet you would say he has walked from Siberia. He wears what must once have been plimsolls but are now just blackened strips of canvas stuffed with brown paper and held together with string. His toes – or at least what once were his toes – protrude obscenely. They are black with filth. His coat is ancient and stained. His breath is foul. But he comes to teach me to speak God's own language and to tell me that Esther was a peach. When he leaves, my mother throws open all the windows. But guiltily. He is, after all, a species of holy man. Cleanliness is said to be next to godliness but at the edges of folk religion filth would appear to denote a quality of piety that is closer to godliness still. At thirteen I don't know enough about Jew hatred and what has been identified by our enemies since the Middle Ages as the *foetor judaicus*. If I did, I would be horrified by how closely my revulsion from my Hebrew teacher resembles the Christian world's revulsion from Jews altogether. But I am no Jewish St Francis and would never be able to clasp this man to my bosom as a brother.

So why do we let him into the house? Because he is the best there is at preparing boys for their bar mitzvahs. And sure enough, although my voice cracks and squeaks, I get to the end of my portion without incident. 'Mazeltov!' Uncles I didn't know I had put their arms around me when it's all over. 'Now you are a man,' they say, no more believing it than I do. An uncle I do know I have – my father's brother Rudolph – plays knock-knock on my yarmulke. 'Who's there?' I ask. 'Alec.' 'Alec who?' 'Alectrician.' It turns out that I am no better at faking a smile as a man than I was as a boy.

But at least, I tell myself, I will no longer have to smell whatever's dying in my Hebrew teacher's gut. An anti-Jewish thought on a day I should be more a Jew than I have ever been.

The next day is the reception at the Broughton Assembly Rooms from which, over the years, I've run out into traffic rather than join one of the conga lines led by my father's sisters. Today, I hope, they will leave me alone.

My speech goes down well. I say *my* speech but my mother wrote half of it, including the opening. 'My dear parents, my dear grandparents, my dear great-grandparents, reverend sirs, friends – my cup of happiness is overflowing to be with you today . . .'

I say *that*? I do. Everyone knows it's a lie. Everyone knows I've never had a cup of happiness with anything in it let alone one that overflows. But, for a Bar Mitzvah Boy, allowances are made. Once I get over this hurdle I am free to deliver my own material which consists of jokes made at the expense of one or two exorbitant aunties on my father's side who I know enjoy a laugh, and my friends who welcome the opportunity to snort and heckle openly. It turns out that I enjoy public speaking and go to bed that night thinking I would like to be a comedian if I don't make it as a novelist or a lyric tenor.

5

EAT, EAT

How old was I when I first discovered that other families sat down to dinner? Five, ten, fifteen, fifty? Dinner was itself a foreign concept. Dinner was what school provided at lunchtime. Anything we consumed after that was tea. But it wasn't so much what other people called the evening meal that astonished me as the fact that they sat down for it. What, around a table? Yes, around a table. In the kitchen? No, in the dining room. You eat in the dining room? Yes, that's why it's called a dining room, you shmuck.

So they didn't just eat dinner, they *dined*.

If I find it hard to conjure memories of family meals it's because there were none. Did my father wake from his evening 'kip' when food arrived? I can only say I don't see him at the table. Later, when I travelled with him, I discovered his passion for transport cafes. I was not to tell on him. His away-from-home eating – the Yiddish word *fressing* gets it best – was a secret we'd share. So it's unlikely he was hungry when he did open his eyes.

What eating we did as a family – my sister, brother and

I – we did at the kitchen table and my mother too was absent from it. However long and hard I close my eyes I cannot see her sitting down with us. 'I'll sit down when you've finished,' she'd say. Why? It wasn't that the table was too small for her. Yes, it was cluttered with letters and photographs and post-cards and some Jewish newspaper or other (unread for weeks), but we could have pushed those away for her, or just put her plate on top of them the way we did ours. Her reason for not sitting was that there were things to go on doing in the kit-chen, not least replenishing our plates long before we'd finished. Eat, eat! But there had to be some deeper psycho-logical explanation for her never joining us at the table, for her hovering over our food like the ghost of some uninvited guest, that was buried deep in Lithuanian, or even Judaean/Samarian traditions of mothering. Was it to demonstrate the sacrifice a mother made for her children? Self-denial was a way of denying us nothing. Never taking the weight off her feet was a way of taking it off ours. For us she would starve and hobble.

Or was the very idea of relaxation alien to her on account of our long history of having to get up, pack our bags, and run for it? There, in the kitchen, my mother stood, listening out for the hoof-beats of Cossacks, the rumbling of tanks, the cries of an angry mob, poised to sweep us up in her arms and carry us to safety at a moment's notice.

I'll write about this one day, I thought. I will make it funny. But will I know how to make it serious? It's one thing to joke about the Cossacks, but do I fully gauge the fears and strains of keeping an ever-watchful eye on a Jewish family so soon after events we find too terrible to name?

Anyway, we ate and she stood. It's a long time since she's been able to stand at all. Whether that's the price she's paid for never being off her feet in her younger days there's no knowing. But for all I haven't seen her out of her bed for years, she is always standing when I think of her.

There was an important part-exception to the family customs I have just outlined. Bagel Sunday. For Bagel Sunday my father would rise from his sleep, collect one or all of us, and head for whichever delicatessen happened to be in favour with us at the time. Birds are never more beautiful than when they're swooping from the sky to grab the worm they've just espied, lions never grander than when they see their dinner loping across the savannah. My father never looked more audacious than when he took us out on the Sunday-morning hunt, not only for the perfect bagel but for the perfect smetana and kes to plaster on it. There is an art to mixing sour cream into cream cheese and I am not going to divulge its secret. Suffice it to say that only a fork as wielded by my father like a wand could blend these two divine components without compromising the lightness integral to the creaminess or the creaminess indispensable to the lightness.

Did my mother join us at the kitchen table for smetana and kes at least? No, not even for that. 'You eat now, I'll eat later.'

One other aspect of Bagel Sunday stays in my mind. On the counters of every delicatessen in the period I'm describing stood a collecting box for Israel. Usually it was made of tin, oblong, blue and white in colour, and showed a map of the Promised Land. We put change into it without thinking. One that I remember well stipulated the planting of trees as the object of our charity. A cynic at school had made the crack that when Israel said trees it meant guns. I repeated this one Sunday when I was in Titanic's buying bagels with my father. He made a dismissive gesture with his hand, like swatting a fly. 'What do you expect?' he said. 'There's a war on.'

As must by now be clear, we were not a Zionistical family.

I wasn't encouraged to join Habonim, the Zionist youth movement that so many anti-Israeli Jews of today attended in their teenage years. Their disillusionment was predictable. They grew up but they didn't want the country to. The harsh realities of state became a personal affront to them. Why couldn't it all stay singing round the campfire and free love?

Gods fail those who demand too much of them. Half the atheists in the world were avid believers once. My father didn't set out to teach me that but it was the lesson of his pragmatism. He harboured no wild hopes of Israel, understood the reasons for its existence, understood it would have to do some harsh things to remain intact, and said only – in between the smetana going into the kes – that there might be a time when we'd be grateful for it.

There are Jews who think we are safe in the world today, will never again need a lifeboat, and accuse those who believe otherwise of whipping up panic to justify tramping over someone else's land. My father would have laughed in their faces. He didn't think we'd ever be safe in the world. No sooner did he hear of a blackshirt rally than he was off with his friends to disrupt it.

I have already alluded to the time he got himself arrested during a demo in London for giving Oswald Mosley's horse a bloody nose. He hadn't meant to attack the horse but it had reared just as he was aiming a punch at Mosley. Leaving aside the hurt to the horse, which my father deeply regretted, and the fact of the ensuing scuffle making it onto the television news, which my mother regretted, this was practical, worldly Judaism that had no time for ideology. You fix the problem as it arises, don't make the mistake of thinking you've fixed it for good, and in the meantime get on with other matters.

I took little interest in Israel at this time but inherited my father's conviction that we would never be entirely safe. I imagine my grandmother's fatalism played a part in this too. The Almighty would look after us, but only when He remembered we existed. Too many dark years – *alles schwarzen jahren* – made it impossible to be sanguine. We had to take responsibility for our own safety.

I have since gone further than my father would have thought wise in calling out those who think Jews lie about their fears in order to disguise the essentially exploitative nature of Zionism. People are entitled to their views of Israel, but they do not deserve to be listened to unless they understand its origins in dire necessity and that for most Jews – excluding, of course, those who would never want me to speak for them – it is as much an emotional as a political entity, a voicing of near-impossible hope, an expression of desperation rooted in a fearful past. To be accused of lying for Israel is therefore not only to be accused of cynical opportunism, it is to be accused of lying about the very nature of Jewish history and memory.

But this is to bring the anger I feel today into the history of what I felt yesterday, when the collecting box on the counter of Titanic's defined the limits of my politics. I squint and see it as a quaint relic of a less wrathful age.

6

THE FORSAKEN MERMAN

For years my poem of choice.

*Read it to me, Ma. And then read me 'The Lady of Shallot'.
Again. And now read me whatever else you've got about people going
mad with loneliness and grief near water.*

You know the story. Everyone knows the story. Once the
Merman sat with his mortal wife on 'a red gold throne in the
heart of the sea'. What could she have wanted more? The salt
weed swayed in the stream. The great whales went sailing by,
round the world for ever and aye. To the sound of the surf she
had the Merman's children and combed their bright hair as
they sat upon her knee. But woman is never happy until she is
unhappy. The lesson my mother taught me. One day, through
the clear green sea, she hears the bells from the little grey
church on the shore. The old religion. The austere allure of
conventionality, calling her back. And now the Merman haunts
the shoreline calling to her, begging her to return, singing

> *There dwells a loved one,*
> *But cruel is she!*

She left lonely for ever
The kings of the sea.

Odd that I should have felt as implicated in the poem as I did.

Odd for a boy who couldn't swim and screamed in the bath to make common cause with a species of fish.

Odd that the specifics of the Merman's abandonment should have pierced me so keenly given that I was a long way from having a wife, let alone losing one.

It would appear that some men are already imagining losing a wife while they're still boys.

And odd, given my willingness to half hanker for the far-away faith of my grandparents, that I should feel no sympathy for Mrs Merman, who leaves her husband and her children in order to sing hymns.

But there's no continuity between who one is in real life and who one is in made-up life. Especially when the made-up life rhymes.

Whatever the oddities, from the moment my mother read me Matthew Arnold's exquisite poem, I *was* the Merman. I loved the seductive music of his desolation, the incantatory sorrow of *left* and *lonely* and *for ever*. Round and round his desolation revolved in my head, as eternal as the surge of the tide. I pictured him as noble but anomalous. A freak. A king of the sea, but what price royalty when you've been abandoned? A fallen monarch, at home neither in the icy ocean, with its roof of amber and pavement of pearl, nor on the still, forbidding land where people troop to church through narrow-paved streets. So a Jewish Merman, though that might be another of my interpolations: I didn't see being Jewish as a problem at the time. The Merman I was, anyway. I'd be the Hunchback of Notre-Dame later. And only a long time after that, Shylock.

How often I thank providence that I was born before the mobile phone made glazed-eyed halfwits of the nation's parents. And for having a mother who was a conscientious educator even by the standards of that more conscientious age and didn't call time on her literary responsibilities to her children the minute she'd pointed out a few comical farmyard animals in a rag book. If ours was a heathen house compared to my grandmother's, it was not an uncultured one. Like her sister, my mother had been compelled to leave school by economic necessity when she was about fourteen, and my father had had even less schooling than that. My father's loss never registered with him, or with us: he was a practical man, he thought with his hands. He would make his way without schooling. So, come to that, would my mother, but she might have made another way had she stayed on. She was not a classical reader of novels; though she enjoyed Dickens and George Eliot, her taste ran more to writers like A. J. Cronin and Nevil Shute. It made an impression on me, of course, to see her engrossed in one novel after another, and to sit with her in the dark as she listened to *A Book at Bedtime*, but it was to her love of poetry that I ascribe much of the word music I go on hearing in my head.

Another of our favourites, 'The Lady of Shalott', stirred me in ways I didn't understand. Did I know what it was about? Did it matter? With undiminished vividness I saw and go on seeing the sound of Lancelot, or do I mean hearing the sight of Sir Lancelot, riding down to Camelot, the entire landscape aquiver, 'And as he rode his armour rung.' I couldn't have said then that the alliteration and assonance combined to create the impression of heroic, leisurely masculinity, but the word picture dazzled me. As, of course, it dazzled the Lady of Shalott herself. We were in this together, she and I. The sight and sound of her nerves jangling jangled mine.

> *She left the web, she left the loom,*
> *She made three paces thro' the room . . .*

What with him ringing by the river and her rattling through her room, I don't know how my little boy's head stayed on its shoulders. But when, as a man, I came to write about arousal *in extremis*, the breathless cadences of the Lady's crazed awakening were the rhythms I heard. Just as when, 'in vacant or in pensive mood', I caught the pitch and coloration of gentler, more reflective music, it was as often as not that of another poem my mother and I read together, Wordsworth's 'I Wandered Lonely as a Cloud'. It wouldn't be fanciful – and no matter if it were – to say these hours of reading with my mother determined the very orchestration of my interior life.

Where my brother and sister fitted into this intimacy I don't know. Maybe they were there, listening as attentively as I was, and I have wiped them from my memory because I want the intimacy to comprehend only her and me. Or they were in the room, drawing or crayoning, for their interests were more pictorial than verbal. My mother, me and words is how I choose to remember it, anyway.

She had a thrilling voice, full of warm vivacity. Years later I would ring her whenever I was unhappy. You have to blame somebody so I blamed her and wanted her to hear the hurt in my voice. *Your fault, Ma. You caused this.* Had it been her ringing me she'd have begun immoderately. Her default position, conversationally, was apocalypticism. '*You'll never believe what's just happened!*' Often, I never understood, never mind believed, what had just happened but found it easier all round to drop into apocalyptic mode myself. '*My God, is it possible? Did he/she/they really do/say/suggest that?*' But the effect of my ringing her was to turn her from a woman facing the end of civilisation single-handedly, to a mother whose baby needed to be hushed, soothed, and maybe even fed. Her voice would descend a hundred decibels to lullaby level. Motherly mirth would return to it and, with mirth, hopefulness. 'Oh, shut up,' she'd laugh when I said I was ready to end it all. She didn't make light of my troubles. She never made light of anything. And she wanted to be certain that I was taking care of myself, not worrying too much, not expecting too much, and eating well – I had looked thin the last time she saw me. Was whatever her name was giving me enough food? But ending it all? Come off it. When all was said and done, everything would turn out all right. Don't ask me where in her cataclysmic nature she found that philosophy. It doesn't say much for me as an independent man, who should have cut the apron strings long before, that after half an hour of being back in the maternal embrace I was indeed soothed, but at least the call did her good too and not impossibly saved her from a stroke. I suppose what I'm saying is that she had a voice for her children that was different from her voice for everything and everybody else. Suffused with love and intelligent concern as it was, this voice proved to be a wonderful instrument for reading poetry to a seven- or eight-year-old boy.

I sometimes wonder if she chose the poems at random or with intent. There was great sadness in those she read to me. A fair share of sadness awaited her, but in her poetry-reading period life was as happy as it could be for a reserved and introspective person. We had no money. She was often ashamed to let people into the house because she thought it was shabby. And my father was always a worry because he worked too hard, earned little, and was improvident with what he did earn. But none of this explained the morbidity count of the poems we read together. Perhaps I am making too much of this and the real explanation lay in the nature of nineteenth-century poetry itself. It was doom-laden. But that begs the question of why nineteenth-century poetry was the poetry she liked best.

There was nothing random in her choice of a poem about a son who is ordered by a devilish woman to prove his devotion to her by cutting out his mother's heart. I can't believe this wouldn't have struck me as blatantly Freudian, not to say propagandist on behalf of mothers, even when I was eight, but I listened with enthralled horror. Crazed with desire, the son plunges a knife into his mother's chest and hurries back to the woman, carrying the heart in what, for some reason, I imagined to be a Shredded Wheat packet. The clue to what happens next is in that verb 'hurry'. Not that there could ever have been much doubt what was going to happen next. He trips – of course he trips – dropping the Shredded Wheat packet from which his mother's heart cries out to him – 'Are you hurt, my son?'

'Give me a break, Ma,' is what I should have said. But whatever scanned, transfixed me.

I have not succeeded in unearthing the title of this poem, or the name of the poet. For a while I thought my mother had made it up. But after I'd alluded to it in a talk I was giving, a member of the audience said she remembered it as a folk story from her Romanian childhood. So there we are. It had come over in my family's luggage.

How to decide whether the poem ever succeeded in doing what my mother wanted it to do? In so far as it was intended to deter me from cutting out her heart it can be accounted a runaway success. But whether I learned never to carry out the wishes of an enchantress or to put my love for my mother before my love for her, is trickier. It's possible the poem had the opposite effect and left me in thrall to the idea of the siren who would set no limits to her erotic demands. Hot in my ear I imagined her distilling her poisonous desires. Fetch me this, get me that. Cup of tea. Slippers. Your mother's vital organs. I was certainly to encounter one or two toxic whisperers in later years, especially during the time I spent in Australia (which is where the sirens swam to after Odysseus rebuffed them, coming ashore at Bondi), and if I never committed murder at their behest that might only be because they never went so far as to demand it. But there are other terrible things a man might do to win a faerie's love –

And, shame on me, I did them all . . .

My mother was right to think of me as susceptible to women and not well able to resist every enticement they put in my way. Perhaps because of all the washing I'd undergone at the hands of women in my early years, my skin was thin and my knees buckled easily. As I moved through the gears of early adolescence my mother was to warn me frequently of the dangers her

My mother and father's wedding day, 1941

61

sex posed to me. What she most feared, I think, was my getting someone pregnant and being saddled with a family from too early an age. She had married at eighteen, my father at twenty-two; she didn't regret her marriage, she loved her husband and without doubt she found herself – found her métier – in motherhood. One, two, three – she loved us all. But you can find yourself and lose yourself at the same time. Both my parents wished they hadn't been rushed into things by the war. And now there was no war, they both wanted their children to take their time and enjoy everything else that life had to offer. My father kept his advice simple. 'Don't do what I did. And use preventatives.' Preventatives! He made them sound like something he carried in his toolkit – a pun I regret – along with Rawlplugs and his tin for mixing glue.

In the event I did exactly what he had done – almost to the month. My mother's way was to keep up the attack on her own sex. If they said they loved me, they could as easily say the same to another boy. If they were too quick to ope' their maiden treasure to me – not quite her words, but nearly – I could be sure they'd already ope'd it for someone else. And anyway, as I'd discover soon enough, sex wasn't all it was cracked up to be.

'You'll find,' she said to me once, 'that there are things other than the usual things. Don't try them.'

'Things?'

'Things!'

We exchanged mysterious looks.

I am still figuring out what she meant, which can only mean that if there are such 'other' things I never did try them.

To be frank, I'm not sure I even tried all the 'usual' things.

More than disease, pregnancy and being tied down in a loveless marriage, what she wanted to save me from was disappointment. The enemy, not just to me but to my brother and sister as well, was expectation. Better not to want too much or aim too high. The sadness that my mother loved in poetry, and indeed in music, was the sadness that waited on dashed hope.

A story I have told a thousand times but have to tell again because I am not comprehensible, my mother is not comprehensible, and maybe Judaism – at least the version of it handed down to me – is not comprehensible without it. Stefan Zweig wrote a novel called *Beware of Pity*. The novel my mother was forever writing in her head, and mine, was *Beware of Hope*.

It is 1960 and I am lying in bed, pretending not to be waiting to hear whether I've been offered a place at Cambridge. I'm on *shpilkes*, that's to say I'm sitting on pins. Barely a day goes by in our house when one of us isn't on *shpilkes*. Needless to say, my mother has been on *shpilkes* for me for weeks. It's she who brings up the telegram. Possibly it's a letter but my memory is insisting it's a telegram. I open it and read it out to her. Yes, I have a place. A silence falls on us. We aren't a whooping family. My mother extends a hand, not to pat my cheek or ruffle my hair or shake my hand, but to retrieve the envelope. She is reading the address. 'Just want to be certain it's for you,' she says.

No cruelty is intended by this. She isn't implying there might be some mistake because I'm undeserving. If there is a mistake, if the telegram has been sent to the wrong person at the wrong address, it is because the universe is spiteful, because fortune as good as this doesn't befall us, because things more often go wrong than right. And from the disappointment attendant on any such misprision or mischance my mother will do anything to protect me.

Better never to love than lose. Better the Merman had forestalled rejection by staying in the water. Better not to let imagination off its leash.

★

It dawned on me early that mothers would rather see their children happy than successful. In the case of my sister I wonder whether this precautionary zeal amounted to cruelty. Of all the ways children could go astray, did it have to matter quite so much that a daughter should be protected from going astray *that* way? What way? You know what way? *That* way ...

But she was born in 1948 when respectable families still feared the scandals a headstrong girl could bring down on them. She was gifted visually, attended an art high school in Manchester with my brother, but he went on to art college and became a painter and she didn't. Like my mother, she too found a vocation in motherhood, but that was later, and also like my mother, and my auntie Joyce, there are things she hasn't done that she might have.

Here is not the time or place to tell the story of the obstacles heaped in the way of whatever career my sister Marly might have chosen for herself. Full of vitality, far more adventurous than me, and far more generous-minded, she could have made a go of university or art college or any other form of further education, and then gone on to do a thousand things. What stopped her? It was the oldest story. Being a girl stopped her. By that I don't mean she lacked courage. I mean our parents lacked courage for her. There was a sense in which they used up all their boldness on Stephen and me. Which isn't to deny that something inhibited us as well. We were simultaneously urged on and held back. The world lay all before us but it was inadvisable to wander too far from home. (And home, I regret to say, meant not only the house but the tribe. Of the tribal fears that circumscribed us, the fear of our marrying out, saying 'I do' to someone who couldn't say it back to us in Hebrew or in Yiddish – someone not from our neck of the woods, if I may so put it – was the most constricting. In my father's case, the most deranged, deafening even when silent. I will come to marrying out as it bore on the immediate family Jacobson in its proper place and when I have mustered the strength for it.) The high ambitions I nursed for myself no doubt originated in the enthusiastic applause that greeted my every baby gesture. Where then I got my fear of pushing too hard at any door, even when that door was already half open, or where my mother got hers, I can't say for sure but I suspect the besieged and watchful nay-saying Jewishness of Lithuania.

Fortunately for my sister, as things panned out she got more than her fair share of our father's Ukranian audacity.

My mother's devotion to poetry didn't only soften me up for love and loss – it won us a television. Sometime in the early 1950s the *Manchester Evening News* ran a competition inviting readers to finish a couplet in praise of television. I don't remember the first line but my mother's follow-up was 'A beam to enlighten our way'. Clever, eh? A shaft of radiant light coming from the television meeting the pleasurable glint in our eye. Enlightenment as in casting light but also as in education. Those were the days. The *Manchester Evening News* liked it and awarded her the telly. We went I think to something like an Ideal Home Exhibition to be formally presented with it by McDonald Hobley and Mary Malcolm, unless it was McDonald Hobley and Lady Isobel Barnett, two of BBC television's earliest and most popular personalities. A photograph of the presentation still exists. How old am I? Nine? Ninety? For some reason I am wearing my school cap. Who made me do that? It occurs to me now that the decision to wear my school cap might have been my own, in order to look I don't know what – more skittish than was my wont, more boyish, more of an urchin, more rakish even . . .

Rakish? In a school cap? I know. I know.

If it's hard to own up to the school cap, it's harder still to own up to what was happening underneath it. Look away now: I can't. For I have a clear memory of Mary Malcolm, unless it was Lady Isobel Barnett, bending down and straightening my cap in a spirit that might have been maternal but could just as easily have been provocative. I would have had no idea at that age what a glad eye was, but I fear I must have tried out something of the sort as a way of showing that the provocation had worked. A glad eye on a small boy's mournful countenance is a ghoulish sight. With luck the person it was intended for was looking elsewhere. But had she seen it, then what? Did I hope she'd run away with me? Hardly my fault. She shouldn't have mussed up my school cap and allowed me to inhale her perfume. 'Yes?' she asked, catching me looking at her in a peculiar manner. Meaning, is there anything further I can do for you, little boy, before I go to award a television to some other family with an over-eroticised schlemiel for a son? In response to which I turned a colour red hitherto unknown to nature.

What a nest of deranged desires a young boy's brain is. And then, after desire has shrunk to the size of a peanut, what a nest of shames.

So where do these accumulated ignominies go to? My theory is that they go nowhere. They simply gather, wait and engender more of the same, each lending abashed credence to the other, establishing a sort of Republic of Abashment, until only the end of memory provides relief.

But what if there is no end of memory?

Never mind how long will a man lie i' the earth ere he rot, how long ere he forgets ...?

I was immensely proud of my mother for winning the television. Not everyone had a mother who could write poetry, and what is more not everyone had a television. Wanting to show it off was the reason I gave for inviting about a hundred kids to what must have been my eleventh birthday party. Much like the Pied Piper dancing the children of Hamelin to a joy-ous land, I led the way to our front garden where I told them to wait a minute or two while I prepared my mother.

Something about my demeanour made her suspicious. 'How many did you say you've invited?'

'Twelve.'

She came to the door to look. A solitary balloon was tied to the knocker.

Attracted by the crowd, another thirty kids had joined them.

'You'll have to tell them that we can't accommodate that number,' my mother said.

'There aren't that many.'

'There are too many.'

'So how many can I have?'

She thought about it. 'Eight. Six. Five.'

Goneril had not been crueller.

'*Five?!* What do I do about the others?'

'You send them home.'

'I can't.'

'You'll have to.'

I could hear the murmur of festive anticipation growing. Were they shouting for me? Were they stamping their feet?

'I can't,' I said, covering my face and running inside.

'I'm really very sorry,' I heard my mother saying to my guests, 'the house just isn't big enough,' and then I remember nothing else.

I locked myself in my room and never left it for a year.

You may think that's exaggeration. It's the opposite. There's a sense in which I never left my room again.

7

INTERLOPER

What? Not even to go to school?

I don't want to talk about school or university. I didn't enjoy either. That's an understatement. I was utterly miserable at the first and hated the second. Not their fault. Mine. This was a golden age for grammar schools and it's always a golden age for Cambridge. But this is my story, not theirs. And in my story, I shrank from them, they didn't shrink from me. So, no. Not the primary school in Cheetham Hill, where I fell in love with a little girl in plaits called Sheila who didn't fall in love with me; not the primary school in Prestwich, which I went to for a year after our family fortunes had improved sufficiently for us to begin the Great Jew Trek North, and where I wrote an end-of-term skit on *Twenty Questions* which the assembled school found funny for the wrong reasons (the name Botticelli wasn't hilarious: it was the mispronunciation – 'Pot of Jelly' – that was hilarious, and the fact of the little girl playing Anona Winn, a brilliantly intuitive contestant on the real *Twenty Questions*, guessing Botticelli before asking a single question); and not the grammar school in White-field where I never once finished a cross-country run; never finished the pencil box assignment I'd been set by Mr 'Chimp' Chisholm the woodwork teacher, no matter that I grooved and shaved it assiduously for four years; never finished the work my auntie started all those years before by going on to speak French; never finished hating the master who slippered me with the gym shoe he called Percy; never finished reading *Don Quixote de la Mancha* in Spanish (never started it if you want the truth, though I owned an elegantly illustrated edition); never forgave the music teacher who wouldn't let me sing in the class choir because, in his words, I had a voice like a frog; never got to be School Captain; never learned to play the recorder; never learned to ask to be excused without turning scarlet; never used a school lavatory without checking there was no one in the cubicles on either side of me; never asked for seconds at the dinner counter; never understood why buying a steak-and-kidney pudding from the pie shop round the corner was considered a detentionable offence; never asked out a girl from our sister school across the road; never met a girl from our sister school across the road; never appeared in a school play; never looked a teacher in the eye and said 'I would rather not'; never got the hang of something or other; never quite gathered, never fully grasped, never wholly learned how to, never fathomed, never figured, never – now I come to think of it – heard anything that was said to me other than that I sang like a frog ...

 ... and no, not Cambridge of which I tried to be a part for a day, going so far as to buy a college scarf, stationery, a teapot, a toasting fork and crumpets★ (for my room had a little gas

---

★ One small footnote for those wondering what became of the crumpets. I discovered them in a cupboard the day I left Cambridge three years later. They didn't look as bad as you might have expected but I decided against keeping them. I could no longer read the writing on the packet but estimated that they were past their sell-by date.

fire, ideal for toasting crumpets on), and then waiting for the young women for whose entertainment and delight I'd bought those crumpets to come to me, which they never did, and what didn't come to me I never went to find, so I never joined the Union or Footlights, never wrote for *Varsity* or *Granta*, never acted or debated, never participated in Rag Week, never went to a May Ball,⋆ never ran along the towpath during Eights Week, never kept my head, never treated triumph and disaster just the same, never found a common or an uncommon touch (and what you haven't found you cannot lose),

---

⋆ That's a lie. I did go to a May Ball in my final year with Barbara, my future wife, danced to the Dave Clark Five, drank a lot of champagne, even punted down to Grantchester afterwards for early-morning breakfast in the heavy rain, she lovely and laughing in her strapless evening gown, I less lovely and not laughing in my sopping wet dinner suit. But to tell of the pleasure I took in her company, and in showing her off, when she was able to get away from Manchester, and to describe the hours of delightful and instructive conversation I enjoyed with my best friend at Cambridge, John McClafferty, would be to water down the annals of comic misery to which I've reduced my undergraduate experience. I cannot say why.

Why it was a bitter farce to me at the time, I understand. Long before writers disclose themselves to the world – and they are doing that whether they write autobiographical novels or essays on the metaphysical poets – they tell the story of their lives to themselves. I was simultaneously the victim and the hero of my own narrative from the earliest age: a boy doomed to introversion like the Lady of Shalott but redeemed by the other person I was, Sir Lancelot of the ringing armour and flashing wit. And obviously I couldn't be the second without the first. As for Cambridge, it stood in well enough for Camelot.

What's harder to understand is why that's still how I tell it. It can only be that writing has been no sort of therapy for me. Progressing from boyish soliloquy to writing proper has not changed the originating myth. In my own eyes I am still a wretch waiting to be saved. But whether that's self-punishing or self-delighting, I am back saying I don't know.

never trusted myself when others doubted me, never filled the unforgiving minute, and therefore – for how could it be otherwise? – never inherited the earth and all that was in it. As for being a Man ...

8

MY FATHER, METHINKS
I SEE MY FATHER

Before the writing of this chapter my father came to me. In a dream not a vision, but some dreams half attain to the visionary, and this dream was one of those.

I knew why he had come. It was to express dissatisfaction with what I'd been writing about school and university. *Was it for you to get so little out of your education – or to* say *you got so little out of your education – that your mother and I worked our fingers to the bone?*

It won't have been all he was displeased with. What was that about his views on intermarriage?

'Dad, I've barely mentioned your views on intermarriage.'

'I think you've said enough to make it clear what you think.'

I didn't dare say, Dad, I haven't started yet.

He shook his head, not at me, *away* from me. Who was I to suppose he hadn't thought hard about the subject? Or didn't know something for himself – growing up in a neighbourhood where such defections were not uncommon – of the pains and sorrows of marrying out? And yes, he knows I don't like that word *out* – as though whatever isn't Jewish is outer-darkness. Allow him to remind me that he's been more a friend of the non-Jewish world than I have. Has more non-Jewish friends. Has spent less time arguing about Israel. Correction: has spent *no* time arguing about Israel. And – yes, *and* – why did I begin my account of him with his death? *Must I be over for you, my son, before I begin?*

I mean to answer all those charges. It's possible that this book exists to do precisely that. But it will take time.

He was sitting cross-legged at a low table strewn with leaves. He was making something with the leaves, a look of intense concentration on his face. Often, when I picture him, or when he comes to me, he is concentrating hard. This is a true account of him. He lost himself in a task, whether important or trivial. He looks up at me without pleasure. Has he read my mind and heard the disdain in that word 'trivial'? Who am I to judge him? Who was I to judge anybody? His long-standing complaint against me was that I was critical of everything. *What do you enjoy, Howard?* I had a pat response to that. I wasn't obliged to enjoy a damned thing. He goes on staring, through the dream-mist, meeting my eyes without fondness. He isn't obliged, his look says, to enjoy *me*. I have written about him, often, sometimes in a fictional form, sometimes not, but not is difficult. He was built on a fictional scale. I hadn't imagined I would hurt him. He's a sport. He takes a joke. And isn't the amount I have written about him a proof of my affection? Love, even. (Why *even*? Because I am a cold fish when it comes to family. As a teenage boy I told girls I'd met five minutes before on the dodgems that I loved them to distraction. But to my family the best I could come up with was 'affection'. I don't think I was alone in this. I had grown up in non-mawkish times.)

73

So what about the things I've said about him? The fun I've had with his fun? Does he or doesn't he mind? It seemed not at first. He wouldn't have read any of it anyway. He was never a reader. But you get to hear what your son's saying about you. 'It's complimentary,' I told him. 'I don't care what it is,' he often said. 'So long as you make a few quid out of me.' Sheer bravado. No man was ever less mercenary. But since he'd never known how to make a quid himself, it pleased him to think that he might be instrumental to my making a few.

From the way he's looking at me now, though, I'd say it grew, it's grown, irksome to him. He hasn't lived his life – or died his death, come to that – to give me material. Very early on in my career I was the subject of a BBC documentary in the *Arena* series. My father had a walk-on role. He was a children's conjuror in his spare time and we had some good footage of him entertaining a party. There was one trick he did specifically for the programme, close up in front of the camera, producing silk scarves from a bucket. What's marvellous about this trick, when it's well performed, is that a profusion of scarves could ever have been housed in the tiny receptacle from which the magician conjures them. A bucket isn't a tiny receptacle. 'It's not a trick to pull a few small things out of a very big thing,' I told him afterwards. 'If anything, that's the opposite to a trick.' He shook his head. What did I know!

What I knew was that I'd wanted him to be in the programme because it wasn't every novelist who had a conjuror for a father. But what I also knew was that I was ashamed of him. Firstly, for not being a very good conjuror. But also, for being a conjuror at all. Pride and shame are not always incompatible.

Recently I met one of my closest school friends who had been living in America for half a century. John Heilpern, a successful, clever, critical man, from a good, by which I mean a professional, well-educated, family. He told me he remembered coming round to my house hoping my father would be home. He loved the tricks.

'You *loved* the tricks?'

'Yes. I loved all the wands and cloaks and white rabbits.'

'There were no white rabbits.'

'You wrote a piece about the white rabbits.'

'It was a lie.'

'Well, I liked it all. Your house was like a stage set.'

'That didn't please my mother.'

'I imagine not. That's mothers.' (Easy for him to say. His home was out of *House & Garden*.) 'But I envied you having a magician father.'

Envied!

'But the tricks were no good,' I reminded him.

'That's not true. Maybe to you if you saw them all the time. But I couldn't see how he did them.'

Envied!!

See! my father is saying. Not everyone turned their nose up at me.

Only he isn't saying 'See', he's saying 'Bleh, bleh, bleh' – the equivalent of sticking his tongue out or thumbing his nose – like a child.

He loved playing the child, inventing words. '*Taugetz*,' he'd say if he thought what I'd said was nonsense. '*Taugetzmeowgetz*.'

My nonsense trumps your nonsense.

What the hell did that mean? *Taugetzmeowgetz*? What language was he speaking? It's just possible he didn't know he'd invented such words and thought he was speaking Yiddish. Zay gesund. Take a shtum powder. Mind your own bitnut (business). Bitnut, bitnut. Keep your big schnozz out. Zol zein. Hak mir nit in kop! Hab seichel (use your brains). See you in Lontish on Wengy. (*Lontish*? London. *Wengy*? Wednesday).

75

Bleh, bleh, bleh. In his own way he was multilingual. Any mood or sound that popped into his head he found a word for or turned into an expression never heard before.

He peopled the world similarly. Any old woman was Granny Noblets. A soprano he would walk into my mother and me listening to on the radio was a Shvitscheheike. 'Dad, that's Elisabeth Schwarzkopf.' 'Wasn't that what I just said?'

When I talk about where my passion for writing comes from I say 'my mother'. From the books and poems she used to read me. But my wife Jenny thinks I do a disservice to my father. From him, she says, I must have learned to play with words.

She never met him. It's one of her greatest regrets. It's mine that he never met her.

He is still focusing on his task, white with concentration, sorting the leaves.

I don't kneel to be on a level with him. I stand, waiting. When he looks up I can see he is angry with me. Yet again, in some way, I've let him down.

The letting down began early. I was a mother's boy. Not my fault, I'd have argued, it was the doing of all those women. Yes, but I'd liked it, hadn't I? I'd let them.

Then there was my long face. He was always apologising for me, he said. People took my expression amiss. 'Cheer up, it may never happen,' they'd say. And I'd reply, 'It already has.' For which, on one occasion, he slapped my face.

I'll kill you for that one day, I thought.

Sons have done more than that for less.

But in the end I accepted his valuation of me. I needed to lighten up.

As for what he needed, it wasn't a leaden son hanging like the albatross round his neck. He had troubles enough. Here is a brief summary of those troubles, of which working his finger to the bone to give his ungrateful, sour-faced son an education was just one –

His upholstery business had gone up in smoke. Actually or figuratively, I can't remember which, but whatever went wrong it was taken as gospel that the fault lay with my father's partner who just happened to be one of my mother's old atheist boyfriends. A partner in 1950s Hightown parlance was a necessary but inevitably destructive part of any business. Everyone had one and everyone owed the fire in the factory, the missing cash, the discrepancies in the books, the pregnant or absconding secretary, to him. The best kind of partner from the point of view of expressing disillusionment, bitterness and rage, was your own brother. Most of my Jewish friends' fathers had brothers they were no longer speaking to. Gentile brothers drifted apart silently and by degrees. Shook hands at their parents' funerals, exchanged a Christmas card, and never gave the other a further thought. A Jew cursed his brother in language no wife or child should ever have been allowed to hear, regularly called on God to open up the earth and send him to eternal hell while vowing never to make reference to him again. *Don't talk to me about that mamzer! May every syllable of his name burn out the tongue of whoever dares pronounce it.* So for my father never to speak to a mere old boyfriend of my mother's again was small potatoes. As I recall, the boyfriend ended up in Strangeways Prison in connection with sundry other matters, which was where my grandfather maintained all atheists belonged.

Shortly afterwards, in the hope, perhaps, that a change of air would create a change of fortune, we moved away from the Hightown/Cheetham Hill borders into a sunshine semi – i.e. a small house with one downstairs room through which the sun no sooner entered than it left – in what would prove to be a culturally colourful cul-de-sac in Prestwich, close to Heaton Park. We were lucky in our neighbours – one of whom was Malcolm Megitt who became my friend and companion in late-adolescent nefariousness until he fell in love with a Swede and chased her all the way to Gothenburg, where he stayed until he could get no more air into his lungs for fifty years; another of whom was Stanley Samuels, the only religious boy in the street, a fellow table-tennis player who practised his forehand drive as we walked along, regardless of the people he drove into the road, and who pretended to hang himself from a gallows he made from the For Sale sign the estate agents had left in the drive; another of whom was the musician Lol Creme who would go on to play with 10cc and Godley and Creme; another of whom hid in a shed at the bottom of his garden and was said to be a conscientious objector who had deserted from the British Army; another of whom had to leave the house and lie on a bench in the park all night whenever his wife's coach-driver lover turned up in a vehicle that was longer than the avenue (we all wondered why he didn't allow the husband to sleep in that); and another of whom owned several market stalls in Wales and Nottinghamshire and would eventually employ my father to collect stock for them from importers in London.

These were to be my father's Ben-Hur years, there and back in a tail-lift chariot between Manchester and London, day after day, going empty and coming back loaded with boxes of *swag* – the professional word for objects of neither use nor loveliness, made in Hong Kong or Romania and destined to be sold on markets in Oswestry and Worksop. At weekends or in the holidays, aged somewhere between pre-adolescence and the full-blown tumorous thing, I would accompany him. I find it hard to remember what we talked about. It couldn't have been The Forsaken Merman. That would have elicited a

Taugetzmeowgetz from him. Mostly he drove in silence – no rude jokes, no bad language, no passing wind – livening up when we got to one of the transport cafes that served the sort of liver-and-onion fry-up he most liked. It was at these cafes, before the advent of motorways, and so more like family restaurants, that I saw at first hand the charm he exerted over women. They knew what he liked to eat and gave him bigger portions than were good for him. They treated me well, telling me I should be proud of my dad, who was a scream, and pinching my cheek, though not in any way that reminded me of Great-grandmother Bobby. Something told me that if I showed any of these women a long face my father would leave me on the hard shoulder of the A6. I made superhuman efforts and squeezed out a sickly smile. Twenty miles on we'd be warmly greeted at another transport cafe. The liver-and-onion fry-up even better here than before. 'You don't have to tell your mother how often we stop,' my father would say to me, man to man.

The sweet juices of masculine betrayal of the woman we both loved coursed through my veins. I became his willing confidant against the other sex.

For some reason, my most vivid recollection of these trips is the hotel we stayed in when we got to London – the Russell Square Hotel in Bloomsbury, which I likened to a palace on account of the terracotta tiles in which it was clad. It seemed so elegantly upper-class English to me that I wondered Jews were allowed to stay there. That agitated sense of exclusiveness that was always lying in wait to exclude me roared in my ears when I heard my father address the porters. He didn't change his accent or intonation exactly – I doubt he'd have known how – but he lowered his voice to a different register, spoke with a deliberation that wasn't native to him, as though one party owed the other a measure of deference but he wasn't sure

79

which, and didn't once say *Taugetzmeowgetz*. On formal occasions, in a restaurant or a function room, I'd seen him straighten himself up like this, and it had upset me. He was my father. He ruled the roost. What was out there that could unsettle him?

Something else upset me – the sight of him in a vest. It took somehow from his authority. He had a powerful chest but his skin was white and hairless except for a single hair that grew about six inches above his navel and which I learned later he'd promised my mother he would never cut.

I laughed when I learned that. Now his promise strikes me as full of erotic charge. One single hair, allowed to grow until it became long enough for Stanley Samuels to have hung himself from, just for her.

Otherwise I liked being away with him, just the two of us. He always got us a good room. The same room, I thought. Cold and grand with a vast oak bureau that had a special drawer for collar bones and cufflinks. I decided that when I grew up and became English I would have a drawer just like it.

I smell that room all these years later whenever I check in to a hotel. No matter how grand the room they give me, it never quite measures up to the room I shared with my father at the Russell Square Hotel, circa 1953.

In the end it wasn't the liver and onions, or the extreme good manners expended on porters that put my father out of action, but the hours behind the wheel. He was ill-paid and exhausted. Fortunately, our neighbours were expanding their operation into wholesale and handed him the opportunity first to work on one of their market stalls and then to take it over altogether. 'Cheap Johnny' – a name he inherited with the stall – was born.

There were essentially two ways of being a market man, or gaffe worker, if you were Jewish, as most market men were then, and if you were Jewish you didn't do fruit and veg or flowers

80

which required an indigenousness to the soil you couldn't lay claim to. The reason you were a market man in the first place was that you couldn't lay claim to anything: you rolled up in your van to bag a space which, in the end, if you were lucky, became yours so long as it suited the toby – that's to say the market superintendent – not to give it to someone else. The first way to go about being a market man thereafter was to be a shtummer, a stay-shtum, say-nothing, purveyor of nylons or woollen gloves which you'd lay out on your stall and wait for someone to buy. The second way was to be a big mouth, a pitcher, a fairground auctioneer with a line of patter that could hold a crowd – an edge, we called it – for the time it took to go through every line you had for sale and sell it. The stage was the back of the van, the jokes were well-worn and repeated ten times a day – 'Who's that in there?' you'd ask a punter, getting her to look in a mirror, and when she said it was her you'd say, 'Thank God for that, for a minute I thought it was me' – your patter was low, your prices even lower, and the straight man who copped all the flak – the butt of every joke, the schlemiel who had to take the candlewick bedspread or non-stick pan-set out to the back of the edge to pretend it had been sold and then bring it back hidden under his shirt, the one with the burning cheeks, the one 'Cheap Johnny' called Charlie – was *me*.

'And you made no effort to hide that you hated every minute of it,' my father says, looking up.

(If 'Who's that in there? Thank God I thought it was me' was my father's shtick, then hating being my father's stooge, giving him the long-face treatment every Saturday on Worksop market, every Monday in the holidays on Retford, every Wednesday on Oswestry and every Friday on Garston, was mine. Couldn't I have raised a smile occasionally? Couldn't I have gone along with the performance?)

'*Do you suppose I didn't hate it half the time too?*' he says.

'*I didn't know you did.*'

'*Getting up at the crack of the dawn, putting up the stall in the freezing cold, looking out for ganovim, telling the same stupid jokes over and over, seeing your verkrimt expression . . .*'

'*I didn't know.*'

'*There's a lot you didn't know. You were too busy being a kunilemelly.*'

'*Don't use that expression. You know I hate it.*'

'*Something else you hate. And I hate that you made a ganze megillah out of everything. Where was your famous sense of humour?*'

'*I'm not going to say you stole it, Dad. I'm not going to say you made all the jokes. I'm not going to say you took up all the room, your shadow was so broad I never got any sunlight.*'

Once, on the East Lancs Road, halfway between Manchester and Liverpool, he jammed on the brakes suddenly, pulled the van over, and ran out into the traffic towards a vehicle he had spotted on its roof in a field on the opposite side of the road, its wheels spinning silently in the moonlight, its engine smoking. I stepped out of my side of the van as though I had weights tied to my feet, afraid to follow him. 'Stay there!' he shouted unnecessarily. But I decided to stomach my own cowardliness and ran out into the traffic. By the time I got to him he was wrenching a door open. He put up a hand to stop me coming any closer. Whatever he'd seen, he didn't want me to see. What use would I have been, aged eleven, anyway? Or any other age, come to that. Mortality was my father's sphere. My role was to stand back and leave the dead to him.

'*That's something else I'm not going to say you stole from me, Dad – unthinking courage, or whatever the word is for what you – a tough Jew from the Ukraine – had in abundance, and I – the mother's boy*

82

*Jew from Lithuania – didn't. Because if I didn't have it, how could
you have stolen it? Unless what I mean by saying I didn't have it is
that I ceded it to you. You did the action, I did the words – was that
our unspoken pact? You used your hands, I used my – call it what you
like, my* kopf, *my head, my imagination. But yes, many were the
times I'd have preferred the courage.*

*'But it wasn't just courage, was it? It was instinctive kindness. You
helped out. You were on the spot when people needed you. Maybe you
were too often and too quickly on the spot. That's what my mother
thought. You were at the whole world's beck and call. Max, the Mr
Fixit for the Universe.*

*'You don't have to answer that, Dad. But I do. If you were Mr
Fixit, was I Mr GoFixityourself?'*

I not only wasn't cut out for emergencies, I wasn't cut out to
be a gaffe worker either. Unless you were one of the shtum-
mers who sold nylons on a quiet corner next to a charity
stall, the gaffes were dog eat dog. Every pitcher was shouting
down every other. Some of them blew whistles. Some of
them broke china. Some of them gave half their stock away
for nothing. It was as though rival theatres had thrown wide
their doors and were openly competing for audiences. Is it
possible I enjoyed it more than I let on? I know I revelled in
the lingua franca of the markets, that fantastic mix of Yiddish
and Hebrew and *leshon hakmah* (the covert language of the
Jews) and Polari and cockney rhyming slang and costermon-
ger insult and Maxims – words simply made up on the spot,
to meet some contingency or other, for the godlike joy of
creation, by my father himself.

Later, when I went off to study English Literature at Cambridge under F. R. Leavis, I would induct my Downing College
contemporaries into the secret patois of the gaffes, teaching
them that bunce meant profit, that a nobbel was a laugh, that

a shneid was a reject and a shmendrik was a fool. 'That's fixed that shmendrik C. P. Snow,' I caught one of my gentile friends saying to another after Leavis's famous demolition of the would-be polymath. Leavis himself, it must be said, pulled no punches in his lecture, but even he didn't go so far as to call Snow a shmendrik.

Dickens was much in our minds at this time, because Leavis was said to be changing his view of him as a mere entertainer, but as I was the one who'd lived a life Dickens would have relished, with a father who was no less improvident but nothing like as reprehensible as his, I felt entitled to pass myself off as vitalistically Dickensian when in truth, like everyone else at my overwrought college, I was straight out of the excruciated school of nineteenth-century fiction, much of which, I sometimes thought, could have been written by my auntie Joyce. 'In catalepsy and dead trance I studiously held the quick of my nature,' Lucy Snowe, the heroine of Charlotte Brontë's *Villette* confides. Which could have been a description of me, too, in my three years of trance at Catalepsy College.

I owe my old man an apology. Forgive me, Dad, give me another go at the gaffes and I promise I'll loosen my hold on the quick of my nature.

But I owe myself an apology too. I wasn't all Lucy Snowe. I wasn't a *verkrimteh* every second of the day. Some days I laughed. Often, looking back, I laugh still more.

Suddenly, reading my mind, my father looks up from what's occupying him.

'It wasn't all misery,' he says.

'I know it wasn't all misery. Who says it was?'

'We had some good times.'

'I know we did.'

'Do you remember that shtarker Smulewitz?'

Lennie Smulewitz! How could I forget Lennie Smulewitz?

My father employed Lennie as a favour after his own flooring business went *mechula*. He was a giant of a man with rippling muscles which he'd built up throwing rolls of lino in the air to pull in punters. It was after one fell on a punter who successfully sued for whiplash that Lennie went *mechula*. My father hadn't trusted him from the off. Something about the way he moved when handling money. He seemed to crouch. It took a lot to arouse my father's suspicions. He could have seen Smulewitz roll a five-pound note into a ball and swallow it and he still would have trusted him to cough it up later. But that crouch worried him. One day – I think it was on Garstang market in Liverpool – he confronted him.

'If you're accusing me of stealing from you, Max, I want a witness.'

My father offered me.

'Not him. He's biased. I want the toby.'

So my father and Smulewitz went into the market superintendent's office where Smulewitz emptied out his pockets. *Gornisht.* Nothing.

'Satisfied?' Smulewitz asked.

My father tells it now, unable to stop laughing. 'Was I getting worried? What do you think? But I knew I'd seen something. So I told him to take off his shoes and socks. Still nothing. Then his shirt, then his trousers. Again nothing. The toby was getting anxious. "This is going a bit far, Max," he said. I told him that Smulewitz likes showing his muscles. He was down to his unterhasen now. "Off," I said. Smulewitz grinned. "OK, Max." Stood with his hands in the air and his legs apart, stark naked. All right, now I was having second thoughts. "Only one place left to look, Max," Smulewitz said. And that was where he made his big mistake. He stuck out his thumb and put it behind his back as if he was going to stick it you know where. If he'd used the other thumb he might have got away with it. But this thumb had a bandage on it. And now I came to think about it, there'd been a bandage on that thumb a long time . . .' My father taps his head. *'Plus, I used a bit of the old what do you call it? You and your mother are not the only trick-cyclists in our house, you know. Why was Lennie Smulewitz acting as though he needed to hide that thumb you know where? Only one reason. "OK, Lennie," I said. "Let's take a look at what's in your bandage." You should have seen his face. It was a picture.'*

'A picture of what?'

'What do you think? Not innocence, that I can tell you.'

'So you got him?'

'Stone dead.'

'Had he really hidden money in his bandage?'

I know he'd hidden money in his bandage. I was standing just outside the toby's office, keeping an eye on the stall, when Smulewitz came out, hanging his head and with no bandage on his thumb. My father followed in high spirits. 'Five tenners rolled around his thumb, inside the bandage,' he announced. He even did a little war dance, like an Apache. Probably something he'd seen in the only film he hadn't slept through. 'Bleh, bleh, bleh!' he said. Which wasn't Apache.

I was in earshot of the whole thing but he's told me his version a thousand times since. I've written so many variations myself, I no longer know whether I'm fictionalising the truth or factualising the fiction. But my father never tires of telling it his way.

I shake my head the way I always do. 'Inside the bandage. Sheesh.'

'Let that be a lesson to you. Don't mess with your old man.'

'So did you call the police?'

'Of course not. He's a Jewish boy.'

One story begets another. 'Do you remember when the pig escaped in Bakewell . . .'

And he's off with another of the great gaffe escapades: the time a pig escaped from the enclosure where the animals were being auctioned and charged our van. Gerald Cohen, one of my father's best and most loved workers, was doing the pitching. Gednut was my father's nonsense name for him. '*Oy gevalt*,' Gednut shouted, 'there's a wild pig attacking the gear.' The crowd scattered but Gednut went on with his patter, showering the pig with free notepads and plastic combs. Seeing the pig seemingly pacified by the plunder, my father approached him with a mirror. 'Who's that in there?' he asked. The pig looked, then, disliking what he saw, trudged back to the pens to be auctioned.

Thereafter, Gednut only had to say 'oink oink' for my father to throw his head back and laugh the laugh of his Ukranian forebears.

'*You're right, I say, we had some fun.*'

'*So why do you always say you hated it? Why can't you remember what you enjoyed?*'

'*It's what I'm like.*'

'*Why can't you remember it isn't only yourself you're disrespecting? Why can't you remember how that makes me feel? This was my occupation. Why do you have to disrespect it?*'

'*I don't disrespect it. I never disrespected it. I said you made mistakes, that's all. I said you made some bad business decisions. I said you trusted people you shouldn't.*'

'*I didn't trust Lennie Smulewitz.*'

'*No, you didn't. But you were careless with money.*'

'*How was I careless with money?*'

'*You left the takings in a phone box.*'

'*Once.*'

'*You dropped pound notes out of your pockets.*'

'*Twice.*'

'*You sold stock for less than it cost you.*'

'*Only a little bit less. But I worked hard to give you the education I didn't have.*'

'*I know and I'm grateful.*'

'But you disrespected that.'

'I didn't mean to.'

'It's part of what you do. You disrespect. You disrespected my magic.'

'I was wrong about your magic.'

'You disrespected me for not having an education like yours, the one I worked to give you.'

'That's not true.'

'You disrespected me for not having your mother's words.'

'I loved your words.'

'Taugetzmeowgetz.'

'It's the truth. I never disrespected your capacity for play. I envied it.'

'For play. You see?'

'I never disrespected you.'

'You patronised me. You belittled me in the act of thinking me a character.'

'What about how you belittled me?'

'When did I belittle you?'

'You slapped my face.'

'For contradicting your mother.'

'Not then.'

'For torturing your brother.'

'Not then.'

'For not dancing. For sulking in a corner with your face on the floor.'

'I didn't like dancing.'

'You didn't like anything. "What's wrong with the kid?" people asked me.'

'What people?'

(I knew what people. Rudolph and Isabel. Netta and Joe. Rita and Harold. Bella. His brother and sisters. And the Weisbergs, the better-class side of the family. The cast of that MGM extravaganza staged every other week at the Broughton Assembly Rooms to celebrate someone's engagement or ruby wedding.)

'The people you wouldn't dance with.'

'That wasn't a dance. It was a hokey-cokey.'

(My greatest dread. The snaking line of uncles and aunties kicking their legs out, a giant centipede of *mishpokhe* – a word that means what it sounds it means: ever extended and extending family – winding its way between the tables, out into the street, out all the way to Kamenetz Podolski and back again, my father among them, beckoning me with a crooked finger, furious.

'It was people having a good time. That was all.'

He gathers the leaves he's been arranging, cradles them in his arms like poker winnings, then lets them go. The wind catches them. I thought they were leaves from a tree, but they are leaves from a book. He rises, gives me a sorrowful little wave, as though with one of his collapsible magic wands, and is gone.

All ghosts are sad, but none as sad as the living who conjure them up.

'NAH, THAT'S JUST THE BROTHER'

My father's right. I disrespect for the fun of it. Even myself. It's a species of self-aggrandisement. I see there comes a moment when a confession – especially a confession of cringing cowardice, ineptitude, gracelessness and, I dare even say, Jewish incompetence – risks looking more like a vaunt than a regret. I am not ennobled by having made a dog's dinner of school and university and regret giving the impression that I think I might be. Stand Grammar, in Whitefield, built in the shadow of a massive, brooding parish church which was originally designed to be a cathedral somewhere else, was no Dotheboys Hall, even if some of the masters were too niggardly with encouragement and too free with Percy. I formed lifelong friendships there. I studied *Jane Eyre* which, among much else, taught me that you don't have to find your replica in a novel to find yourself, and Wordsworth's *Prelude* which taught me that morality was an immanent, breathing force, as present in the streets I walked as in the lakes and mountains further north. I learned a little Latin. Forgot a lot of French. And went with others in my class to Paris one year and Barcelona the next. We had a debating society, thanks to which I acquired the essential art of rehearsing an argument in which I didn't necessarily believe, and a music society where I heard a Mahler symphony for the first time. And we did comprehension exercises every week, learning to distinguish what was said from what was meant, why a judgement was a richer thing than an opinion, and what tone could tell us that literal statement could not. The school, in other words, subscribed to a high idea of thought and educated citizenship and I was lucky to be a beneficiary.

As for the custom of dispatching the Jews to a balcony room during the singing of morning hymns, it is a matter about which, more than half a century later, I continue to have conflicting views. I say 'dispatched' but for all I knew this brief daily exile was practised at the Jews' own request. I'm not sure whether I'd have joined in Christian hymns without a qualm but there were some of us who certainly would not. Did it do us any harm to be segregated in this way? Did it do the rest of the school any harm to see us as a segregated minority? We knew what *they* were doing. We heard them. But they could only guess at what was going on in our room where one inept young Hebrew teacher after another failed to keep us quiet. 'Will the Jewish boys have the manners to shut up?!' the headmaster on occasions shouted up.

Jews had no manners. Was that good for any of us to be told?

One lasting effect for me has been the sentimentalising of alienation. I loved some of those hymns for the very reason that they were denied me and drifted up into our noisy room as though from another world. Why 'Let us now praise famous men' lodged in my heart I can't explain. Could have been the Ralph Vaughan Williams setting. Or the odd conjunction of worldly fame and godliness. Maybe I even imagined being famous one day and not being praised by such an assembly as this because I was of the wrong faith. For the singing of the school song, 'Forty Years On', we of the wrong faith were called back out onto the balcony, where we stood conspicuously, 'the cynosure of all eyes', bearing in our confused souls responsibility for the smallest infractions on the head's charge sheet of petty wrongs – even the missing toilet rolls were my fault – and consumed with sorrow for those who would not be with us forty years from now. Feeble of foot and rheumatic of shoulder myself now, I still weep when I hear 'Forty Years On', and if I have to thank Stand Grammar for that, all right, I do.

On the other hand, yes, the PE teacher found a way of getting round my excuse note one Wednesday morning and, discovering that I and several other Jewish boys were wearing our underpants under our shorts, made us run around the gym bollock-naked. Funny that what I remember most about that episode is not his ordering us to undress, right there in the middle of the gym, but his inspection, going from boy to boy, pulling at the waistbands of our shorts so he could the better see inside. Why we kept our underwear on in the first place I cannot now explain. Comfort? Natural modesty? Provocation? The deep yet obscure impression left by circumcision? But then why we were expected *not* to wear underwear I can't explain either.

And why didn't I find the courage to say, 'Like what you see, you monstrous, Jew-hating, perverted prick?'

And yes, the geography master held up by one corner, as though it were contaminated, my map of the cornfields of Manitoba and jested to the class that a spider could have done a neater job, though in fairness to him he didn't attribute my inelegance to any specific racial incompetence, a precaution that our woodwork teacher, 'Chimp' Chisholm – so named because he had bad breath and long arms – would have been wise to take when he showed around that pencil box I'd been working on for the whole time I'd been at school and wondered aloud 'why Jewboys were so gammy-handed'. Once reported to my father who, as I've said, had been an upholsterer, and to the cabinet-maker fathers of a couple of friends, this observation generated much heat and controversy and very nearly, but for a well-planed apology to the Jewish nation, cost 'Chimp' Chisholm his job. While it's true that our fathers' professions proved the misguidedness of his judgement in general, he was hardly wide of the mark in relation to me. I was as clumsy with a chisel as with a drawing pencil. And how different, when it came to stereotyping, was my joke that while the Christian boys were taking home double-wardrobes and three-piece suites after two terms of woodwork, I and my co-religionists (I doubt I would have used that phrase) were still having trouble with the lids of our pencil boxes after four years?

Note to myself as novelist: A Jew can be too cute about his Jewishness.

Otherwise, but for the occasional rebellion staged by more Orthodox pupils against the highly charged religious symbol we were compelled to wear ...

... let me rewind. On our school caps and on the pockets of our blazers was embroidered a cross, not any old cross consisting of limbs of equal length, but the Christian cross – not quite a crucifix, because it didn't have Jesus on it, but close. It never occurred to my parents to worry about it and I certainly didn't feel it reminded me of my people's blood-guilt every time I put on my school uniform, but then it went with my family's quiescence and gratitude to go along with things the way they were. Had we been compelled to wear an illustration of medieval Jews crucifying Christian babies we might have thought twice before doing so, but otherwise, *otherwise*, we weren't prepared to rock the boat. Parents more religious than we were, however, did take offence and unpicked the embroidery with their own hands, returning the cross to its unoffending, pre-Christian geometry. An unseemly row ensued, with one retiring and scholarly Orthodox boy bearing the brunt of the school's insensitive anger. The school capitulated in the end, but it was noticeable that whenever a teacher lost his rag and hit out, it was always the gentle Elias who copped it. Whatever else this incident in our simmering war with Stand Grammar achieved, it taught me that the world is unjust and the meek are invariably the first to suffer its injustice.

Otherwise – *otherwise* – excepting the English teacher who couldn't stop himself remarking that whenever the Jews were absent for Jewish festivals they came back to school with a Saint-Tropez suntan, meaning either that we spent more time on the beach than in the synagogue (an expensive beach, was the clear implication) or that, as the chosen people, God caused the sun to shine on us indoors (hardly our fault if He did); and excepting the odd encounter in the playground with a boy from Radcliffe or Fishpool or somewhere equally benighted who wondered if Jews still had residual tails and if so could he feel the stump; and once, maybe twice, being accused of Jewing someone in the matter of swapping marbles or cigarette cards advantageously to myself; and being hit on the way home by a stone thrown by the prefab boys who lived on the other side of the Heaton Park wall, who called us 'Dirty Jews' but never, I thought meant it, and anyway we threw back with equal gusto, and called them 'Dirty Something-or-Others' in return; and every now and then being told to go back to where we came from, to which we made many a witty riposte, such as 'Do you mean Altrincham?'; *otherwise*, the school years skipped by without further inflammatory racial incident.

For all the watchfulness instilled in us by our parents, it didn't feel perilous to be Jewish in fifties Manchester. If anything, I'd say this was an easier time for a Jew to be growing up than the present. I don't recall anyone accusing us of having run the Slave Trade. Or of harvesting the organs of Palestinians. Even the money charge had fallen quiet in the aftermath of the war. If anyone got hot under the collar about Jewish bankers it was us; a newspaper photograph of a Jewish plutocrat puffing on a cigar in the back of a chauffeur-driven car being enough for us to cover our faces or stay inside for a week.

I say a quiet had fallen after the war, but it was a quiet of willed ignorance as much as anything else. Holocaust survivors found refuge in silence for many years, but so did everyone else, Jew and Gentile. It was really only with the publication of Lord Russell of Liverpool's *The Scourge of the Swastika* in 1954 that details of what had happened in the camps began to circulate. And perversely, though that evoked horror and compassion, it also, I believe, marked the slow beginning of a backlash against them. With the Holocaust as history came the Holocaust as hoax. And little by little came the revulsion from pity. By the time of the Six Day War, barely more than a dozen years after Lord Russell of Liverpool's book, there was no small willingness to go from sorrowing over the Jews as victims of violence to admonishing them for practising something just as heinous themselves.

To live at the centre of such changes, at the very time we were growing out of boyhood, was not to be fully aware of them. *The Scourge of the Swastika*, which we passed around when we were thirteen or so, scrambled our brains, the photographs of naked women prisoners and the detailed accounts of sadomasochistic practices in the camps disturbed us almost as much as the eyewitness accounts of extermination, choking our affective processes. I discussed the book with two Jewish friends. One was a religious introvert, the other a wilder precocious boy for whom no subject was out of bounds. As I recall, we spoke only about the crimes against the Jews the book recorded. The warped eroticism beneath was like a tune each of us wasn't sure the other heard and none of us knew the name of. A secret element to being Jewish had entered our lives.

But those were Jewish street friends not Jewish school friends. To the latter I spoke differently and of different things. Why, I am not sure. It might have been that while the street was where we lived as in the shtetls of old, still cabined and confined, school was the means of our escape. For that reason it was also a more ironic place. However angered we were by 'Chimp' Chisholm and the gym teacher who couldn't keep his eyes from the contents of our shorts, we joshed one another freely about our parents' and indeed our own hypersensitivity to anti-Semitism, inventing a whole mythology of Jew haters and Jew hating to account for every ailment and setback. Blister on your foot? Anti-Semitism. Refused a kiss after school on the no. 35 bus home? Anti-Semitism.

To have used the word any other way, unless there was urgent reason to, would have embarrassed us. *Anti-Semitism.* To this day I feel a country-cousin when I say it. *Anti-Semitism* – its utterance turns me into the very Jew anti-Semites deride. If I can possibly avoid saying the word, I do. Best to save it for when it's genuinely needed, when the offence, by very virtue of its innocent-seeming denials, truly merits it. Assuming we will know when that is.

My best friends at Stand Grammar were also my most serious rivals. Gabriel Jacobs and John Heilpern. Gabriel had, and still has, an intricate and even scientific mind. Nothing seemed too abstruse for him. He was also a brilliant linguist and musician. He'd spend a weekend in Barcelona and come back speaking fluent Spanish. He'd listen to a song once and be able to sing it back. Perhaps because I read as someone who wanted to write, and so needed to possess the soul of the literature I loved, and he read in order to understand it, we didn't talk about our feeling for art that much, though we did once go together to see *I Pagliacci* and *Cavalleria Rusticana* — Gabriel following the libretto in Italian while I hummed along and secretly wept. So if literature wasn't his bag and languages and science weren't mine, what did we find to be rivals about? Everything else. Astronomy engaged us for a while, though I knew I was playing away and ceded the ground to him altogether when he had a telescope installed in his bedroom. Bodybuilding, with the aim of looking like our muscular boxer friend Mike Passant, and arming ourselves against bullies who might kick sand in our faces on the beach, not that we ever went to the beach, followed a similar pattern. We both sent away for chest expanders and 5-spring hand-grippers. I was bigger built than him and expected to win this one hands down. I could see my chest turning triangular while his remained obstinately thin and rectilinear. But then one day he invited me into his bedroom. The telescope had gone. In its place was a gymnasium — bars on the walls, coconut mats on the floor, ropes hanging from the ceiling, and a pommel horse that had been reupholstered in red leather by his father. The only thing it lacked was a *farbissener* gym teacher to look inside our shorts. I went home and threw my chest expanders away.

One long-running competition entailed making lists of books we'd read or thought about reading, extended to books we'd seen in bookshop windows, and finally went on ad absurdum to books we vaguely knew about. I believe we both cheated at last, writing down the names of books we hadn't heard of.

I still recall the names of some of the books on Gabriel's list. *Tschiffely's Ride*, about a journey on horseback through Central American rainforest and jungle. *The Kon-Tiki Expedition*, about crossing the Pacific Ocean by raft. And there was one about the Raj which must have been what determined him to travel by road to India ten years later at the invitation of a waiter he met in an Indian restaurant in Manchester. Of the books on my list I remember only *Too Late the Phalarope* by Alan Paton, and that's because it's a novel. Even when it came to knowing about books I wouldn't go on to read, the books I knew about were always novels. From my earliest days non-fiction held little fascination for me. What wasn't made up – what hadn't been hammered out in the hot forge of the imagination – didn't count as literature and barely even counted as a book. Steinbeck's *Of Mice and Men* began on my 'heard of' list and then, after I saw the film, progressed to the status of 'book I must read'. 'Tell me about the rabbits, George,' is a line I carry about in my head still, perhaps because it's about the universal hunger for the deceptions and consolations of a story. *Tell me, tell me . . . Never mind if it's true. Just spin it for me, George.* In fact, though I wasn't able to put it to myself in so many words at the time, stories weren't just better than the truth, they were somehow truer than the truth. I had reached the age when my auntie Joyce's spinsterishness was a bother to me. But while the thought of her being on her own forever touched me, I didn't find it so poignant as the prospect of loneliness that faced Catherine Sloper, the heroine of Henry James's short novel *Washington Square*, who is abandoned by the man she loved, and left to sit and stitch – 'for life, as it were'. I wasn't old enough yet for James, and I struggled with the novel, but the anguished finality of that phrase taught me that life became more tragic when it was 'told'.

Notice that at no point did this competition involve us in actually discussing any of the books on our lists. That would have spoilt the purity of our endeavour. Later on we were rivals for the attentions of girls. About them, I am ashamed to admit, our conversations did at times become more detailed. But yet again Gabriel seized the initiative thanks to his parents buying him a sports car. It was pathetic of me, I knew, to employ the chat-up line 'My friend drives an MG Midget', but I was desperate. I might as well not have bothered. The girls couldn't wait to meet my friend.

My rivalry with John Heilpern was of a different order, both culturally and socially. It's possible his personal confidence was so high that he didn't know we were rivals. But we were the writers in our school and I can't believe he didn't keep as close an eye on the marks I got for my essays as I kept on his. We discussed the theatre, Wesker's *Chicken Soup and Barley*; John Osborne, whose *Look Back in Anger* was shaking everything up and about whom John would go on to write a magisterial biography; and the waspish theatre criticism of Kenneth Tynan in whom I think John saw something of himself. As often as not we walked the second half of the cross-country run together, complaining of a stitch, discussing *The Return of the Native*, which we agreed laid the irony on a bit thick, and Graham Greene's *The Power and the Glory*, which we thought we might not have been Catholic enough fully to appreciate, and Evelyn Waugh's *The Ordeal of Gilbert Pinfold*, which John thought lacked the brilliance of *Scoop* and I thought lacked the blackness of *A Handful of Dust*, bluffing all the way (because I, at least, had returned *Gilbert Pinfold* to the library unread), and landing back at school mightily pleased with ourselves intellectually, but cold and wet, long after the gym teacher – cursed be his name – had gone home. Our reluctance to enter into the physical side of school life resulted in our having to sit on the hall platform, where everyone could see us, polishing the trophies neither of us had the slightest interest in winning, though John, I now recall, did come to excel at shot-putting. Had he and Gabriel enjoyed the rivalry I enjoyed with them both, John's successes as a shot-putter would have resulted in Gabriel ripping out the gym from his bedroom and laying a sports field.

Thus far I have omitted all mention of table tennis which provided me with a sort of ancillary and yet satisfying life from about my thirteenth year. For a shy, interior boy, table tennis was just the thing to make me shyer and more interior still, while making it look as though I was normal. If I blushed, I could pass the redness off as perspiration. If I had to look away in embarrassment I could pretend I was looking for the ball. I would go on to write a mock-heroic novel about table tennis – *The Mighty Walzer* – which is sufficiently autobiographical to deter me from telling in any detail the story of my ascent through the ranks of kitchen-table enthusiasts playing against their mothers, to joining a club team in the Manchester League, where, reader, I once topped the third division averages, to winning tournaments (I was Manchester Closed Junior Champion *twice*), to representing my county, to getting an England trial (though not, alas, making the England team), to representing Cambridge against Oxford and winning – a triumph that could only have been sweeter had Gabriel Jacobs and John Heilpern been on the Oxford team.

Table tennis had for me, as it had for most players, a compulsive quality, not only in the playing but in the narrating: the analysing of what went wrong; the repeating of what went right; the instant reminiscing and memorialising of every point won and lost. Statistics count in all sports, but in no

100

other game are they enshrined in the memories of players for so long. To this day I meet men who remember the last game we played more than half a century ago and can reel off the exact score including deuces and disputed net calls. There's a Yiddish word, nebbish, meaning someone pitiful and nerdy, that well describes me at the time and many of those I played against. The game attracted nebbishes because of its actual and mental interiority – so much concentration on a small ball hit across a small table to such small interest from anybody else. You slapped your thigh with your bat, hunched your shoulders, crouched over your serve, urged yourself to 'Come on', and disappeared into a world no bigger than the ball. Away matches, usually played midweek on dark winter nights, took me to all corners of Manchester, to works canteens and social clubs and church halls, to post office sorting rooms, bus depots and YMCAs. Neither Marco Polo nor Ulysses ventured so far or saw such things as I did. But there, exactly, was the sadness and the comedy: in the efforts we were prepared to make; in the sense of intrepidity as we crammed into the car to get wherever we were going, excited by the glow from the dashboard in the dark Manchester night; in the importance we attached to every game; in the grandiosity of our dreams, compared to the actuality of the spectacle, the meagreness of the returns, the indifference of the world. There we would be, hunting out the little ball on our hands and knees every time it rolled under a social-hall bench or behind a school radiator, but in our heads the crowd was roaring on its support and women with wild eyes and full red lips were waiting to welcome us back up off the floor with laurel wreaths and moist kisses.

The refusal of my school to acknowledge my success rankles still. Every morning at assembly, after the Jewish boys had trooped back out, the headmaster would invite us to applaud the fact that one among us had almost scored a goal for the third reserves of a football club none of us had heard of, and yet there was I, ranked briefly among the country's top ten junior table-tennis players, and not a mention. My parents wondered – yes, you've guessed it – if this could have been anti-Semitism in action, like 'Chiseler' Chisholm and my pencil box. I thought not. For all that there were many Jewish club teams in Manchester and some of the world's greatest players were Jews from Hungary and Austria, table tennis was hardly an expression of the Jewish soul. More to do with the way our school viewed itself, I thought, in the tradition of Dr Arnold's Rugby. Though then again, if sport was supposed to further Christian manliness, I could see why ping pong might not have figured in their moral calculations. So, all right – giving the terms their broadest interpretations – the school's silence might well have been, if not anti-Jewish, then pro-Christian.

John Heilpern was also a good table-tennis player though he never took it as seriously as I did. His apparent insouciance aggravated the rivalry on my side. It gave him the air of a gifted amateur who could pick up an interest or leave it alone – I have a feeling he didn't even play table tennis in shorts – while I, to my own eye, had to labour hotly ever to achieve anything. He lived not far from me – I could have hit a table-tennis ball from my bedroom into his – but across a palpable barrier of class. Park Road. There were detached houses on Park Road with leaded windows and double garages. Even the trees outside John's house exuded assurance. Yes, Jews lived there, but they weren't our sort of Jews. I took deep breaths when I went to call on him and straightened my jacket. His parents made me welcome right enough but I wondered how they saw me. Come to that, I wondered how John himself saw me. What did he make of the noise and the clutter in which I lived? If he didn't see me as a rival was that because I didn't have the social wherewithal or antecedence to make me any sort of threat? We both dreamed of greatness but the greatness I dreamed of must have been a lesser thing than his for the simple reason that I started from so much more humble a base. Not because he was supercilious but because he came from the other side of Park Road, he must have looked down on me and my peasant parents.

Let's not get into the psychology of this dread. I bow my head. In an email he sent me recently he told me he'd adored my parents. I had to read that again. I am still reading it. *Adored*!

I weep to read it.

We knocked up together in the local Jewish clubs, and every now and then went away for a weekend in each other's company to a coaching school in Burnley – Ken Stanley's Coaching Academy, situated above a Burton's in the centre of town. Here, we drank club soda, swallowed glucose tablets and practised serving at a matchbox for hours on end. Had we only encountered matchboxes at the other side of the table when we played competitively we'd have carried all before us. As it was, Ken Stanley sharpened up our games, I went on to win a few junior tournaments and John moved on to matters that interested him more.

He went to Oxford and edited *The Isis*. I went to Cambridge and edited nothing. He would leave Oxford already well on his way to becoming a successful journalist for the *Observer*, where he would interview the likes of John Gielgud and Graham Greene, while I would leave Cambridge on my way to being an unsuccessful academic. A dozen or so years later he published a book about the director Peter Brook. It attracted more notice than it is fair a book by a rival should. You could say it acted as a spur. How much further ahead of me could I allow him to get? Clive James wrote a funny poem celebrating the fact that the book of his enemy had been remaindered. A more painful and funnier version still, in my view, would have been 'The book of my best friend has been remaindered'. I wondered if one way of catching up with my best friend would be to write a funny and painful book about this very question. The trouble was, this wasn't the kind of book I had it in mind to write. But rivalry as a subject, and the perils of allowing rivalry to fester until it becomes indistinguishable from envy, hung about in the darker corners of my mind. Let's be clear, though: finding a way of writing in the face of, and about, John's alarming success, wasn't my first problem. Finding a way of writing at all was.

Because Gabriel and I were not heading in the same direction professionally, we had less reserve and fewer secrets. And neither of us was capable of the hauteur John could manage even when he was serving at matchboxes. Whereas John lived north of the Park Road divide, Gabriel lived south, no nearer to me measured in miles, but far closer measured in social status and assurance. John and I never hit the town together. Sometimes, as sixth-formers allowed to study in the Central Library, we met for a quiet lunch at a Ceylon Tea House on Oxford Road, did Tony Hancock and Frankie Howerd imitations, and smoked Stuyvesants. Some days I had the feeling that we were marking out our different career paths. But what John did in the evening I never knew. My relations with Gabriel were more boisterous and less chaste. Given the size of his sports car in which we trawled the town for girls together, it was probably for the best that we rarely found any. We confided intimacies, put rude words to popular songs, and made each other laugh. He was one of those laughers who truly did crease himself, folding at the middle like a collapsible chair. After a falling-out that lasted more than thirty years, Gabriel and I have resumed our friendship and making him fold at the middle is once again the pleasure to me it was. When Dudley Moore went to Hollywood, Peter Cook looked like a man without a mission. Who else would ever appreciate him as Dudley had? I make no comparisons as to comic genius, but when Gabriel and I turned our backs on each other I felt as I imagined Peter Cook must have felt. There are some friendships whose dynamic requires one of you be hilarious and the other to have hysterics. My unspoken deal with Gabriel was that I got him to laugh and he got the girls.

Gabriel also played the clarinet, but you'll have guessed that. Jazz was big with a number of my Jewish friends. They bought records, went to jazz clubs, played instruments, and mentioned names talismanically. I'd heard of none of them. Coltrane? Nah. Buddy Somebody? Nah. Benny Goodman, yes, but only because he sounded Jewish and shared a name with someone I played table tennis with. It struck me that for Gabriel and co jazz was a way of defreezing Jewish culture. Gabriel's mother had sung with a Manchester dance band which to me accounted for a certain louche quality to Gabriel's intelligence. His mother had loosened him up. The nearest I had to a torch singer in my family was one of my grandfather's sisters who taught pianoforte, and Zaide who had played in a klezmer band in Lithuania. While jazz did nothing for me, anything that evoked the old world – any old world but preferably *my* old world – brought me to the edge of tears. Leo Fuld singing 'Where Can I Go?'. Tauber singing 'Goodnight Vienna'. Even Sophie Tucker singing 'Some of These Days'. At the time I just thought I was the schmaltz merchant of our group and did my best to keep my emotionalism secret. But what I realise now is that I was simply the most Jewish. Probably the least Jewishly informed but definitely the most Jewish in the heartstrings.

The strictly Orthodox look down on stomach or bagel Jews who return to Judaism only when they eat. But there's more than one way to express one's religion. My way was through tears. Unless those tears weren't so much an expression of Jewishness, as milestones on the road to finding it. I cried as a blind man gropes his way in the blackness, but with this difference: the blind man knows where he wants to get to, whereas I sobbed and stumbled towards being a Jew without having the first idea where I was going.

I never played a musical instrument, but my brother Stephen did. The four years' difference in our age was half a lifetime culturally. I don't know whether the jazz thing had blown itself out by the time he was old enough to want to play something, but I'm pretty sure he never cried to Leo Fuld or ever missed Vienna. He taught himself guitar, and joined a band made up of Jewish boys his age from Jewish Prestwich. They practised in our house when I was studying for my A levels which allowed me to conceal my pique under the righteous rage of a distracted scholar. I don't recall yelling for them to shut up and saying 'It's not even as though you're good musicians' but I must have. The first group was called the Whirlwinds, more of a performing than a recording band though it did both. I think my unmusical father was their roadie for a while. Then the Whirlwinds disbanded and became the Mockingbirds. By the time of the third coming my brother had left Manchester to study art in Liverpool. That third band was 10cc, which gives you some idea of the quality of the musicianship. Thus I had shouted 'Quiet, you bunch of no-hopers!' to Lol Creme, Kevin Godley, Graham Gouldman, Stephen Jacobson and others of that ilk. In my house, the Manchester Beat! And beginning to snake their way from the bottom of the road to our front door, the fans, the beautiful fans. Not only could I play no instrument, I had no musical enthusiasms of this youthful kind. Musically, I was old beyond my years, loving the 'September Song', and dying a thousand deaths with Kirsten Flagstad. But that didn't stop me being envious of my brother's army of teenage admirers. After a bleak first term at Cambridge, in which I hadn't seen a girl, I returned home, got out of a taxi and found my way blocked by near-hysterical fans. One called out 'Steve Jacobson!' and screamed. A second said, 'Nah, that's just the brother,' but she must have seen the expression on my face because, after whispering to a friend, she had the decency to scream a little bit for me.

10

THE LOST TRIBE

I've done my best by school, but Cambridge goes on defeating me. I'd been warned that the exclusivism of Cambridge could very easily prove daunting to a working-class Jew. So what was I supposed to do, I'd asked, spend the rest of my life working in a bagel shop in Prestwich? Of course I wouldn't be daunted. In the event what proved daunting was the paranoid conviction – I had been a prey to it at Stand Grammar, too, when the other boys returned from the holidays having forged secret connections without me while they were away – that everyone had made friends with everyone else at some prior time and in some secret place, and that I, whenever I entered a room or joined a conversation, was looked upon as an intruder. There was some anteroom where life's participants-to-be had gathered on some signal I had missed, and where the alliances and friendships necessary for a happy future, let alone a successful collegiate present, were formed. I can see them now in those first fraught days of term, gathering by the college gates or on the chapel steps, re-establishing old acquaintance, recalling the long summer evenings they'd enjoyed in one another's company in a bar in Taormina close to where Lawrence wrote *Lady Chatterley's Lover*. How warm were their embraces. How lovely their delight in being together again, here, in their undergraduate gowns, like bats gathering in the rafters, among the yellowing stones of Downing College. There was to be no second chance for me. Without their shared history there was nothing I could join them in. What I'd missed I'd missed forever.

That these glamorous clued-up socialites in cord trousers and Viyella shirts were no more in the swim of things than I was, I only realised when that knowledge came too late to be of use to me. By then I was too much of an outsider even to enjoy the company of outsiders like myself.

So yes – whatever fancy psychic name I gave it, I suffered all the sense of exclusion I'd been warned I would. I was a working-class Jew. I should have found a job in a bagel shop in Prestwich.

I had gone to Downing College for a very particular purpose: to study English under Dr F. R. Leavis – at that time the most formidable literary critic teaching at an English university. I had been introduced to his work in the sixth form at Stand by a slightly older boy, David Ellis, who later became a professor at the University of Kent and wrote the elegantly elegiac *Memoirs of a Leavisite*, and by a teacher who had himself been taught by Leavis – the connection was passed on in this way, as though by monks infiltrating monasteries – and who bore what I now recognise to be the imprimatur of election: a voice you had to incline your ear to catch, a lean frame taut with critical attentiveness, and a way of being disappointed in everything you said that somehow encouraged you to do better rather than change the course of your studies and revert to woodwork. In addition, this particular teacher had uncannily pink fingernails at the end of attenuated El Greco fingers which he'd place on my desk as though they were candles made of the most priceless wax. I smell the scent of them still. The scent of purity of mind. Thus perfumed, I read the first sentence of the book which showed me my future course in life. Many a young priest must have started out on his career in the same spirit of devotion. To call the opening words oracular fails of justice to their deliberate, even mischievous plainness. It was as though one's nerve were being tested. The book was *The Great Tradition* and it was prefaced with a quotation from Dr Johnson – '. . . *not dogmatically but deliberately* . . .' – then began, 'The great English novelists are Jane Austen, George Eliot, Henry James, and Joseph Conrad – to stop for a moment at that comparatively safe point in history.'

Music to my ears, all of it. Not just the judgements which, but for the omission of Dickens, I happened to share, but the casual provocativeness; the Johnsonian quote, forestalling the dogmatism charge which had pursued Leavis all his career; the subversive narrowness of the list, one in the eye for those muscular populists who had been the bane of my life at school because they hated any man who hated any book; the pause at a 'comparatively safe point in history', as though what he'd written in those two and a half lines wasn't already explosive enough; and the implied assurance that plenty more danger was on the way. It was like watching a boxer come out of his corner with his fists high, light on his feet, winking at his corner, devilish. Yes, this was for me.

I began my storming of Fortress Downing badly. A reader who has come this far would expect me to say that, but it's true. A knowledgeable friend – had I made one in those first fraught days before teaching began – might have put me straight in the matter of who at the college was who, but my fellow freshmen were too fondly recalling taking tea in Keat's house in Rome to have any time for me. So I blundered in, telling Leavis when I encountered him in the college grounds that I was looking forward to term beginning and that meanwhile I was rereading *The Dunciad*. This was my first meeting with him so I didn't know how to interpret any of his expressions, but thought him discouraging. I went on smiling at him when we ran into each other by the college gates, occasionally quoting Pope, and he went on returning my greeting with the same lack of interest. I wondered if I'd sounded too enthusiastic about *The Dunciad* and told him, the next time we met, that I was going off it. I received a blank acknowledgement. He was not, I realised, going to be easy to please. The next week, term began in earnest and a person not at all like the person I'd been talking to turned up at Leavis's seminar room and distributed practical criticism sheets. If this was Dr Leavis, then who had I been discussing *The Dunciad* with? I discovered, in due course, that it was a college porter, I believe called Tony.

Some mistakes you never fully recover from. I should really have written about it for *Varsity*, the student paper, but I couldn't be certain they'd understand the play I made with personal agony. And what if Leavis himself were to have read it? He hadn't as yet rethought his position on Dickens so I didn't know where he stood on comic writing broader than Jane Austen's or Henry James's. Three years later I wrote a knockabout piece called 'The Ogre of Downing Castle' – John Heilpern was somehow in a position to commission it from Oxford – which was a response to the pious outrage caused by Leavis's rampaging lecture on C. P. Snow as novelist, thinker and proponent of *The Two Cultures*. As it turned out, Leavis liked it, or told me he liked it, signed a book for me by way of thanks and warned me to be careful how openly I supported him in a world which generally didn't. So maybe he would have enjoyed a funny article about confusing him with a college porter who didn't much care for *The Dunciad*.

I revered Leavis and still do. He could be as tedious as any old soldier reliving his war memories when the subject, say, of his antique spat with T. S. Eliot came up, which it did at least once in every three seminars. The details are abstruse and personal but might be boiled down to Leavis believing Eliot abandoned him when they were taking on the literary establishment in the matter of Milton's greatness. 'He's a worm,' Leavis would always find a way of concluding, meaning Eliot, not Milton. To many an American student the opportunity to hear F. R. Leavis call T. S. Eliot a worm was worth the cost of a bus ride across Cambridge, and not impossibly an airfare from Boston. They would gatecrash our college seminars, let ambitious adulation shine from their faces in the way only American scholars can, and ask the question that would lead Leavis into that thicket of regret and recrimination from which the only escape was the code word 'Worm'. Because I didn't want the entirety of these precious seminars consumed in this way, I took it on myself to request 'foreigners' to refrain from asking such stupid questions as 'Dr Leavis, can you tell us your view of T. S. Eliot?' Some accounts of this fractious period in the history of our civilisation allude to shadowy groups of Stasi-like bully boys who shielded Leavis from awkward scrutiny, allowed no dissension from the canon, and in other ways prohibited free speech. Mystery solved: chief among those shadowy Stasi-like bully boys was me.

Undistracted by bland visitors and bitter memories, Leavis could get on with teaching us how to read. I still hear him – no, in truth I still *see* him – reciting Shelley's immensely subtle evaluation of Wordsworth's genius in *Peter Bell the Third*. '*He had as much imagination / As a pint-pot ...*' But if we thought that that was Wordsworth done and dusted, wait for this –

Yet his was individual mind,
And new created all he saw . . .

Leavis's eyes – themselves once said to be hypnotically Shelleyean – flamed as he declaimed that all-saving 'Yet'; and I don't expect ever again to hear 'individual mind' given such momentous emphasis. What made a poet individual, and what made his creations all his own, were vital considerations for Leavis. He paid a debt to Eliot here, often quoting from his essay on the eighteenth century – 'Sensibility alters from generation to generation in everybody, whether we will or no; but expression is only altered by a man of genius.'

He spoke and wrote wonderfully well himself about tradition as a living, changing continuum, but it was the men and women of genius who altered expression he believed it was his life's work to champion – hence his see-sawing between Eliot and Lawrence whose contributions were so vital but whose geniuses were so antithetical.

Hence, too, his deep appreciation of what Shelley saw in Wordsworth.

'New created all he saw . . . *new created*!' Did we get that? There was no prior *seeing* that the poet had to internalise into art. Creation *was* seeing.

The way that great poetry found its way to meaning – a world away from 'statement' – was at the heart of his teaching and explained the high importance that literature had for him. He could blow hot and cold on Shelley and was never colder than when comparing a speech from Shelley's play *The Cenci* –

O
My God! Can it be possible I have
To die so suddenly . . .

113

– with Claudio's 'Aye but to die and go we know not where' from *Measure for Measure*. We pored over the well-worn sheets on which Leavis had reproduced the two passages. The point of the exercise was not to show that Shelley was a lesser poet than Shakespeare. What the explicitness of the Shelley helped us to hear was the linguistic tactility of the Shakespeare, the slow accretion of icy dread as the experience of cold confinement line by line suffocates Claudio and all but makes a poet of him.

Of the calumnies Leavis's work attracted in equal measure to the devotion he inspired, the most enduring have been those that impute a proscriptive narrowness and insularity to him. 'The great English novelists are . . .' – doesn't that prove it?

Only to the tone deaf. 'The great English novelists are' raises a standard. Here, here, is what writing in English can achieve. This, this, is what, imaginatively, 'English' means. It does not imply that no other novelist, writing in English or any other language, is worth our attention. And those who heard him lecture, or just ruminate in his morning seminars, will remember how he encouraged the widest possible reading, how effortlessly he would quote from Dante or Nietzsche or Mallarmé.

But I wasn't here for Mallarmé. I was here for the full English. Just the word 'English' as Leavis understood and employed it was enough to thrill me, the little Jew from Manchester. Cambridge kept me at arm's length, but as long as I was listening to Leavis I forgot there was a 'Cambridge'. It was as though I'd finally scaled that wall from the other side of which, in earlier days, the prefab boys had thrown stones at us. There was nothing insular about the idea of 'English' if you came from a shtetl in Lithuania.

By comparison with the flash bang wallop of George Steiner who was teaching across the city in Churchill College, Leavis could certainly appear inward-looking. There is a way in which theirs was a story of two wars. Steiner, who gathered

114

all literature to him like a magpie, while questioning the value of all of it in the light of the Holocaust, was decidedly excitable in the post-Hitlerian manner of European intellectuals. If there was a name to drop, Steiner dropped it. If there was an obscure still-to-be-published Balkan novel to be found, Steiner not only found it but discussed it in the language in which it had yet to be written. Leavis, on the other hand, was a casualty of an earlier war from which he'd emerged gassed and vatic. His urgencies were an earlier generation's. The well-being of English civilisation and letters after the cataclysm was enterprise enough for Leavis. The problem of evil, as Steiner would go on to address it, was beyond solution. For Leavis the great questions were more specifically located. The job he set himself was that of tribal prophet and salvager. Hence, again, the importance to him of Lawrence and Eliot, the former so earnest in his search for whatever might yet flower from the ruins, the latter in his articulation of what might yet be articulated. And hence that provocative opening sentence of *The Great Tradition*. It wasn't a ranking exercise. It was an attempt at remembering and reconnection. *This* was the conversation we'd been having before the Great War. *This* was what creativity had looked like. If England was ever to be England again, these were our formative voices.

As a mid-century Jew I might have been expected to find Steiner's voice more sympathetic. *My* hopes hadn't perished with the death of Edwardian England. Let's be honest: my hopes hadn't perished at all. But the nearest thing to the destruction of the Jewish people had taken place where Steiner had pitched his tent intellectually. Yet I heard more in Leavis's voice that I recognised and found sympathetic than in Steiner's. 'Neither of the Leavises was at all posh,' David Ellis writes, 'and that created an atmosphere at Downing that suited me. I found it a congenial home in a university whose predominantly public school ethos filled me with a social discomfort I never entirely got rid of during my whole time there.' David Ellis and I had been to the same school but I had the added discomfort of being a Jew, so I found Leavis's provincial, outsider status doubly congenial.

Steiner was not a product of the English public school system. It was his internationalism I found alarming. I encountered him only once at that time and he was quick to pick me for what I was. I had gone to one of his seminars, I no longer remember on what subject, and had asked a question which I also forget. I must have been incensed because as a rule I was too shy to ask a question. No sooner did I speak than he too grew incensed. 'I will not tolerate,' he said, 'being dragged into this provincial circus.' However faltering my memory of the occasion, I can vouch for 'provincial circus'. The thing he picked me for, I had not the slightest doubt, was a Leavisite thrower of custard pies.

Unless, unless, he'd picked me for the other thing I was ... But in that case, oughtn't he to have extended the hand of brotherhood?

Looking back, I wonder whether I had absorbed a bit of Lawrentian anti-Semitism and transferred it to Steiner, seeing in him something of Loerke, the 'wizard rat' in *Women in Love* whose cosmopolitan nihilism both fascinates and appals Lawrence. The provinciality for which Steiner had no time was, in my understanding of it, the very English particularity I found in Leavis. You got to the big questions, I believed, by a subtle interrogation of the little ones; you arrived at everywhere only by revering somewhere. 'Whoever saves the life of one man saves the whole world.' If I felt that to be a lesson I learned from the way Leavis read, it is ironic to recall — at least in the context of Steiner — that its origin is the Talmud.

So while I was inclined to think that studying English literature with Leavis at Downing was a million miles from being Jewish in Cheetham Hill, and did all I could to make no new Jewish connections – pooh-poohing all solicitations from the Cambridge Jewish Society for example – I was probably misguided. My Leavisite passion for the actual would only lead me back to things Jewish in the end.

Because of the name Leavis, and the biblical echoes in Leavisite, some people wonder if he was a Jew himself or had Jewish connections. Jew himself no. But his wife was born Queenie Roth, daughter of Morris Roth, hosier and draper, and Jane Davis – a Jewish family from Edmonton who, it is said, sat shiva for her, that is to say mourned her as one mourns the dead, when she married Leavis. I was taught by her briefly, but while she was rumoured to have a soft spot for her husband's Jewish pupils – Morris Shapira, who directed studies at Downing at that time, was a case in point – I never felt she had one for me.

In Shapira I encountered sophistication of a sort that was entirely new to me. Gay, elegant, shyer even than I was, possessed of what I took to be the most elegant taste in draperies, carpets, kitchenware, audio equipment, familiar with every word Henry James wrote, and I guessed contrapuntally ignorant of the environs of Cheetham Hill, Hightown, Prestwich or anywhere else Mancunian, he made me feel ashamed of my background as Leavis never did.

Although we were companioned in excruciations, we grew to be friends of sorts a few years after we both left Downing, I because I'd graduated, he because the college's hateful post-Leavis politics – removing all trace of FRL and his unmannerly controversies – made it impossible for him to stay. We found ourselves in Melbourne at the same time in the early 1970s, he on an academic exchange, I pushing a wheelbarrow. He cut a strange figure in the city's bars and billiard halls in the sarong he'd decided was the right thing for the climate. But he was much loved by Australian students and colleagues who called him Mozza, roughed him up playfully at parties and even threw the odd glass of low-quality claret at him. I won't go so far as to say that Melbourne all at once made him easy-going, but it was plain that he liked being with people who didn't frighten easily. Given what was to happen to him when he returned to his lectureship at the University of Kent, it's a tragedy he didn't stay.

'We don't need Nietzsche to tell us to live dangerously,' Leavis used to say. Morris Shapira certainly didn't. He must have had a taste for what I think is called 'rough trade'. He invited someone he met at a bus stop back to his apartment in Canterbury – I picture Henry James's 'bad-faced stranger' encountered in a house of quiet – and that was that.

It all swirls around now. Was Downing a house of quiet? Were we innocent of the passions we aroused and innocent of self-knowledge half the time, mere attendant disciples at the Passion of St Leavis, undeserving of the connection, not ready, never ready, to join him on his pilgrimage? Was that what Morris Shapira was doing there – trying to show us a way out, whispering in our ear, like a Jewish Satan, that there were other routes? Well, not his, that was for sure. The longer I go on thinking about Downing the more I realise I haven't the first idea what happened there.

Morris Shapira, above all, I think about often. Once, at a seminar in his Cambridge apartment, he put on a record of the Nadia Boulanger Ensemble singing Monteverdi madrigals, I don't recall why. I spent years trying to lay hands on that record and eventually found it as a compact disc. I play it when I want to recall him, in particular the exquisite madrigal for five voices, 'Lasciatemi morire'. And then I weep for him and wish I'd known him better and longer. And weep for me too, wishing I'd been someone else.

It was at Cambridge that the melancholy boy I'd always been turned into the fully-fledged depressive man.

Did I actually suffer from depression? I don't think I have a right to claim that exactly. There was no crisis of the sort John Stuart Mill underwent. I didn't reach the point of believing I had nothing left to live for. Nor did I approach that 'utter hopelessness' Dr Johnson describes and of which he feared the only outcome would be 'madness'. But I awoke each morning to a piercing realisation that life was and always would be disappointing, that everything I had hoped for was unlikely to come about, and that even if some of it did come about I was in the wrong place to enjoy it. So where would the right place have been? There you have me.

That I had reached the age of nineteen without writing more than a flimsy pamphlet about the Leavis/Snow controversy and the odd sentence of what might just turn out to be the novel I had for so many years believed I had it in me – more than that, had a *duty* – to write, was part of the problem, but whether it was a cause or a symptom I lacked the clear-sightedness or the courage to decide. But every day began the same, as though something I had gone to sleep with had been lost in the night and all that remained was the same old despairing consciousness of uselessness and failure. If the day was cold and wet, it mirrored the state of my soul. If the sun shone it reproached me for having squandered hope and opportunity. You can take only so much desolation without a part of you dying. In my case it was buoyancy. I went through Cambridge without merriment or joy.

A Downing acquaintance to whom, for no reason I can explain, I once described this condition, told me he'd had a Jewish friend at school who'd spoken of his experience of waking in identical terms. Was it a racial thing? he wondered innocently. Were Jews sad because of what they'd endured, or because they were always far from home, or because they'd learned the folly of daring to hope? Explanations of this sort struck me as treacherous, since they evoked the figure of the Wandering Jew, cursed for all eternity because he'd taunted Jesus on the way to the Cross. I found it hard to accept that the grief of waking was a punishment for a crime thousands of years old. But I went on wondering if the bitter, bottomless sense of wasted opportunity which accompanied that grief, whether as cause or effect, could indeed have been a Jewish legacy. Nothing to do with Christ but with that sense of higher calling – the requirement that we be a light unto nations, the conviction that God had chosen us for sacred purpose – of which we were bound ever to fall short.

Of all literary educations said to be bad for you, a literary education at the hands of F. R. Leavis was sometimes said to be the worst. The proof of that being how hard to write Leavis's students found it, indeed how contemptuous of 'actual' writing they often were. Morris Shapira looked at me in the strangest way after I wrote 'The Ogre of Downing Castle'. His eyes seemed to slide off his face. It was as if he didn't know me. This was not the sort of thing Downing men did. Morris himself wrote almost nothing and when, after years of editing and selection, he did put together a collection of Henry James's criticism it came out with a preface by Leavis. The rumour was that Morris couldn't do that part himself. I have no way now of verifying that. But that we believed it at the time testified to how we too – we Leavis men – felt we had been trained to have sensibilities so fine that no articulation could violate them. And certainly very little violated mine.

Nonetheless, I believe we do ourselves a disservice. Yes, maybe the Lawrentian phrase 'life-affirming' didn't always get the rough treatment it deserved – all art is life-affirming, even art that tries hard to be life-denying; and yes, Leavis set a high and sometimes unforgiving standard as a critic, but have I not said that it was because I was already an unforgiving and hyper-critical boy that I wanted to be taught by him? Most of my fellow students were the same. We weren't there to scribble. We were there to be discriminating. But that didn't mean I had shut the door on scribbling altogether. Indeed, my friend John McClafferty and I co-wrote a slangy pilot for a TV comedy sitcom based on my market experiences, put it in a binder, took it to an agent in the autumn of 1962, and still await its explosion onto the screen.

I don't accept that Leavis inhibited creative genius. What he did was make us see what a rare thing creative genius was, and how it needed to be distinguished from creative mediocrity. He was not to be blamed if many of us came also to see, under his tuition, wherein we were deficient. And who's to say that just as many of us didn't try harder as a consequence? Besides, falling silent before great works could just be the best of all apprenticeships for a writer. How do you learn to write? By first learning how to read.

But apprenticeships often pall. Too many years go by learning your trade when all you want is to go out into the world to practise it. And who was stopping me? I was stopping me. It was in my nature – or at least my Lithuanian nature – to judge myself and be disheartened. Since I couldn't be Dickens, I couldn't be anybody. Which, I consoled myself by thinking, at least meant I didn't make a fool of myself. Unless to be as tongue-tied as I allowed myself to be *is* to make a fool of oneself. And that's my Ukranian nature speaking.

That I didn't succumb to a still greater malady and die of loneliness at Cambridge I owe to two people. John McClafferty and my girlfriend Barbara Starr. McClafferty – whom I did not consent to calling Claffers, as others did; I preferred the stern Highland music of McClafferty – was not among those who seemed to have met everyone else already. I found him alarming at first not on account of who he knew but *what* he knew. He had done part of a degree at a Scottish university before coming South and I was at pains to persuade myself that his partial degree was the reason he was so much better educated than me about everything. In my heart, though, I knew that McClafferty would have come out of kindergarten better educated than me. He educated himself as naturally as other men breathe. Without appearing to have made any effort, he went to bed every night more knowledgeable – in the best sense of that word: made wise by what he'd come to know, enthused and enlarged by the experience of reading and looking, looking at the breathing world as well as looking at art – than when he'd risen in the morning. Sixty years on, he remains the most comprehensively interested and interesting person I have ever known. Infinite in his curiosity and variety, and age has not withered him. We still meet for lunch and I still fantasise about a time when I will have read more, seen more, thought more, since we last met, than he has. It won't, of course, ever happen. Instead, he will have acquired another language, visited another remote monastery, changed his mind about another classic (he recently confided to me that he thought *Middlemarch* had longueurs!!!), gone to another art class and painted another painting.

I did what I could to distract him while we were studying. For one year we shared a house on Parker's Piece. My room was directly above his and when I could bear to read no more I would tie a knot in the cord from my dressing gown, dangle it out of my window and make it swing loudly against his. He would resist these blandishments for hours at a time but eventually he would relent, open his window and shout up, 'Man alive, what now?' 'Hoots, hoots, McClafferty,' I would call back. Which was code for wondering if he fancied a curry. He always did.

He was awarded a very good degree. I wasn't. There is some justice in the world.

Hoot, hoots, McClafferty.

Barbara Starr was a hairdresser from Manchester with whom I'd fallen in love on a trip back home in my second year at Downing. I'd known her from a distance, thought she was alluring in the Ingrid Bergman style, but lost my head when I saw her doing a Shirley Bassey impersonation on a table at a party. Her fingers touched the ceiling. I looked up and fell in love, first with her fingers, and then with the rest of her. Though I believed her to be beyond me, I made her laugh and somehow persuaded her to go out with me.

She visited me at Cambridge when she could and when she couldn't we corresponded several times a day, I on mimsy college stationery, she on scented blue paper which I could smell as I approached the porter's lodge to collect my mail. So could Tony. 'I'm surprised these don't make their own way to you,' he said, handing me the day's bundle. But I was living in digs by now and couldn't risk going back there with the latest letters in my pocket, for fear I'd faint in the middle of Parker's Piece, overwhelmed by their promise. For the whole of my final year I sat in the college library and read what she had written with a fervour that could have led to blindness.

In the event I kept my sight but lost my mind.

IN OUT, IN OUT, SHAKE
IT ALL ABOUT

I was the last boy in my circle of school friends to go out with
a girl. And just about the first to marry.

Gabriel, John, Harry, Malcolm, Mike, Stuart, Ivor – as our
number thins out, I feel I must wear their names like amulets,
the living and the dead. We are down to about fifty per cent.
They were all at my wedding. Malcolm danced with my aunties. Just before he died, two years ago, he rang me up from
Gothenburg to sing to me. His chest was ruined and I couldn't
make out the words, but I knew it was a love song to our
youth. John Heilpern was my best man. As I write I learn that
he has died in New York. If I stop to bow my head for him I
fear I won't be able to lift it again. Harry Cowen had previ-
ously gone out with the bride. He was the most political of us,
voted Labour all his life, did wonderful comic imitations of
our friends, and died after two weeks of quiet weeping in
2017. Those of us who saw him just before his death cannot
get over the sadness of it. Whatever he confided to his wife
and daughter and stepdaughter at the end, to us it was as

though there was nothing to say that his tears couldn't say for him. We were all coming to an end. We'd had our time. A more discreet goodbye to our joint adventure is hard to imagine. It was in Harry's boisterous company, anyway, that I first set eyes on Barbara. Too grown up for him, I thought. Too grown up for any of us. How had it happened that one minute we were little boys and then we were going out with real women who wore pencil skirts and high-heeled shoes? Some of us were anyway. The old mystery. I had only to turn aside for a second for everything to have changed when I turned back. This time they had all gone to some sort of Jewish holiday camp or pretend kibbutz on the south coast for the summer. Felixstowe rings a bell. I don't know why I hadn't gone with them. Required for market duties, I can only surmise. 'Lady over here and a lady over there – come on, Charlie, chop-chop, or is that long face of yours too heavy to carry?' while Gabriel, Harry, Ivor, John, Malcolm, Mike, Stuart were buying Babycham for barmaids. Six weeks later they were back with deep voices, beards, haystacks of pubic hair, and girls who'd grown into women.

I am still trying to catch up.

My mother must have cottoned on. 'There's plenty of time,' she once enigmatically declared.

'For what?'

'Making mistakes.'

There was one mistake all my friends' parents were afraid of. Getting the wrong girl pregnant. And who was the wrong girl? At this stage, all of them. But in particular – you know . . .

If my parents worried less about this initially it was because I was unlikely to get a girl pregnant buried alive in my room, sobbing over Kirsten Flagstad's rapturous conflation of Love and Death and Jussi Björling warming Mimi's freezing little fingers. But my mother was too shrewd not to see what followed from such gorgeous abstinence: the first time I spoke to a girl – and she wouldn't have to be a Mimi or an Isolde – I'd ask her to marry me. She and my father were happily married, she assured me, which was always the prelude to her telling me that, happy or not, they'd married too soon. Look at us, stuck in Manchester, with no education, no money and no prospects. They didn't want that to happen to me.

No chance of that, I laughed, though no one else would have called it a laugh.

Unable to distinguish between premonitory adolescence, phantom adolescence and the thing itself, I date what can only sadistically be called my erotic life from the age of about six when I began to feel the absence of a girlfriend as an anguish. Between the ages of seven and ten I ruined every hard-earned family holiday in Blackpool or Morecambe with my tantrums and tears. My parents shtupped me with ice cream and toffee apple and candyfloss, hoping one of those would bring a smile to my face. No dice. What I was crying for was the prepubescent, post-toddler equivalent of a mistress, many a suitable candidate for which position I passed and appraised as we walked along the promenade but lacked the boldness to address. I passed my tenth, eleventh and twelfth years alternating between Wagner's 'Liebestod' and a lighter operatic trance, in which either duty on my part or consumption on theirs dragged me nightly from the arms of buxom waitresses in Heidelberg or wasted artists' models in Montmartre. The years between thirteen and sixteen were not much of an advance. My father feared I would never come out of my room. Yes, a boy needed his privacy but my taste in music was causing him concern as was the amount of time I spent buried in books. In fact I read less, in the conventional sense, than he imagined. Mainly I would lie in bed and obsessively spell out the spines of all the books on my shelves, either to try to picture my own name on a spine one day or to make my head spin (there's a Yiddish word for this: *kopdreyenish*) by reciting titles and authors backwards. *Wenk Eisiam Tahw* by Semaj Yrneh. *Omortson* by Dranoc Hpesoj. *Amme* by Netsua Enaj. Dranoc and Netsua — those that didn't come out sounding Hungarian came out sounding Japanese. How many Japanese novelists, I used to lie there and wonder, sounded English when you read their names backwards?

It crossed my mind to tell my father that this, rather than actually reading books, was how I whiled my life away, but I suspected that would only have made him worry about me more.

Shyness was a problem he tried to help me eradicate in myself by forcing me into whatever I owned that looked like party clothes and pushing me out of the front door. There was always music coming from someone's house on our street and my father assumed that once I was out I would do as he'd have done and make a beeline for it. The possibility that I would huddle snail-like under the privet hedge in our front garden until it was time to return, pretending I'd had a whale of a time, never crossed his mind. Tell enough lies early enough and you're bound to end up a novelist. In answer to the question 'So how was it?' I invented balls that would have put St Petersburg society to shame. Pip came up with a gold coach after he returned from a day in Miss Havisham's company. I beat that by a mile. I conjured a circus complete with dancing bears and a rabbi dressed as the Pope swinging from a trapeze ... What, at number 19, a sunshine semi just like ours? Yes, but they had cellars with an underground swimming pool and a car park big enough for three Rolls-Royces — but still I couldn't conjure a girlfriend.

For my seventeenth birthday my mother bought me driving lessons and changed my life. I was no longer needed on the gaffes. My father was losing too much money to continue with the market stall and had begun to 'do the knowledge' necessary to become a black-cab driver. This meant that I was free to take a holiday job driving for Walls Ice Cream, initially delivering catering packs to hotels along the Ribble Valley in a three-ton truck whose gears I couldn't double-declutch and so could be heard crashing from Clitheroe to Bowland, and later, once they'd decided I was better suited to driving something more manageable, selling directly to the public from a mini fitted out with a refrigerator and chimes. The mini was too small to stand up in so I had to climb out in all weathers in my yellow charlady's pinafore and serve rock-hard wafers from the boot, sometimes while holding an umbrella, for it is one of the ironies of the ice-cream business that more people answer the chime of 'Greensleeves' when it's cold and wet than when it's hot and dry. You won't be surprised to learn that I asked to be put back in the three-ton truck, not only to stay dry and recover a bit of dignity but because it enabled me to join the other van drivers at an uninhibited transport cafe in the centre of Bolton. We ate the same meal every day: two steak-and-kidney puddings swimming in boiling gravy, the joke being that they resembled women's breasts. One thing leading to another they'd discuss their love lives, bragging about their conquests of the night before who as often as not turned out to be their own wives. Until then it had never occurred to me that a man might include the mother of his children as a notch on his belt. This was not, I believed, something Jewish men did. Nothing prohibiting such a thing appeared on any tablet the Lord handed down to Moses; just not the way we talked about the women to whom we were bound in holy wedlock. That there were other ways a Jewish man might disrespect his wife, I would soon discover. But not this.

'Now what about thee, Howard?' my fellow drivers would ask. 'Bet you're having a good time of it. Single chap like you.'

'Ho, ho, what!' I'd answer, which could have meant I was or I wasn't. But in truth I was having a better time than I'd had thanks to my mother's gift of driving lessons. *From* a vehicle I could talk to young women and *in* a vehicle I could talk to them without blushing. Between sixth form and Cambridge I became one of the young gallants of Manchester. One of the young gallants of Nottingham, too, on account of my friend Malcolm Meggit reading somewhere that Nottingham's lace factories employed countless young women who had nothing else to do in the early evenings but gather in the city centre and wait for Jewish boys from Manchester to come charging through in their dormobiles. It's possible we chose the wrong nights, but there were no more women to be seen in Nottingham than we could encounter back home cruising round Albert Square. Malcolm couldn't yet drive himself so relied on me to get us around the country. 'Leicester,' he said to me a few nights later. 'Why Leicester?' 'Hosiery.' After the same result he urged me to drive us to Northampton where more than a million women were said to be employed in the manufacture of shoes.

I told him I had a puncture in three tyres.

Being one of the young gallants of Cambridge turned out to be a trickier proposition, partly for the reason that we weren't allowed a car but also because there were no young women in Cambridge to be gallant to. This has been denied by many of the men – 'man' being Cambridge argot for 'boy' – who were there the same time I was. In their recollection the place swarmed with tottie – tottie being Cambridge argot for 'girl'. When they mention names I shake my head. They weren't what I meant by young women. My mother's present of driving lessons took me to parts of Manchester where, from the wound-down window of my father's dormobile, I chatted with secretaries and receptionists who dressed in anticipation of a business meeting leading to something else, had manicures every morning, and carried themselves like mannequins from Lucy Clayton's, a legendary Manchester model agency that taught deportment by getting its girls to walk with a book on their heads. Put briefly, no Cambridge woman I encountered — that's an important qualification: no Cambridge woman *I* encountered — had what could remotely be called deportment. Yes, they carried books, but not on their heads.

Enter Barbara, who carried books both ways, had elevation, style and a sense of humour, and was free at the time I needed her to be. What Cambridge had been unable to supply, Manchester did. She was unhappy in love when I linked up with her, or had been unhappy in love as a consequence of which her parents had shipped her off to Israel where the change of language and climate did the trick. To my Cambridge friends who wanted to know more about this girl I'd fallen for, I showed photographs of her staring sultrily out over Lake Galilee in a tight skirt the like of which was never seen on anyone studying English at Newnham or Girton. The photograph of her laughing wickedly in the back of Yossel's banana delivery truck outside a kibbutz in the Negev I wasn't allowed to show around. It never left her mother's mantelpiece. Yossel was built like a banana delivery truck himself and had a moustache that bristled as Omar Sharif's had when he came riding out of the desert like a mirage in *Lawrence of Arabia*. It was my impression that Barbara's mother much preferred Yossel to me and believed he'd have made her daughter a better husband and her a better son-in-law. A judgement with which, in retrospect, and on both counts, I can find absolutely no fault.

There was one small obstacle in the way of Barbara and I

happily pledging our troth. Hold on to your hats. **She wasn't officially Jewish.**

That's to say she wasn't entirely, wasn't adequately, wasn't from crown to heel, wasn't in every drop of blood, wasn't under every painted toenail and behind every mascaraed eyelash, wasn't – I was going to say the real McCoy, but that's to add insult to injury – let's just say *Jewish* Jewish.

She could have been half as Jewish and still Jewish enough for me, God knows. Her father was the genuine article – a tall, modest, good-looking Jew with curly dark hair, a profitable market stall (he was somewhere between a shtummer and a pitcher), revolutionary instincts – he had set out to fight Franco in the thirties but was refused entry to Spain on a technicality – and a bad back. The back might have been the technicality. You had only to hear him complain about his back to know how Jewish he was, or why the Republicans might have had second thoughts about recruiting him. You forgive a bad back in a tall Jew. It is a holy affliction, somewhere between a badge of honour and the mark of Cain. If he wasn't in the garden, resting on a shovel, he was in bed with a hot-water bottle. Neither I nor my parents thought he'd make me anything other than a good Jewish father-in-law. The problem was – speaking only halachically, that's to say as regards Jewish law – his wife. Barbara's mother Mary was – well, what is there to tell you that her name doesn't? Mary. She ran a Jewish home, koshered meat, lit Friday-night candles, and played kalooki. But *Mary* . . .

Her maiden name wasn't McCoy but it could have been.

'What more can you want?' I asked my father, when he wondered whether Barbara and I were serious about each other. 'She's more Jewish than you bloody are.'

I was right there. If being Jewish meant knowing anything about being Jewish, then my father wasn't Jewish in the slightest. But he was Jewish in another way. He was Jewish by objection.

What happens now can only be understood with reference to what went on in my father's house in the pre-war years, and that can only be understood with reference to the Jewish exile in Babylon in 598 BCE or thereabouts. We fear marrying out because it's only by marrying in that any vestige of us – scattered across the globe – remains. If we'd assimilated in Babylon this memoir would never have been written, and there would have been nothing for my father's family to have fallen out over. There are parties to that falling-out who are still alive so I must be careful what I say. Let it suffice, then, that this one did that, that that one did the other, that tears were spilled, that things were said that could never adequately be unsaid, that mothers went away, that babies stayed behind, and that my father's soul was marked forever by what happens when a non-Jewish man drops his trousers in a Jewish family, or a non-Jewish woman ... enough. He had nightmares most nights. He cried out in his sleep. He had lived through the shame of scandal and couldn't face living through another.

'It's only a scandal if you let it be,' I said. 'Shame is your choice.'

If there was one subject I could lecture my father about, it was shame. *Shande* in Yiddish. I was the *shande* meister.

But he knew what he knew. 'No,' he answered. 'This is *your* choice. You're the one doing the marrying out.'

'Just tell me why that's so important to you.'

'Why is marrying out so important to me? Because it's not marrying in?'

'And why is marrying in so important to you?'

'Because it's not marrying out.'

His Jewishness was a perfect circle of know-nothingness. Who was a Jew? A person who married in. What aspect of Jewishness was lost when a Jew married out? The marrying in aspect.

He knew so little of Jewish law and ritual that he was eleven or twelve before he discovered that the Passover table his family set every year wasn't set for his birthday. I find this so sad a tale to tell I can barely tell it. But here goes:

His birthday fell more or less when Passover did, and as his parents could not afford to throw a party for him they pretended the Seder meal was in his honour. *How is this night different from all other nights? Because on this night little Maxie is another year older.* But one Seder Night his mother, forgetting, sent him out to get something or other from the neighbours. Bitter herbs? The bitterest herbs there were? And there – not exactly in one glance, but piecing together the details as they dawned on him – my father saw that another party identical to his had been prepared, the same saltwater soup, the same hard-boiled egg, the same shank bone, the same matzohs covered with a cloth. What more evidence did he need that the party back home wasn't his and never had been? The guests sitting round the neighbour's table looked up at him and wondered at his tears. But he couldn't tell them. He hurried home, spoke to no one, and went to bed.

Worse had happened to him. He'd been born a twin but lost his brother when he was too young to remember – that's if you're ever too young to remember. This, my mother believed, was the reason he cried out in his sleep.

Thus, anyway, my father's litany of loss and tsorres.

Whether I'd have gone on to make a life-or-death fight of the marrying-out business I never discovered. I was coming to the end of my time at Cambridge and growing angry with myself for having wasted my student years; angry with Cambridge for being Cambridge; angry with the general tenor of embarrassment that pervaded my college; angry with the rugger types who didn't have the decency to be embarrassed; angry with my moral tutor for never remembering my name and calling me Finkelstein and Strulovitch and Hindenburg; angry with Leavis's critics; angry with Leavis for getting me into this; angry with being angry – so another fight with my father seemed neither here nor there. But I'd have lost because he had unassailable allies – Barbara's parents.

They too, as it happened, didn't want any marrying out. And the solution was simple. Make Barbara – who was already, in all but the finer points of Judaism, Jewish – Jewish in the few small officious ways she wasn't. And while they were at it, make Mary Jewish too. And Barbara's sister Irene. Make 'em all Jewish and there'd be no harm in my marrying all three.

And make me Jewish too, I joked, which no one found amusing.

To my future in-laws I was not so much a problem as an opportunity. The real Jewishness of which my father comprehended nothing was the same real Jewishness they wanted for themselves. There's a procedure for it so long as you're not too picky, i.e. so long as you understand that a conversion to Liberal Jewishness makes you anathema to the Orthodox.

I speak as though I know something of ultra-Orthodoxy from experience but that would be to give a false impression. In the Manchester I grew up in there were only two streets of recognisably ultra-Orthodox Jews – *frummers*, we called them, or *frummies* if we were feeling affectionate. I recall my father once driving us up the first and down the second in order to show us – well, I wasn't sure what. That Jews came in many forms? That there were Jews far holier than us? That wouldn't have been difficult. I wonder now if it could have been pride he was feeling. Behold, we are still here, refusing to capitulate to a hostile world and unapologetically living the life we've lived for centuries. *We*? Well, what if that too were part of it? That in the rapt self-absorption of those pale, other-worldly, scurrying medieval figures my father recognised something of himself.

I hope he did. Blessed are those who don't disown.

That's an odd word to employ, I realise. *Disown*. In what sense were the fiercely and demonstrably religious ever owned by us or us by them?

That question goes to the heart of being an emancipated Jew, but for years I shied from exploring it. No, no, absolutely no, nothing bound us. More recently I've grown uncomfortable with my contempt. Why was it so important to distinguish myself from them? Why, still, can't I let them be?

From the Orthodox themselves I expect no answering perturbation. They know what being Jewish is and what it's not. But it's precisely because their side is so sure of its inviolability that our side, I argue, shouldn't be. I can't say I recognise a kinship with them, or even an obligation to them, but I hear a distant tune. Why would I feel so uncomfortable and even angry when, at a luggage carousel in an airport, say, I see a group of Haredim in full throwback regalia, if I didn't recognise some far familial tie? I wouldn't be uncomfortable if they were neopagans in their nightgowns on their way to Stonehenge for the winter solstice, or a group of Jehovah's Witnesses waiting for their Brooks Brothers suit packs.

Recently I read an Isaac Babel story describing the 'long bony backs ... and tragic yellow beards' of the Hasids of Volhynia and Galicia, in whom there was 'no warm pulsing of blood' but whose 'capacity for suffering was full of a sombre greatness'. I doff my cap to Babel. He loved the warm, wild animal beauty of the Cossacks. But that didn't stop him admiring a different sort of nobility.

What are words for if not to make you think again? *A sombre greatness.*

*

Before I leave the subject of in/out, in/out, Jewish/Gentile hokey-cokey, I must mention my father's putting himself through it all again with my brother some time later. And this time there were no ameliorating factors. My brother's wife-to-be could not lay claim to Galilee, kosher hens or kalooki. When dissuasion failed, my father went into hyper-*verklempt* mode, locked his jaw, stared at ceilings, made a 'finished' gesture with his hands – finished not just with my brother but the whole world, and vowed not to attend the wedding. It was at this point that my magnificent sister, who knew my father's strong and weak spots better than any of us, since she'd been at the sharp end of them both, hit upon a ruse of genius. Ask him to perform his magic at the reception, she suggested to my brother. Tell him only one thing upsets you more than the thought of his not attending your wedding, and that is the thought of his not doing tricks at it.

This my brother did. Whereupon, hey presto, bimsalabim, abracadabra, armed with his collapsible wand, his bucket of silk handkerchiefs, and a dozen decks of dodgy cards, my father rescinded his interdiction, allowing it to be inferred that, in his considered view, however terrible intermarriage was, not spreading innocent amazement with his illusions was worse.

There are two views to be taken of this. I veer towards the more ecumenical of them. When the chips were down, my father dug deep into his pragmatic magnanimity and put giving people a good time before religious literalism. Imagine Shylock releasing Antonio from his debt and offering to sing Hebrew melodies at Portia's wedding.

To return to my future wife's conversion: while I completed my Leavis thing at Cambridge, she and her family were completing their learning-to-be-even-more-Jewish thing in Manchester. They were handed over for tuition to the son of a well-regarded

Liberal rabbi, a man so well regarded by his congregation indeed that he would soon run off with one of them – which is exactly the sort of laxity the Orthodox would say they keep themselves to themselves in order to prevent. Conversion turned out to be a piece of cake. How could it have been otherwise? They were more than halfway there before they began, what with Mary knowing how to kosher a hen, Barbara having looked out over Galilee, and her father being troubled with a bad back. It wasn't long before I was standing with my bride under the chuppah, saying 'I do', stamping on a glass, and receiving two hundred and fifty mazel tovs. Thus did everyone, at least for the time being, get what they wanted.

Three months later we were on a boat for Australia.

'Australia!'

I explained I'd been offered a good job there.

'A job? Do you have to go to *yenevelt* to get a job?'

Strictly speaking *yenevelt* is the world to come. But the word was popularly used to designate somewhere far, far away. Exaggeration was built into it. *Yenevelt* could mean round the corner if your parents didn't want you to go there. By any standards, though, Australia really was *yenevelt*.

'Are there no jobs any nearer?'

As a matter of fact, there weren't. Not for a Leavisite with a poor degree. Leavis was right to claim that many a good 'man' had wrecked a promising career by being too obviously an adherent of his teaching. 'Be careful,' he'd warned me in hushed tones when I'd presented him with 'The Ogre of Downing Castle'. To be hugger-mugger with Leavis against a world of philistines excited me. The biblical association wasn't accidental. I'd entered Cambridge a persecuted Jew. I left it a persecuted Leavisite.

But while it was true that Leavis's pupils weren't universally liked, it was no less true that there were places where they were revered. And the English department at Sydney University – or at least a section of it – was, in this period of its history, one such holy place. Professor Samuel L. Goldberg, a Joyce scholar from Melbourne – which it might help to think of, at least in the middle 1960s, as the Athens to Sydney's Acapulco – had only recently arrived in the latter charged with the task of waking up what had been a Lotos Land of drowsy, over-tenured beach bums, half-hearted careerists, amateurs and anthologisers who had no time for a sentence such as 'The great English novelists are . . .' on the grounds of its proscriptiveness, its Anglocentricity, its promotion of the principle of discrimination, its assumption of the importance of literature, and the length of its words.

The sun shone, the beer flowed, and why should it matter to anyone that some Pommy Puritan considered George Eliot a better novelist than George Meredith? Live and let live – just don't let him live here. What the new professor felt was needed to stir things up was a principled, not to say contemptuous, discriminator like himself, but ice-cold as only the English could be, while at the same time scorching hot from the fires of Leavis's teaching. I lower my eyes in modesty, but after a brief exchange of knowing letters the job was mine. All I had to do was get there.

It cost Barbara and me ten pounds each to migrate. For that we got a four-week round-the-world cruise in a two-person cabin on the *Oriana*, in return for which we had to agree to stay in Australia for two years. We had taken a tearful farewell of our parents who thought they would never clap eyes on us again. My mother couldn't bear to come to the station to see us board the boat train. My father bought us a cine camera to film the trip but wanted to shoot us leaving. This was difficult to negotiate. 'You've still got the camera,' I shouted as the train pulled away. My father, who wasn't built for running, ran after it. I hung out of a window with my arms outstretched. My father couldn't bear to let go of the camera. The shot of me possibly falling out of the train trying to grab the camera that was filming me possibly falling out of the train was too good to miss. And my father wasn't even versed in the theories of *la nouvelle vague*. Finally, he accepted that the train was too fast for him and tossed the camera to me. I still don't know how I managed to grab hold of it.

'Good catch,' Barbara said.

How wrong she was.

12

YENEVELT

I had an unexpected botanical reaction to Australia. I opened like a flower the day I arrived. And I closed again the day I left.

On a hard, electric-blue day in February the SS *Oriana* slid through the Heads. The wind was hot. We could just make out the arch of the bridge, as full of promise as a rainbow. Seagulls twice the size of any I had ever seen in England hovered over us. 'Waltzing Matilda' was playing on the boat's loudspeaker system. Yachtsmen in small crafts shouted us in, as though they'd been here for weeks, wondering what was keeping us. People lined the quay, waving flags and carrying pieces of cardboard with names on. It was an absurdly theatrical entrance, like sailing onto a stage. I felt the urge to cry. I filmed Barbara with her hair blowing, waving back at people she didn't know. That was a great difference between us. She was a promiscuous waver. I waved rarely and reluctantly. She filmed me dabbing my cheeks – 'Sea spray,' I told her – and trying hard, after so many days on the undulating rubber mattress that was the Indian Ocean, to keep the contents of my stomach to myself. The ground would stay unsteady beneath my feet for the rest of my time here. But only a small part of that could be ascribed to seasickness.

Professor Goldberg – Sam – was waiting for us at the quay. Though he was said to have a devilish mind, he seemed an innocuous enough figure, short and round with a mouth like a cherub's. Was he wearing shorts down to his knees? He might have been. Otherwise there was nothing overtly Australian about him. I can't say I saw the devilishness of his internal workings all at once either, but among the innocents with whom I'd mixed at Cambridge I had encountered one or two academics who knew their way around the politics of literature and he reminded me of them. By the politics of literature I don't mean understanding how to secure advancement through publication; I mean deploying the subtleties acquired in reading to gain mastery of those who don't read as well, or who fear being known as a book is known. When I got to spend more time with him I'd be fascinated by the way he peeled an apple, in a single spiral of peel, as though leaving nothing to chance. Sometimes I would feel as the apple must have felt. Or indeed a poem when he'd finished with it. But for now I thought of him as a protector.

'You will stay with us tonight,' he said, 'and before that, if you're up for it' – he noticed me swaying – 'have dinner with the department.'

The department. There, in two words, was the drama – speaking only academically – that would engross the whole of my time at Sydney. Because we didn't in fact have dinner with the department. We had dinner only with Sam's departmental allies. Within an hour of my arrival I wasn't only enmeshed in the politics of Sydney University English Department, I was bound by silken ties of loyalty to people I hadn't known earlier that day and was swearing undying enmity to people I was yet to meet. In the course of the next two or three years there'd be some changing places, but not much. I would go off some on our side – or at least they would go off me – but I never saw much reason to alter the views of the opposition into which I was inculcated that night.

I was surprised to discover this appetite for intrigue in myself. I shouldn't have been. Mischief and satire are part of a writer's equipment, especially a writer who has yet to write. In the absence of a novel, you need to find something to do with the words you spin. And Sydney was to *become* my novel. I would turn it into an actual one years later – *Redback*, I called it – but it wasn't much liked, even by me. I think it never succeeded in rising above its mischievous and maybe even malevolent intentions.

In my defence – not for what I would write about Sydney later but for the alacrity with which I fell into line – I call two glass flagons of wine to the stand. I drank more that first night at Sam's house than I had in three years at Cambridge and, before that, nineteen years in Manchester. But more to the point I drank in a spirit that answered to all my expectations of cultivated depravity: in the company of vivacious and curious people, all too clever by half, all steeped in literature, sarcastic, cruel, alert, opinionated, unforgiving, scurrilous and – so long as you were on their side – flattering. But remember, this was 1965. The great Australian wine revolution had not yet happened. I was offered red or white. Claret or Riesling. And both came in glass flagons capacious enough, had they contained diesel, to power my father's van from Prestwich to Oswestry. As it was, they powered me still further, out of my old constrained life into whole new freedoms: an unashamed volubility, opinions about all manner of things I didn't have when I set out from Southampton, a preposterously judgemental vocabulary I didn't recognise as my own – could I really have pronounced *Lolita* a nasty novel and *Wuthering Heights* a lousy one? – an elaborate air of gallantry that would turn far too quickly to flirtatiousness ... but that's enough. Of my three sometimes triumphant, sometimes inglorious years at Sydney I have already written and spoken more than I should.

Of the departmental colleagues I would grow closest to – the encyclopedist of science fiction, Peter Nicholls, and the short-story writer, Peter Shrubb – I have not spoken enough. Both belonged to the less ideologically driven wing of *the department*, which meant I could charge them with faint-heartedness and they could charge me with the opposite. Peter Nicholls I would go on to see a lot of, in London and later in Melbourne. I called him Pishkie in deference to his entirely accidental Jewish looks. He had an incorrigible sybaritic charm and a warm tobacco-driven laugh. His perception, that the minor characters in literature engaged me more than the major ones, that I had more to say about clowns and night-watchmen than kings and generals, stays with me, though I'm still not sure if I should take it as a compliment or an insult. Peter Shrubb, together with his wife Liane – he a deceptively equable Claude Rains lookalike, she a quicksilver, sabre-toothed Jewish woman who had, I think, been born in Vienna – took on the role of surrogate parents to Barbara and me, inviting us often to their house in Wahroonga, a half-bush suburb on Sydney's North Shore, where we would listen to Mozart, discuss Jane Austen, play carpet bowls and swim (that's to say Barbara would swim) in their pool. With them we enjoyed a bourgeois Sydney life that was largely disconnected from the university and its misdeeds. We felt safe and loved there, if you leave out the hairy huntsmen spiders which would lower themselves from the guest-room ceiling on silver filaments and wake us with their circus antics. 'They're harmless,' Peter would assure us when we emerged pale and shaking

143

after a sleepless night. 'They aren't poisonous.' But it wasn't venom that we feared; what unnerved us was the fact that they had faces big enough for us to see what they were thinking. I fell out with Peter years later because, I am ashamed to admit, he wasn't sufficiently admiring of my first novel. My real father didn't have the words to appraise anything I wrote. Peter did. So go on, Peter – you're in literary loco parentis – praise my prose. He couldn't possibly have known what I needed from him. Who ever does? We made it up, partially. But it's all too late now. What distance doesn't harm, time does.

I loved Sydney beyond words: the panoramic, watery beauty of it, the conviviality of it, the wit and cleverness of it, the freedom of it, the sadness of it – because someone is always leaving and being left, because the natural forgetfulness of things is exacerbated by time and distance and will always strike the leavers or the left as betrayal, and because the infinite promise of its natural beauty, to say nothing of the beauty of its inhabitants, can never be fully integrated into a life that must have its quiet days as well as its tempestuous ones, else a person will go mad. And maybe, just a little bit, I did go mad.

I found a self there I liked better than any I'd found in Manchester or Cambridge. And also a self far worse. But at least it was out in the world. I turned my face to the sun. I forgot to be shy. I forgot to be depressed. I forgot to regard being Jewish as a problem. To be honest, I forgot to be Jewish, so little of an issue was it. I forgot I was meant to be a writer. Why write when life was so beautiful? Or so combative, come to that? Why write a novel when I could stir things up with a snide review of Raymond Williams's book on Tragedy for the *Bulletin*, a dismantling of *The Melbourne Critical Review* and its failure with *Mansfield Park* for the Sydney student newspaper, *Honi Soit*, and a boyishly dismissive article about the poet Yevtushenko for the *Sydney Morning Herald* (the sum total of

144

my creative efforts over two and a half years). Novel? I forgot why I wanted to write one. I forgot my friends back home and couldn't put faces to their names when they wrote to me. I forgot to ring my parents. I forgot to be a good husband. I forgot that I wasn't the world's best drinker and drank too much – more Riesling and Claret from two-gallon flagons to begin with and later from bottles with actual necks as the Australian wine industry, and I in tandem with it, grew more refined. I forgot that it gave Barbara no particular pleasure to scrape me off the floor, drive me home, and contrive to get me up the stairs.

We had found a fourth-floor apartment on Sydney's North Shore with a balcony overlooking Lavender Bay from which we would eventually watch the magnificent shell-shaped sails of the Opera House take shape and fill with wind. They could have been a metaphor for me. Each morning, as often as not the worse for wear, I walked down a cliff face dotted with wild flowers, and boarded a little white ferry that took me to Circular Quay, a seedy, threatening place at night, but which, when the morning sun came charging in from the harbour, felt almost like an Italian piazza, a place to buy fresh cheese, olives and salami, listen to a busker, meet a friend, catch a train or take a bus to the university. It was more than the city's hub; to me, precisely to the degree that it was glamorous and yet not, run-down and yet snazzy, it was the city's soul. I liked to think I was run-down and snazzy myself. I let my hair grow and wore a black leather jacket. They called me Ringo Starr, Fuckin' Poofter and Jesus Christ. For a Christian country, Australia didn't show the Saviour much respect. For a gay country, it didn't show homosexuals – or those it took to be homosexuals – that much respect either. But then it hadn't yet got around to discovering it was a gay country. Not that I was complaining. Once I was punched for looking like Jesus

Christ. A small price to pay for resembling the Son of God. And it was good to have a name. At Cambridge they hadn't called me anything.

Cambridge? Where was that again? *Yenevelt*.

Sydney gave me a second bite at student life. There were times I forgot I was supposed to be a teacher. I treated those I taught as though they were my friends, which wasn't always a good idea, but some were within their rights to think they were teaching me – particularly Dick Nichols who took us sailing and could hum all Beethoven's Late Quartets, and Terry Collits who got me to listen to records of Brahms's Clarinet Quintet and then list the clarinettists in ascending order of virtuosity and plangency. The thing Australians called the Cultural Cringe – that inferiority complex born of distance and European condescension – made the brightest of them compensate furiously, turning deprivation into a sort of intellectual gluttony that put those of us born with art and music all around us to eternal shame. All I had to offer in return was a Mancunian bluffness which I overdid, the fact of having been close to Leavis, which, to heighten its mystery, I underdid, and the clowning I'd developed a taste for in the course of telling the guests at my bar mitzvah reception that my cup of happiness was overflowing to be with them. How far it became the profession of academic to deliver lectures on *Tess of the D'Urbervilles* in the manner of a northern working men's club comedian is not for me to say; but Sydney and Manchester shared a vigorous proletarian scepticism that wasn't abashed by idealism, and I found the quick, iconoclastic humour of Sydney undergraduates very much to my liking. They gave back, anyway, as much, if not more, than they took. I found them inspirational. Thanks to them – there were eight hundred in Second Year Humanities at my first lecture – I discovered myself capable of doing what I had never been able to do for my father on Worksop or Oswestry markets, namely make a noise, pull a crowd, make them listen, make them laugh, sell a line, make them come back for more – in short, show off. *Tess of the D'Urbervilles* turned out to be my plunder line. I tore pages out and threw them to the punters. Over the following months, having secured my edge, I'd get on to the big shticks – *Little Dorrit, Nostromo, Women in Love.*

It wasn't seemly but I'd done seemly. At Cambridge I'd been so seemly I was invisible. Australia gave me a chance to be someone else.

Cheap Johnny had come to Sydney.

That I could subject the classics to such rough treatment yet still rub the seeming stern abstemiousness of *The Great Tradition* into the faces of the old slack Sydney pluralists whom Sam Goldberg had been hired to put out to graze, bemused and angered them. Was literature sacred to Leavisites or wasn't it?

But they were the ones who laughed last, laziest and longest. In what was to become known as 'The Split', Sydney University English Department would divide into Course 'A' and Course 'B', with Course 'A' being more picky about what it taught – on the principle that some books merited and repaid study more than others – and Course 'B' offering to be more libertarian. Ironically, students applying to read English were asked to choose in the matter of whether they should be asked to choose. If you felt uncomfortable with the idea of 'evaluation' – expending greater curricular energy on the novels of George Eliot, say, than the novels of George Meredith – then Course 'B' was for you. Attaching more or less value to this or that writer – indeed attaching any value to anything – was anathema to Course 'B', for whose proponents 'evaluation' was the dirtiest word in the critical tool bag. We who taught Course 'A' wore it, of course, as a badge of pride. The 'Split' finally made it to the front page of the Sydney papers. I sat next to people on ferries who were wondering who the hell F. R. Leavis was. I could a tale unfold, I thought, but kept my counsel. A ten-minute ferry ride from McMahons Point to Circular Quay was nothing like long enough to explain how *The Great Tradition*, written in Cambridge in 1948, had wrought murderous division in a Sydney English department in the 1960s. In the end the Academic Board or some such body stepped in to restore order and, for reasons buried deep in Sydney politics, and maybe taking into account one or two issues of personal propriety, decided in favour of the Lotos Eaters. Leavis was back in his box. Some books weren't better than others after all – whatever 'better' meant – and those who thought they were should start looking for employment somewhere 'better' if they could find it. One by one, the Melbournites crept back to Melbourne and any stray Mancunian was advised to think of going on a longer journey still.

Thus, a little less than three years after unpacking our tea chests of Swedish wine glasses and cutlery we were putting them away again. The triumph of Course 'B' wasn't the only reason to beat an ignominious retreat. In so far as my unbridled 'evaluating' played any part in outlawing the practice from the Sydney University English Department for several years, except in pockets of bold resistance, I have blood on my hands; but in truth I was only ever academic small fry and overzealous discrimination was the least of my sins. Must I admit to the others? I behaved as badly as any discordant, over-susceptible twenty-two-year-old, living far from home, promoted above his station and uncertain what to do next, could be expected to behave. That Barbara, who originally loved Sydney as much as I had, couldn't wait to leave it in the end and has never returned, tells you all you need to know. She came full of energy and hope, expecting happiness and adventure. She took on the role of wife and companion to an immature and often bumptious lecturer with humour and patience. She read the books I was teaching and discussed my lectures with me. She entertained my colleagues. She made better friends of my friends than I did. At any party, hers was the laughter that rang the loudest. She cut a dash in Sydney, strode the city, swam in the sea, turned her face to the sun and flowered no less than I did, but with this difference – I lost my dignity; she kept hers.

I hope the passage of time makes it possible for me to say this without any disparagement of the love Barbara and I had felt for each other, but it was a bad day for her when she met me. I was in all respects the wrong man for her, the wrong man for any woman, the wrong man for marriage, the wrong man for me. I'm profoundly sorry, Barbara. Someone should have warned you. Beware the bashful who suddenly discover the joys of extroversion. Beware the frog who thinks he has become a prince. Above all, beware the unfulfilled writer who is discontented every day he doesn't write a sentence and finds substitutes for writing in aggression, alcohol, cigarettes, late nights, infidelity and, with a terrible inevitability, falling in love with a student. Yes, that tedious old tale.

It might be that this is where all thwarted ambition leads, but while it was happening I believed I was taking the frustrated writer's glamorous road to ruin. Even the circumstances of my dereliction were not only well known to literature but in a sense *literary*. I had read Dante's *Inferno* at Cambridge and been overwhelmed by the story of Paolo and Francesca who fell in love while reading about Lancelot, himself, of course, an adulterer. 'When we read of Lancelot's kisses,' Francesca tells Dante, 'Paolo kissed my mouth all trembling – *la bocca mi baciò tutto tremante.* That day we read no more.' That the next round of lovers will read of Paolo's's trembling kiss, planted while reading of Lancelot's trembling kiss, and do likewise, goes without saying. From the fatal whirligig of love and literature there is no escape.

Barbara's father would hold my reading, particularly my reading of D. H. Lawrence, responsible for my cruelty to his daughter. But he had the wrong writer. If anyone was to blame it was Dickens. I lectured on *Great Expectations* and *David Copperfield* at Sydney. The heroes of both novels describe a consciousness of there always being 'something wanting', a restless yearning that finds consolation in romantic love, though romantic love cannot assuage it. I had no right to ascribe this melancholy discontent to Dickens himself, but I did. He wrote about it too often and too inwardly, it seemed to me, not to be a fellow sufferer. The inference I drew was that some such sentimental affliction inhered to the practice of writing as surely as the ambition to entertain and enthral, and was the reason writers made themselves and everybody around them unhappy. Very well – I might not yet have written anything but I was progessing well with making myself and everybody around me unhappy.

Explain it how you will, my affair with Anna Sergeyevna, as I named her, after Chekhov's heartbreaking *The Lady with the Dog*, belongs to the history of my becoming a writer. This isn't to say I *wrote* her. But she engaged parts of my imagination that I would eventually go on to write with.

She was exceptionally – to my eye unattainably – lovely. And very much of this flagrant city I had grown to love – at once demure and brash, a Hellene far from home herself, but utterly Australian, a card player with deft hands and dry, sarcastic wit, petite and perfect, dressed not like a student at all but in the summery style of the women who shopped in the expensive eastern suburbs of Vaucluse and Double Bay, dazzling like a tropical moth, and somehow impermanent, an illusion that might not be there the next day, too precious to hold, too impatient to wait, a glimmer of light on the water, like phosphorescence.

Had Pip seen her, while he was looking out to sea wondering why his life always felt incomplete, he too would have fallen for her ... and to hell not only with Joe and Biddy, to hell with Estella too.

'To really love two women at the same time, truly love them, is the most destructive and terrible thing that can happen to a man.' *Happen* to a man, note. The words are Hemingway's, penned in 1964, just as I was 'truly loving' two women myself. 'When you are with one, you love her,' he bemoaned. 'And with the other, you love her. And together, you love them both. You lie and hate it and it destroys you.' I blush for Hemingway's self-pity, self-ignorance and self-aggrandisement as a way of not blushing for my own. That said, the heart is indeed a rogue organ, and will love and betray at the same time, if you allow it.

There is no expiating a crime one cannot reconcile oneself to thinking of as criminal. And regret is too feeble and ungenerous a word to do justice to all actors in this particular drama of the heart. When I have written my last word as a novelist I might know how to talk about what happened.

My plans to return to England with Barbara were thrown into temporary disarray by the stirrings of war in the Middle East. Nasser was mobilising his army along its borders with Israel and had closed the Straits of Tiran to Israeli shipping. Jordan and Syria were sabre-rattling. A fear that this finally would be the war to destroy Israel gripped Jews everywhere. Even those of my Australian friends who would be calling for just such destruction ten years later, or however long it took for their first Marxist fix to kick in, were expressing concern. In answer to Israel's appeal, young Jews everywhere were signing up to give whatever help they could. I asked Barbara if she thought I should volunteer.

'To do what? Give lectures on Thomas Hardy?'

Did she hate me that much?

'I don't know. Fly a jet? Drive a jeep?'

She didn't bother to answer. I didn't doubt she was remembering Yossel her banana-man and wishing she'd stayed with him in the Negev.

A letter from my mother showed how serious the situation had become. I've said we were a non-Zionistical family. With my father I'd discussed the lifeboat option, and with my mother I couldn't recall discussing Israel at all. So her aerogram that began 'The Israeli troubles predominate in all our thoughts' shocked me. 'Yesterday,' she continued, 'Marly and Irene went to get the necessary papers to go to Israel. I haven't signed Marly's yet. The response to the appeal has been fantastic. An emergency meeting held a few days ago was so well attended that an extra hall was needed to accommodate the crowds and still there were hundreds left outside. Max was one of the stewards (with armband) to help control the crowd and also in case of trouble . . .'

My father in an armband I could easily picture. But Marly, who would have been no more than nineteen, flying into danger with my mother's blessing – this suggested another level of emergency altogether. I wondered if my mother half saw Marly's going to Israel as a way of ending the fighting between her and my father over her latest non-Jewish boyfriend – 'It could easily have led to murder, and I'm not exaggerating' – and which had entered the savage silent stage, with my father refusing to stay in the same room with her.

Unlike my father's war with Marly, Israel's war with Egypt and the other Arab countries ended more quickly than anyone could have imagined. It turned from jubilation to sourness more quickly than anyone could have imagined too. At a stroke Israel went from perceived victim to perceived bully. I, who knew nothing of politics, learned a simple lesson. Liberals cannot abide a victor.

As far as our plans to return to England were concerned, the matter was soon sorted. With the Suez Canal closed we would have to take the long route round the Cape, that was all.

On the morning of the day we were to sail away I sat on a bench on Lavender Bay and let my feelings have their way with me. Sorrowed is the only word for it. I sorrowed for the poignant beauty of the place, so far in miles and in imagination from any beauty I had known before, and now about to be strange to me again. For the light of the sky which seemed to emanate from a source as immeasurably distant as the planets, and for the splintered blue of the harbour far, far below, which you could imagine as sapphires rolled between the breasts of mermaids. Sorrowed as I had not sorrowed since the death of my beloved grandmother who had nothing, expected nothing, and waited patiently for the Almighty to disclose his plans for her. Sorrowed for fidelity sworn and forsworn. For all those lurches of joy and fear I'd suffered here. For the writer I hadn't become. For the men I'd wrestled with and called 'Bastard' like an Aussie born; for the women who must have wished my mother had read me less sentimental poetry; for feelings I'd trashed, my own no less than anyone else's. I made irreconcilable promises and left like a criminal leaving the scene of a crime.

13

'MY CAREER GOES BUNG'

I steal my chapter heading from the Australian novelist Miles Franklin's sequel to *My Brilliant Career*. She had a flair for titles. It openly purported to be an autobiography while being a novel, unless it was openly purporting to be a novel while being an autobiography. Who can you trust in this business?

I left Australia in 1967 and went back again – this time by plane and this time on my own – five years later. Given that I would gladly have skipped the intervening years while I was living them, I see no reason not to skip them now. Briefly then: this is a Tale of Three Cities – Manchester, London and Cambridge. In all three it was the Worst of Times.

To be back in Manchester, aged twenty-five, with nothing written but a few dozen lectures, no further degree, and no prospect of another job, felt like a retrogression to the worst years of childhood. The rain it rained every day and within a month it was as though I'd never seen a blue sky let alone sailed to work on a ferry. How long before I'd be a boy at school again, listening to the Gentile boys singing 'Forty Years On'?

For all the restoration of a provisional harmony between Barbara and me on the boat back, I knew I wasn't forgiven. But where did one wrongdoing end and another begin? I did not honour the assurances I'd given when I left Australia – perversely imagining that not to honour them would count as an erasure of the transgression – but nor did I forget the person I'd made those promises to. Put bluntly, I moped between errancies, pulling out my beard the way a caged bird pulls out its feathers, reading one Dostoevsky novel after another – having decided my preference for Tolstoy was misplaced and that I was more the idiot Prince Myshkin and the criminal Raskolnikov than the idealists Constantin Levin or Pierre Bezukhov – and accompanying Barbara and her parents to casinos in the evening where I lost the last of my money on the roulette wheel. Had Dostoevsky not already written *The Gambler*, I would have.

I also put in a few hours a week teaching English at a Jewish school in Cheetham Hill where I got into hot water for making the boys I taught find out who Jesus Christ was and write an essay showing they understood why it was disrespectful, and maybe even anti-Semitic, to call him Yoshkie. When word of this got out I was regarded by some members of the Manchester Jewish community as an anti-Semite myself. And it's just possible that at that time I was. I had to lay blame for my reduced moral circumstances somewhere.

Of this period there is only one happy event to report: our son Conrad was conceived. He was born in London in 1968, Barbara and I having agreed to quit Manchester before I regressed even further into my own infancy. We moved into a house in Finchley with my old friend John McClafferty, his Polish wife Maria, and another Downing College contemporary to whom I haven't spoken a word since. Because he was born late on Christmas Eve, Conrad just missed out on being put in a crib, adorned with holly and crowned the Baby Jesus, an honour reserved for the first boy or girl to be born on Christmas Day. A West Indian baby beat him to it. We took it well and Conrad didn't seem to mind he'd missed out either. He wore glasses from an early age which gave him a comically erudite air. Our friends called him Chomsky, more in deference to his cleverness than any extreme views on Zionism he might have held.

So how did sharing a house with my best and third-best friend from Cambridge plus a newborn baby go? Don't ask. It took only three weeks for each of us to be putting coloured collars round our own bottles of milk. But I had to pay a third of the rent, so it was supply teaching again.

At the school in Bethnal Green at which I taught English to day-release hairdressers, a science teacher called Ernst accused me of being anthropocentric. Funny how often in my short life I'd been accused of being somethingcentric. In Sydney they'd called me Anglocentric, egocentric, phallocentric, Leaviscentric. They could have added harbourcentric. I thought Ernst had a point – I didn't look above me or below me enough; I couldn't take my eyes away from people – but the poet Pope had written that the proper study of mankind was man and I agreed with him. That made me logocentric as well, Ernst said. The pupils had smaller vocabularies and called me Tiny Tim. Not the Dickens character but the musician. He sang in a high falsetto voice and played the ukulele. I could see what they were getting at. Tiny Tim looked dishevelled and deranged. Me too.

It turns out that all along I was Judaeocentric, but I was a long way from knowing that then and, if anything, felt the opposite. What I didn't know was that the further from being a Jew I was, the further I was, too, from being a writer.

★

Delighted as they were to have a grandchild, my parents weren't happy about the way I looked.

'Did anything happen in Sydney?' my mother asked me once.

'Ma, lots of things happened in Sydney.'

'No, you know what I mean. Did anything bad happen?'

I shook my head and laughed.

'So what are your plans now?' my father wanted to know.

'Looking around. Keeping my eyes open for a job.'

He then said something that astonished me. 'You aren't thinking of going back to Australia?'

'I have no plans to,' I said.

'*You* have no plans to? What about Barbara?'

Christ! Where was this going?

'*We* have no plans to,' I corrected.

'Good,' he said. 'We'd find that hard. Your mother missed you a lot.'

I took that to be as close as he would ever get to saying, '*I* missed you a lot.' Which was unfair of me. I was more on guard against intimacies than he was. If my father was reserved with me, I had to be the reason. I didn't invite the warmth in which reserve could melt. Many was the time, in conversation with my father, that I felt we had only just met. He must have felt the same. I imagined him lying in bed with my mother asking her who the hell I was.

On another occasion he asked me how my book was going. I found the question intensely embarrassing. 'All right,' I lied.

Could I have made up the question that followed? 'What kind of book is it?'

By our standards this was more than a conversation, it was an inquisition. If he did speak those words, I can't position him speaking them. Can't see where he was sitting, can't see the expression in his eyes, can't hear his voice in them.

But I do recall my answering, 'It's a novel.'

And I do see him nodding. *A novel . . . Hmmm . . .*

This unexpected and exceptional to-and-fro of ideas creates a hiatus in this narrative that must be filled –

A FATHER AND SON DISCUSS LITERATURE

I have already alluded to the ongoing altercation I had with my father, from about my twelfth year, regarding the second-hand books I smuggled into my bedroom by the filthy boxload from a little market stall in Shudehill in the centre of Manchester. The principle my father couldn't grasp was that you didn't buy a book only to read it and that you were therefore not obliged to finish one before you bought another.

'When will you know you've got enough?' he asked.

'Never,' I said. 'There's no such things as enough books.'

'Well, I'll know,' he said. 'When your mother can't get into your bedroom to clean.'

'Then I suppose I'll have to leave home.'

'As long as you take them with you.'

Easy for me to make fun of him about books. He probably never read one. But over the years, as my library grew and I moved from house to house, I regularly called on him to make me shelves and he never once refused. He built me shelves for the flat Barbara and I lived in briefly on our return to Manchester; he would go on to build me more in Cambridge, London, Cornwall. He would have flown out to Australia to build me shelves had I asked him. Elegant shelves they were too, made of the best timbers and employing the latest techniques and fittings for adjusting shelves.

'So this novel . . . ?'

'This novel what?'

'How much longer is it going to take?'

I'd been lying about my novel. I'd said I was writing one at Cambridge and I barely wrote three pages in three years. Scarcely a letter from my mother went by when I was in Sydney without her asking how the novel was progressing, and I'd replied yes, slowly, but yes ... But ask me now what novel I'd so much as started in Sydney and I would not have been able to answer. Jews don't do confessionals, otherwise – *Forgive me, Rabbi, for I have sinned. There is no novel.* That I didn't feel a heel, or worse a lying dog, I attribute to a conviction I nursed that I was a novelist by simple virtue of wanting to be one. The novel itself was a piece of literal irrelevance. I thought novel, breathed novel, saw and heard the world, as I saw and heard myself, as novel.

The question 'How much longer is it going to take?' brought back to mind his asking me how I'd know when I had enough books.

'Some things are about feel, Dad. You just know. You know when you've mastered a trick. There's no time limit.'

No time limit to finishing, maybe. But what about a time limit to starting?

'But with me,' my father said, 'if I can't master a trick I go to someone who can. Do you have anyone you can go to?'

'Like a senior magician?'

'That sort of thing.'

'I couldn't bear to show anyone what I'm writing.'

'Why not?'

'Because only I know what I'm trying to do, so only I know how to sort it out. The solution to a trick is in the trick, the solution to my writing is in my writing.'

'And if you can't find the solution?'

I wanted to say, 'I kill myself,' but I said instead, 'I just go on until I do.'

'Then you might never finish.'

'It's possible.'

'Sheesh, that will have been a lot of work for nothing.'

He was proud when I did have a published novel to show him, though it would be another thirteen or fourteen years on from this conversation. I dedicated it to him and my mother. I felt they'd waited long enough for it. He kept it in his possession for several weeks before saying anything. What he finally did say was 'It's very nice of you, Howard, to go to the trouble of getting a copy specially printed with our names on it.'

Perhaps for the first time in all the years we'd been father and son I wanted to put my arms around him.

But he had another surprise for me two or three weeks later. 'I don't mind telling you I've been struggling,' he confessed, 'but I think I'm getting the hang of it. You know where it says "All rights reserved"?'

Yes, I knew where it said that. On the same page it gave the address of the publisher and the book's ISBN number and the date of publication. The only page I hadn't written.

I nodded. Yes, I knew where it said that.

'That means no one else can say they wrote it. Am I right?'

'Yes,' I said. 'You're right.'

Not long before he died he presented me with a cyclostyled ten-page booklet entitled *Uncle Max's Magic and Puzzle Book*. 'You're not the only writer in the family,' he said.

Thus were we united in literature at last.

London went the way of Manchester. I was running out of cities to be unhappy in. My longing to be back in Australia had grown into a madness. I was sleeping badly and waking worse. My usual, indeterminate morning melancholy was now shot through with site-specific cravings. The first shaft of light on a wintry day, the merest hint of sun, the smell of freshly baked biscuits (a store in Sydney baked its own biscuits), the sound of laughter that for some reason evoked the laughter that would float across Lavender Bay from Luna Park, a smile or a broad splash of lipstick on a woman's face (could Australian lipstick have been redder than English?) – any one of these could stop me in my tracks, any two would bring me to my knees.

I'd let my hair grow wild and my always long face lengthen even further. If I wasn't having a crack-up I don't know what I was having. People backed away from me on the Tube. It's possible Tiny Tim had the same effect. Tiny Tim! How the mighty had fallen. Once upon a time they'd called me Ringo Starr.

Then Wilbur Sanders, a high-flying New Zealand academic I'd known in Sydney became Director of Studies at a Cambridge College and offered me a part-time supervising job. Though I knew that every day I taught was a day I didn't write, I leapt at it. Soon, going backwards yet again, Barbara and I were in Cambridge.

My friendship with Wilbur would grow to be important. He prised something open in me. Initially, it surprised me we were friends at all, so wide was the cultural chasm over which we met. He wore jeans, I didn't. He hung stuff off his belt, like a backwoodsman, I didn't. He sang in choirs, I didn't. He walked for miles, I didn't. He enjoyed real ale, I didn't. He was published, I wasn't. He meant what he said, I didn't. I made jokes, he didn't. But somehow, in that paradoxical way that Shakespeare loved to make play with – as when the vilest things in Cleopatra so became her that the holy priests blessed her when she was riggish – the very extremity of our differences collapsed them and made them likenesses. And probably never more so, as it happened, than when we were discussing Cleopatra.

We gave Shakespeare seminars together. He a genuine scholar as well as a critic, knowing what he was talking about; I making forays out of my own ignorance which the easily impressed took to be intuition, but which I knew was just ignorance. We were a foil to each other, however it worked. I needed to be in the presence of an ordered and scholarly intellect, and it's possible that my being not at all ordered or scholarly freed something up in him, much as Eliza Doolittle freed up something in Henry Higgins. He believed in me anyway. Believed I should be writing and, when I casually let it be known that I considered Shakespeare to be the first and greatest of English novelists, suggested I start by writing about that.

Over and above these seminars, which didn't bring in sufficient for me to support my little family, I gave individual classes – supervisions, in Cambridge parlance – to Wilbur's students. Supervising doesn't suit everybody whichever side of the supervision you're on. Wilbur enjoyed them because he thrived on the intimacy of the encounter. In the matter of teaching he was a sort of naturist. I was more buttoned up. I'd hated being supervised as a student, so tense did the one-to-one contact become when both parties to it were diffident and apologetic. And I hated supervising for the same reason. Should a student be a minute late I'd find myself praying he'd forgotten, slept in, or met with a very minor accident. Supervising not paying the rent either, I made another of those self-destructive leaps into the ashes of the past and took a stall on Cambridge market.

Humbugs. Handbags, actually, but people unfamiliar with the unholy mess Mancunians make of their vowels thought they heard me say humbugs. So flummoxed by my pronunciation was a group of visiting Australian friends that they searched Cambridge for a humbug stall and gave up on me when they failed to find one. That's the only reminiscence of my handbag days I am prepared to make, beyond saying that I chose bags not swag because Barbara's father had a bag stall himself on Stockport market and could get me started, provided I was willing to cart the boxes on the train from Manchester. No van? Couldn't afford a van.

Thus, seven years after I'd left Cambridge as an unhappy student was I back as an unhappy teacher, shlepper of cardboard boxes, and humbug salesman. Wasn't there a novel, finally, in it? Far too many years later there would be, but at the time I found my life too minutely demeaning to narrate. Let H. G. Wells and Arnold Bennett tackle the retail trade; I was too grand in my non-accomplishment to have truck with any of that.

But if writing about it was unenticing, living it was unendurable. Barbara and I talked things over and agreed it was best all round if I left. I don't say she took pity on me – as far as she was concerned Cambridge market was my comeuppance, for squandering my chances to make a successful academic career in Sydney, for mooning about lovesick when I should have been writing novels or authoring learned papers – but she could see I was in too a bad way to be a husband to her or a father to Conrad. I found someone reliable to run the stall which, after two years, was now doing well enough to give Barbara a living. I would help myself to a couple of tartan travel bags from stock and take off. We didn't discuss what I would take off to do or where I would go to do it.

14

BAH HUMBUG

I rang my mother to tell her my intentions.

She received the news gravely. No expostulations. Just a muted sadness.

'I'm not happy about this,' she said.

'Me neither.'

'I knew something wasn't right.'

'You always know something isn't right.'

'How is Barbara taking it?'

'She's not exactly delighted. But I think she'll be relieved when I'm finally gone. I've been giving her a hard time. I'm not much fun to be with.'

'It's not your job to be fun to be with.'

'What's it my job to be?'

'A husband. A father. You can't just get up and leave your child.'

I didn't need to be told that. 'Ma, I can't go on selling handbags.'

'Humbugs? When did you start selling humbugs?'

'Stop it, Ma. I'm desperate.'

She fell silent. I could hear what she was thinking. Weren't we all desperate at sometime in our lives? That wasn't a licence for just cutting and running. If everybody left their families when they were feeling desperate . . .

Was she telling me that she too had sometimes thought of 'cutting and running'? But she hadn't. Whatever she had felt, she had stayed. That was the difference. I remembered the head pains that had plagued her when she was younger. Terrible migraines that kept her in her bed for days at a time. Could those have been *I'm desperate to get the hell out of here* migraines? Well, she hadn't complained of them for years. So, if migraines passed, maybe the desperation would pass too. But then again, maybe it wouldn't.

'I feel my head is going to blow off, Ma.'

'Can't you just separate in that case and stay nearby? Must it be Australia again? Does it have to be so far?'

I reminded her that she'd given me *The Moon and Sixpence* to read when I was fifteen or sixteen. *The Moon and Sixpence* is a novel by Somerset Maugham about a well-heeled stockbroker who drops everything, his career, his marriage, his children, in order to go to Paris to become a painter. It is widely considered to be inspired, if that's the word, by the life of Paul Gauguin, also a stockbroker, who left his family to live and paint in Tahiti.

'I didn't give it to you to read so you could run away from your responsibilities.'

'Not consciously you didn't, I'm sure. I didn't have responsibilities then, anyway. But why did you give it to me?'

'I liked the story. I thought you might.'

'I did. How could I not? It's about a man who runs away to make great art. I've always wanted to make great art, Ma.'

'I don't think great art is making you very happy.'

'That's because I haven't made it yet.'

165

'I don't think *wanting* to make great art is making you very happy.'

'You don't do it to be happy. We've had this conversation.'

And we had, countless times. Like all boys who read, I'd dipped my toes into existentialism. Happiness was for the small of mind I'd insisted, echoing Paul Morel's words to his mother in *Sons and Lovers*. 'Damn your happiness! So long as life's full, it doesn't matter whether it's happy or not.' Unhappiness wasn't just a failure to be happy. It was an heroic end in itself. A description of the hero's philosopher-father in Joseph Conrad's novel *Victory* was always on my lips. 'One could not refuse him a measure of greatness, for he was unhappy in a way unknown to mediocre souls.' I aspired precisely to that greatness. I had the face for it. But mothers are mothers and mine wouldn't have minded had I aspired to mediocrity instead. Whenever she motioned admiringly at someone else's material happiness I thumbed my nose. The conversation that ensued might as well have been scripted. 'Who wants that?' I'd say. 'I'd rather have an interesting, miserable life than a boring, mediocre, happy one.' 'What about an interesting, happy life?' 'No such thing. It's the misery that creates the interest.' 'You describe to me, then, what you want from life.' 'I want to be fulfilled. I want to write. Blame yourself. You taught me to love literature. Now only writing it will fulfil me.' 'Then write it.'

Back in the present, my mother still didn't see what going to Australia had to do with writing, especially given how little of it she now knew I'd done the first time round. She had a point. Did I really want to go back to Australia to write or was I just after another crack at that happiness I told her I despised? There is a good way of knowing when you're lying to yourself. Close your eyes and describe what you see.

Well?

Me on a ferry.

And?

Me on another ferry.

'I have to do this, Ma,' I said.

'How are Barbara and Conrad going to manage?'

'Exactly as they're managing now. I have a friend who will run the stall more efficiently than I any longer can. I'm taking nothing.'

'Then how will *you* manage?'

'I don't know. Get a teaching job.'

'Do Mary and Leslie know?'

'Yes. Leslie says my behaviour is only to be expected of someone who reads D. H. Lawrence, an Arabist who wrote dirty books.'

'Was D. H. Lawrence an Arabist?'

'No. He's confusing him with T. E. Lawrence. But he's probably right about the dirty books. I've always been easily influenced, Ma, you know that.'

'I do know that . . .' She stopped there, thinking of everything else she knew about me.

'Do you want me to come up and see you before I go?' I asked.

'No. It would be too upsetting.'

'Are you sure?'

'Certain.'

'I'll write to you.'

'You won't.'

'I promise I will. Look after yourself.'

Silence. Suddenly Manchester felt a long way from Cambridge. Then she said, 'Try to be happy.'

So back to *yenevelt* it was.

Melbourne, not Sydney. Most of my old friends had decamped after the Goldberg fiasco. It was from Melbourne that the failed revolution to rouse the Sydney University English Department from its slumbers had been plotted; now the chastened conspirators were back, to a city they had always preferred anyway, bringing with them a younger generation of the hurt and wounded who'd made the bad career move of preferring George Eliot to George Meredith. Other than its Italian restaurants, Melbourne had only one advantage over Sydney in my view: where everybody in Sydney aspired to have a boat, everybody in Melbourne aspired to write a novel. So in that sense, at least, I would be with my own.

I packed my bags and hugged Barbara a long goodbye. No amount of conversing or agreeing or apologising can prepare you for this. The actual moment of saying the words and turning away is an agony I am not sure humans are built to withstand. I don't know what kept me upright. I walked Conrad to his kindergarten, kissed him, kissed his face, kissed his comic-genius glasses, told him Daddy would be away for a little while, and stood at the school railings watching him disappear.

And yes, it went through my mind that to be unhappy in a way unknown to mediocre souls wasn't all it was cracked up to be.

Wilbur drove me to the airport where we clung to each other as we never had before. He must have thought he was embracing a dead man.

15

Am I in Melbourne

or do I dream it? How I got here I have no memory. My old friend and student Terry Collits – Tet to those who love him – collects me off the plane, warns me that whatever of our glorious Sydney past I am hoping to find, I won't find it, and puts me to bed in his house in Carlton. I sleep for days.

When I wake I am in a strange apartment, being cared for by a vivacious New Zealand academic who talks about writing novels as much as I do, the difference being that she is actually writing one. She has two delightful daughters aged about ten and seven who call me Huddy and play board games with me. Suddy – as it seems only fair I call their mother – tells me we met a week or so ago, and have even had lunch out in Carlton. Lasagne. That rings true. I love lasagne. It appears that I am keen on her.

Things go even hazier now. Could it be that I am working as a labourer? A foreman at a building site sacks me for spilling a wheelbarrow of cement. I sack myself from a job driving round the state of Victoria selling educational books. And now I am teaching at a technical college in a suburb of Melbourne called Sunshine North, a dead-flat oily sprawl of closed-down factories, empty machinery yards and cheaply thrown-up railway houses that might just be a suppressed memory of Salford. The pupils, from an inaccessible, mountainous region of Central-Southern Europe, are herded into any class that has a spare desk, regardless of age, gender or whether they speak a word of English. One hot afternoon they clamber over me to get out through the classroom window and begin dancing on the bubbling tarmac of the playground in a spontaneous Balkan rendition of West Side Story. Though none of this is happening in any version of reality I recognise, I hand in my notice just in case it is.

Why I am not lecturing at one of Melbourne's countless tertiary institutions I cannot explain, but in clearer moments I put it down to a) perfidy on the part of old Sydney colleagues; b) the advent of Theory and its accompanying hostility to old-style amateur evaluators of literature like me; c) a mistrust of Cambridge-educated Englishmen who think they can just swan in and steal the best jobs; d) anti-Semitism. This last charge I only ever mean self-mockingly, unless I'm drunk, when I mean it absolutely. Suddy thinks I am being ridiculous, as does Tet who proves he at least isn't anti-Semitic by emptying a friendly flagon of red wine over me. To others he explains away my outbursts as proceeding from 'two thousand years of bitterness' – a phrase which has the virtue of being simultaneously comic and conciliatory even if biblically it's only approximate.

Suddy and I appear to have moved in with Tet and his incandescent companion Mez, but I have no memory of how that's come about or why. Whatever advantages were intended by it are vitiated by the arguments Suddy and I are now having, caused, in her view, by my telling all her friends to get out a) for not supporting my applications for professorships, and b) for being anti-Semitic. I doubt this is a fair description of my behaviour but can't support what I haven't done with hard evidence. When our arguments get out of hand I retire to my room to read a novel (Slaughter-house Five) while Suddy storms downstairs to write one. She types at a speed commensurate with her annoyance, each tap of the keys another missile, I believe, thrown at me.

It must be towards the end of my stay that Mez invites me to a conference on the subject of Women's Literature or Women in Literature organised by Melbourne University where she is tutoring and I am not. Most of the novels I read when I was young were written by women and told of the travails of being a girl. They didn't seem much different to me from the travails of being a boy. I say something along these lines from the floor at the first session to the annoyance of one woman, apparently a mature student of Mez's, who tries to have me removed from the room. It transpires that she is a person of many tribulations and sees the conference as an opportunity to show what she is made of. 'Like you, Huddy,' Mez says.

I have a feeling I like being called Huddy. It means I am not me. But I am not sure I like being compared to the woman who wants me expelled from the conference.

I am still dream-writing, but if I screw up my eyes I see her as I'd seen her the night before, as delegates were turning up at the bar. I'd been at the pool table with my friend Jimbo, a splenetic sociologist with a love of literature unusual in a social scientist and a laugh that explodes without any warning, or indeed without any apparent cause, like a crack of thunder from a quiet night sky. We've been meeting most Friday lunchtimes at the Clyde Hotel on Cardigan Street where we engage in an incessant beer-and-book-filled raillery - a sort of urban pentathlon comprising darts, table tennis, marbles, pool and sarcasm, with literature thrown in as a tie-breaker should one be needed. Tonight's game of pool is looking good for me when I notice her arrive - all flurry and fury, like a hurricane blowing in, tall, big-boned, with strong paper-shredder teeth and a jaw as dangerous as a machete - and see the sort of trouble I liked. 'Now her ...' I say to Jimbo.

He shakes his head and chalks his cue. 'You're on your own there, mate.'

I wait for all his all-destroying, all-alleviating laugh. It doesn't come.

The following day the mystery woman again demands that the organisers forcibly remove me from the conference. Whereupon the fog half clears and I see what Melbourne has all along been storing up for me ...

Six years later, and still daggers drawn, we will be married in a registry office in Wolverhampton.

16

THREE MATES AND A MYSTIC

In the clear light of day, I'll say this for Melbourne – catatonic I might have been, but I *nearly* wrote a novel there.

Carlton – the inner-city suburb into which I was deposited when I arrived and where I stayed the whole time I was in Melbourne – was a voluble, street-café Bohemia, beloved of writers, painters, designers, film-makers, academics, musicians, pool players and pisspots, the last being no less prized for their artistry than any of the others. Suddy buzzed around the streets in her Volkswagen like a maddened fly, writing about everything that happened to her even as it was happening, only stopping at traffic lights to amend her punctuation. Did her industry rub off on me? Put it this way: it made me ashamed of my lack of it.

The drinking helped, too. That's not the paradox it sounds. Australian men, uniquely in my experience, approached the high emotionalism of art, shed tears and found beauty even, in riot. It was in Carlton, anyway, over interminable beers, that I sat in the sun and argued ferociously with Jimbo who devoured contemporary fiction faster than contemporary novelists could write it. Here that Tet, Brahms-lover, wine-thrower, and the best amateur Falstaff that anyone in Melbourne could remember, shaped the thoughts that would finally lead to a prize-winning book on Conrad. And here that I met Geoff Missen, an eminent geographer who liked a spliff, broke his nose playing rugby, cooked marvellous South East Asian food, told the filthiest jokes, and aspired to paint like Matisse.

Of the few hallucinatory pages I scribbled in the time I was in Melbourne – mostly about a gammy-handed Jew pushing wheelbarrows of hot cement across a school playground where a chorus of giant Montenegrins sang 'When you're a Jet you're a Jet all the way' – I showed none to anybody. But I described them to my friends over beers and made them laugh. I was met with no discouragement. Of course I was writing a novel. Weren't we all writing and painting something? To the novel I did publish years later, they would respond enthusiastically. Even Tet, who had turned post-Colonial by then, found a good word to say. 'Bit Jewish for me, but I pissed myself,' I recall Geoff writing to tell me. Melbourne was a dream but I didn't dream this triumvirate of companions. Geoff died three years ago. Tet longer ago than that. Only Jimbo survives to write me combative demurrals in a spidery hand.

A fourth, altogether more shadowy figure tugs at the edges of my memory of Melbourne. Allen Afterman, an American poet who was teaching in the Melbourne Law School, specialising in corporate law, when I met him. Anyone who looked less like the author of *Company Directors and Controllers* would be impossible to imagine. A boulevardier more like. A bit of Simon, a bit of Garfunkel, a bit of Leonard Cohen. We were the same age. Both Jewish. Both far from home, he having been born in Los Angeles and lectured in New Zealand as well as Australia, I a boy from Manchester living in a dream and lecturing nowhere. Both in jobs we didn't want to be in, though he was a successful academic with books to his name and I was a sometime publisher's rep, supply teacher, builder and decorator, who'd published nothing. We went to parties and watched cricket together, laughed a lot, each needing to light up the other's face, each needing to be wise, each needing to be funny. I thought he was handsome and wondered where such a dazzling Jewish chum had been all my life.

He told me he was giving up the law for poetry. He didn't say Jewish poetry. I must have told him the only thing I'd ever wanted to do was write novels. I didn't say Jewish novels. We were entirely Jewish in our rivalry and expressiveness but I don't recall Jewishness being a subject between us. It was as though it was a book we were, for the moment at least, keeping to ourselves. He fades from my memory as furtively as he enters it. One minute he's there, then he's not, and the whole drama of our friendship takes place in the time he's not. Here is why I am filled with regrets. He was my chance to get to know a Jew who, by all appearances, was as secular as I was, a part-time, half-accidental literary Jew, who would turn out to be no such thing, who must have long had it in him – who must have been brewing it while we sat together laughing over beers and Four'n Twenty pies at the MCG – to go the whole, spiritual Kabbalic hog. Wrong animal, but this is no longer jokesville. Afterman went to the Holy Land and became a mystic.

Not all at once. First he went to the country. 'I travel extensively,' he wrote in a note submitted to *Contemporary Authors*, in 1981, 'and currently live on a cattle ranch/fruit orchard in the far south coast mountains of New South Wales.' *Currently*. Not a word you use unless you mean to be somewhere else before long. Far south coast is telling too. Far from what? There's a town called Eden down there. I wouldn't put it past him to have decided that was just the place for he and his beautiful architect girlfriend Susan to wake each day into the wonder of their love for each other. Afterman in Paradise. Afterman before the Fallofman.

But doing what? Growing fruit? Herding cattle? Do Jewish boys from LA know their way around a cow? Let me answer that by analogy. Jewish boys from Manchester don't. So we were miles apart. Unless we weren't. Here's the retrospective fascination he holds for me. I don't as a rule hit it off with Jewish mystics and Kabbalists and they don't as a rule hit it off with me. So why had this been different? Had I recognised something in him I coveted? Or maybe something I already possessed but had no idea how to access. Could Afterman have helped me see into the life of things? And that would explain, too, why I am so angry with myself for having missed a chance with him.

A chance to do what? Or, better, a chance to *be* what?

I have no answer to either question.

How about: *be a Jew*?

We were two Wandering Jews when I met him, but he decided to return to the home he hadn't inhabited for centuries – some sort of commune in the Upper Galilee, a journey inward as much as anything else, in the course of which he farmed, grew fruit, sang gypsy songs, penned more poems, wrote a book about the Kabbala, that most mystic of Jewish mystic texts that searches out language to heal a fractured world, and then in 1990 or thereabouts died, aged fifty.

I see him with his eyes closed, perfected but reduced, the light of merriment gone from his face, a Jew without jokes. Perhaps for the very reason that that isn't the end I expect for myself, he stands as an example and reproach to me. He made good, as it never occurred to me to try to make good, on his birthright. I say I missed out on what he might have taught but I would never have listened. I am too much the nay-saying joker. I don't have time for Kabbalic poetry or secret languages or wise men or gurus. I don't worship. I am not that kind of Jew. I am not that kind of anybody. Never have been.

And then I remember F. R. Leavis. No Jew, but was he not, for me, a sort of prophet? And was I not, to him, a sort of disciple?

And now look at what I have this very moment found on the front cover of Allen Afterman's collection of poems *Desire for White*, to go beside FRL ...

Why, even their Adam's apples are the same ...

17

AND THE END OF ALL OUR EXPLORING WILL BE TO ARRIVE WHERE WE STARTED

Well, here's a turn-up for the books – I am back teaching at a university. All right, it's a polytechnic but in a few years it will be a university. There's a race on: will it become a university before I write a novel?

Suddy is in Cambridge on sabbatical with her girls and I, the eternal lodger, have been billeted with them for a month or so before landing Wolverhampton, a remarkable turnaround for which I must thank 'a fulsome eulogy' – as its recipient later described it – from Wilbur. And that's not all I have to thank him for. He's pushing hard at the idea that we write a book on Shakespeare together. No more slouching, Jacobson. I am rereading the plays, taking yards of notes and firming up my case for *Hamlet* as the first campus novel – Hamlet only being 'down' from the University of Wittenberg to attend his father's funeral and yes – before he can get back to his studies - his mother's wedding. Barbara is married to a man who treats Conrad well. Conrad himself is looking more and more like Chomsky, but with wit. And my parents seem to be blooming. All's well with the world.

Not quite so well with Wolverhampton. I have a prehistory with the place which should have made me think twice before accepting the job. It was at Wolverhampton that I attended England trials as a boy table-tennis star* but failed to make the cut. For some years I could no more bear to hear the word Wolverhampton than the name of the kid who edged me out. Livesey, was it? George Livesey?

To many, Wolverhampton is renowned for having been the constituency of Enoch Powell who made his notorious River of Blood speech just down the road in Birmingham in 1968, predicting race riots on an apocalyptic scale and 'the River Tiber foaming with much blood'. When I told people I was teaching in Wolverhampton, they would ascribe my comic-book gloom to Rivers of Blood anxiety. But despite Powell's prognostications, I found no incarnadined Tiber, just a dismal canal and the blightedness that afflicts most Midlands towns. Wolverhampton suffered from an indescribable municipal dullness, that was all. I wouldn't have minded post-industrial squalor. I had grown up in a poor part of the north of England. I was used to urban ugliness. And I knew how sprawl and smoke and deprivation could make the pulses race. The trouble was, Wolverhampton had no pulse. Faced with the utter forlornness of the place, the soullessness of its architecture, the mediocrity of its amenities, the sense that it had run out before it had begun, the absence, ever, of a single person on the streets who appeared to have an interesting job or be on an intriguing errand, my lifeblood ebbed away. What did people do here? My guess was process applications for dog licences.

* 'The Prestwich Hitter' – not the Prestwich Hitler as an elderly relative read it – was how the *Manchester Evening News* referred to me on its sports page.

Am I to be trusted on this? Although I had always understood myself as a town dweller who found a dusty street more congenial than a leafy lane, it was part of the literary tradition I espoused to view cities and post-industrial provincial life altogether with a revulsion sometimes verging on a madness akin to Lady Chatterley's when she drove through Tevershall and found 'The utter negation of natural beauty, the utter negation of the gladness of life, the utter absence of the instinct for shapely beauty ... The stacks of soap in the grocers' shop ... ugly, ugly, ugly ...'

It went with the territory, for a teacher of literature in the days I taught it — when reading was meant to restore our 'intuitive faculty' — to share Lady Chatterley's nerve-shredded revulsion. We were all Ruskinians of sorts. We too bewailed the death of Shakespeare's England, destroyed by industry, commerce, greed and architectural mediocrity.

So was I merely adding Wolverhampton to the songbook of the too easily appalled? Put another way, had my education made me unfit to tolerate the mundane ugliness that less neurasthenic members of society found ways of living with? Lady Chatterley's mental state had many causes, but should soap in shop windows have produced such shock waves of terror in her? Should the civic dullness of Wolverhampton have produced such a revulsion in me?

And what was I doing plonking myself in the middle of this soulless place anyway? Find yourself a little country cottage, people who knew Wolverhampton had advised me. Drive straight through the town without looking left or right. In ten minutes you'll be in Shropshire. Bridgnorth is nice, so is Albrighton or Much Wenlock. Get yourself a strong pair of walking boots and a dog. This, as it turned out, was exactly what everyone else who taught humanities at the poly had done. There was nothing to have stopped me doing the same;

I didn't have to live in a cold-water flat on the top floor of a gigantic Gothic-horror inner-city Victorian lodging house with no bathroom facilities of my own – I who under normal circumstances would not have chosen to share a doormat let alone a bath. But I was alone and had no need of a garden with a view of the Long Mynd, an apple orchard or a pond for the children to fish in. And I wasn't going to be here long, was I?

I taught there conscientiously at first. By very virtue of their uncertainty as to what they were doing there, what a polytechnic course in the humanities was meant to provide, what they would do with themselves afterwards, the students endeared themselves to me. They were a million miles from the sophisticated, anguished students I gave anything not to supervise in Cambridge. They were poorer, less clued-in, in their own eyes less entitled. They were owed a break. Let's be honest: they were owed better than me. That being the case, I tried to find a better me to give them.

It didn't last. Nothing does when you believe – however vaingloriously – that what you're doing is miles from what you are meant to be doing. Yes, I had a Shakespeare book to write with Wilbur, but already, before I'd even started, I had misgivings: what if it too wasn't what I was meant to be doing?

I was to remain in Wolverhampton, on and off, for seven years. Was that bravery or cowardice? If I close my eyes I can still see the sodden green carpet on the floor of the shared bathroom, see it, smell it, and hear it squelch. Neither bravery nor cowardice will explain why I tolerated that. To find a word that will, I need to excavate the vocabulary of psychosis. I had not rented a *farshtinkener* flat to live in; I had rented a cell in which to expiate my sins, the most egregious of them all being my tendency to turn everywhere I lived into a cell in which to expiate my sins.

Wolverhampton was an act of self-immolation.

Wolverhampton was at once the proof that I couldn't live gracefully, didn't deserve to live gracefully, and the punishment for it.

Today it would be called self-harming. And yet, without Wolverhampton – my St Petersburg, my Malaysian Archipelago, my Elsinore – where would I have been?

18

THE NIGHT THE BED FELL

Had things panned out differently, I might have added to the above list of inspirational equivalents 'Columbus, Ohio' – birthplace of the American *humorist* James Thurber.

Why Thurber has popped back into my mind I can't explain, though the question to be answered is why he ever popped out. He was a favourite of my mother's and I suddenly see her, sitting up in bed laughing, holding a copy of *My Life and Hard Times* (I have the very copy on my bookshelves), tears streaming down her face. I say 'see' her but I heard her first and because I didn't know what the noise was, and my father was away, I'd knocked on her bedroom door to check she was all right. How old I was I don't know, but I see myself as I am now, feeble of foot and rheumatic of shoulder, pushing open her bedroom door to say, I'm sorry, Ma, if I've misrepresented you as the great morbid influence on my life, when you probably read me just as much Thurber as Arnold and Tennyson. You taught me to love his comedy of spiralling calamitousness, and even made me envious of his ability to make you laugh so loudly that you struggled to catch your breath. Wasn't that *my* job?

Having seen what he could do to my mother, I briefly aspired to be the James Thurber of Jewish Manchester. Ask me why the aspiration was brief and I struggle to answer. Grandiosity, was it? Long before I'd heard of F. R. Leavis, I'd been bitten by the novel bug. Only novels counted, and while I liked novels that were funny, I liked them most when they were funny to serious purpose. *Humorists* like Thurber, I thought, were funny to funny purpose. The clue was in the word. *Humor.* American for frolicsome, whimsical, zany, light. I was wrong – not about America but about Thurber. Getting people to see the depths in what appeared superficial wasn't only the fight of his life but that of other writers who admired him, numbered among whom was T. S. Eliot, who found him sombre and profound. Of himself Thurber wrote with exasperation: 'I am surprised that so few people see the figure of seriousness in the carpet of my humor and comedy.'

The image of the figure in the carpet is not accidentally Jamesian. He believed himself to be in the same business.

So how was it that I, a fellow Jamesian who also prized laughter highly, failed, as I grew older, to honour what had made me laugh in Thurber? Answering an unsympathetic critic, Thurber turned another elegant phrase. The critic, he said, 'confused my armor with its chink'. I did the same. All great stylists tend at some point to be parodies of themselves. If Thurber occasionally overdid the whimsicality, that was because it was integral to the seriousness of his ambition, which was to locate 'the emotional chaos' in the familiar.

There is no knowing whether I would have had even modest success had I embarked on a similar course. But I am not proud of what stopped me trying: that deadly mix of snobbery and shame which made me recoil from the familiar. I wanted to write about what I didn't know as a way of denying what I did. And so, in my time at least, there was no Thurber of Jewish Manchester.

19

MAGNANIMITY

I fled Wolverhampton every weekend I could, dividing my weekends between Manchester and Cambridge. My father was taxi driving now. He was known to other drivers as the Godfather. Though he was a short man he was a strong man, with arms like a blacksmith's. I'm not saying he used them to enforce his new authority in the trade as a Somebody and a Busybody – the Yiddish words for which are *macher* and *kochleffel* respectively – but he had a loud voice and liked to win an argument. My mother, too, seemed to be enjoying her new role as Wife to the Godfather, which, as far as I could tell, entailed going out in sequinned cocktail dresses to dinner dances where she did foxtrots with detectives. A strange thing happens when there's less than twenty years between you and your mother: a day arrives when she looks younger than you do. She was certainly having more fun than I was. My father told me that Manchester taxi drivers and the Manchester and Salford police force enjoyed warm relations since each was in a position to help the other. 'We both keep a close eye on the town,' he said grandly. I didn't say I thought he should keep a close eye on a particular police superintendent who, at a dance I attended, appeared to be keeping a close eye on my mother. The superintendent in question collared me at the bar. 'You the son?' he asked. I nodded. 'Bloody fine woman, your mother,' he went on.

I agreed with him but stopped short at allowing him to enumerate her charms.

Still and all, I figured that the acquaintance could be useful if I ever got caught speeding out of Wolverhampton. Or burning the flat down.

When she wasn't dancing with police superintendents my mother was running a shop in a precinct in a badly neglected area of Manchester. Just Fancy, she'd called it, another of those puns which in earlier days won us televisions. Fancy goods, swag, tchotchkes, shmondries, machareikehs – why did Jews, whose ethical seriousness had changed the world for good and ill, have so many words for trivial, pointless objects? As a family we'd begun by showing the profoundest contempt for the rubbish my father had sold on his market stall, but little by little we'd come around to filling the house with it.

'Swag's viral,' I wrote somewhere. Now my father was no longer a market man, my mother's shop enabled us to maintain our shmondrie count.

Though I liked visiting the shop when I was in Manchester to stock up on short-life light bulbs and teaspoons that bent in boiling water, I found the precinct hard on the eye and on the nerves. Half the other shops had closed long ago. Before she could go home at night my mother had to bring down multi-alarmed steel shutters forbidding enough to keep category A convicts apart. Gangs of toddlers ran wild, calling one another 'cunts'. Girls barely out of their school uniforms wheeled their babies in wagon-train formation. Staff stole. Even staff my mother had employed for years and grown close to. And

188

yet she thrived here until at last hers was the only shop left standing and the precinct became too dangerous in daylight hours, never mind the evening. Besides, she had always had bad legs and it was becoming time she took the weight off them. Until then she had run the shop with an enthusiasm that astonished me. She wasn't squeamish or snobbish. She looked down on no one. Indeed, she found it a relief not to be looked down *upon*. The lower bourgeois life of Jewish Prestwich had never been to her taste. She felt her neighbours, and some members of the family, judged her for not dressing expensively, not driving a good car, not being certain which Jewish festival fell when, and not having an immaculate home. 'Our house has more hatch than wall,' I heard her telling a friend over the phone once, 'and my meshuggener husband has invisible wire for his tricks strung between every doorknob in the house. And yet he wonders why I don't invite his sisters round. The place is a death trap.' But there were people she did invite round, and they were always sad, deserving cases she'd collected at the precinct.

Peace had broken out at home. My sister and my father were no longer arguing about her boyfriends. As well as becoming a taxi driver my father was giving more and more time to his magic, not only entertaining diners at the famed Kwok Man Chinese restaurant on Oxford Road in return for free duck and pancakes, but travelling to magic conventions in America and Canada from which he would return with suitcases packed with new and often hair-raisingly expensive tricks not all of which he was able to master. He was unapologetic about the money he was spending. He had a new attitude to life, to himself and to his deserts, encapsulated in a jaunty couplet he must have picked up from the genie in a pantomime he'd been to as a boy.

I've done my work as I've been told
And now I'm worth my bag of gold.

Magic, he boasted, was now bringing in a living. He had turned, in his own words, 'semi-professional', which meant prestidigitating for Jewish toddlers several nights a week and getting his petrol paid for. His latest trick – this one not for toddlers – entailed levitating my mother had she only agreed to being levitated. 'I don't like heights,' she reminded him, citing her unwillingness to go to the top of Blackpool Tower or catch a plane. In the absence of my mother in person he procured a sex-doll (I beg you not to ask me where), dressed her in clothes purloined from my mother's wardrobe, and having, as he believed, perfected the effect, performed it onstage at a gala

'You're not the only writer in this family'

190

night organised by the Manchester branch of the Order of the Magi. The master-stroke was – or should have been – the bicycle foot pump he'd adapted to blow the doll up surreptitiously so that it (or should I say 'she'?) would rise, slowly, to a height of six or seven feet. If only he'd worked out how to surreptitiously stop the foot pump once it had started. Unable to control the flow of air, short of stabbing the doll in the heart with a kitchen knife, he was reduced to watching as it grew rounder and rounder, lighter and lighter, until it floated to the ceiling where it burst on contact with the stage lights, sending my mother's intimate wardrobe cascading down on an audience prepared to believe that this was exactly what my father – as much a comedian as a magician – had always intended.

My mother buried her face in her hands. She, too, those around her must have thought, was highly delighted by the spectacle.

Did she ever do that, I occasionally wonder, when she heard me speak in public?

Marly looked after my father's engagement diary, packed his equipment for him, dressed as a clown, and acted as his assistant. The change in their relations was wonderful to behold. When I ask Marly to explain it from his position, she can't. He just fell back into loving her. And when I ask her to explain it from hers the answer is pretty much the same. But I marvelled at her capacity for forgiveness. My mother had once feared he would kill her or, if not her, the man she was going out with. Once, he did indeed go in search of him and when he found him beat him up. It's my suspicion that it was only my mother's connections with the Law that kept him off the charge sheet. Yet here was Marly now in motley and forever at his side. They were similar – that might account for it. They got on with life, didn't harbour grudges, laughed stuff off. She even drove a black cab for a while, one of the first women in Manchester to do so. And then – it always struck me as a sort of compliment to my father – married another black-cab driver. Jewish, thank God, though by this time that was not quite the issue it had been. Maybe my father had heard the voice of God while striking a top hat with his wand. *Lozein, Max. Leave it alone now. Abracadabra* . . .

As for my brother, his foray into intermarriage was working out fine. He too, I think, had forgiven my father the fierceness of his opposition to his union. Or if not forgiven it, painted it out. And Janet? For Stephen's sake, the same. They had moved to Bristol, to paint, design, sew, embroider, teach, design furniture, and otherwise live the artist's life. Other people's idylls are rarely what they seem, but theirs came close and still does. I envied them. But then I envied everybody. Old school friends I once pitied for never making it out of Manchester now struck me as lords of creation. Manchester! The lucky devils. 'So where are you now, Howard?' they'd ask when I ran into them. 'Shropshire,' I'd answer. 'Not far from Much Wenlock.'

Unless they meant 'Where are you in your novel?' in which case the answer would have been 'I'm at a difficult stage and don't like talking about it.'

With the Shakespeare book, however, I was progressing. The plan was for Wil and I to write two essays each, entirely independently – he on *Coriolanus* and *Macbeth*, I on *Hamlet* and *Antony and Cleopatra* – and then we'd try an introduction together. Though a novel was for me the apex of creation, and the writing of it a near-priestly vocation, I was surprised to discover that a critical essay could demand an attention that was comparably rapt, not to say religious. Could it be that after all I was writing as novelists wrote? A day that began without my knowing where I was going would end with reflections of which I hadn't thought myself capable and stories I didn't recognise as coming from me. I saw things in the plays in the course of writing about them that reading and watching alone would never have yielded. Writing, I came to realise, was a mode of thinking and noticing. Novel or work of criticism, maybe they were not so different: you lowered yourself into language and let the words assert authority over you. How could it be otherwise? Words were not your private property, they contained the accumulated history of your culture and maybe even, as D. H. Lawrence wouldn't have been afraid to say, the *race*. Start to write and you were at once in a conversation with countless souls who'd written before you. Whole hours would go by without my thinking about myself. Had I got up to look at my reflection in a mirror, I wouldn't have recognised me. And this was just half a book of criticism. Only imagine how marvellous it would be if one day a half a book became a whole book, a couple of essays became a novel, and I became . . . Well, what? A whole man?

I'd bought a new typewriter and come up with a title, unless Wilbur had. *Shakespeare's Magnanimity*, from a phrase by Hazlitt. It bore a provocatively unprovocative subtitle – *Four Tragic Heroes, Their Friends and Families.*

Theory had not yet decimated English departments in universities throughout the world, but you could smell it coming in from the Channel like an insalubrious warm wind bearing foreign bodies inimical to what the English meant by English Literature. Our title was a deliberate refusal of theoretic language. An ironic promise of a plain man's reading of Shakespeare, ironic because our reading was far from plain, as evidenced by the book's absence, when it did appear, from the bestseller lists.

For his part, Wilbur was beginning to write novels too. He would show me draft chapters, which I read reluctantly. I was already sharing a bathroom in Wolverhampton; I had no desire to share Wilbur's learning to write fiction. Workshopping, was this called? It all felt a bit amateur to me, which was rich considering how little I had to share with anyone. But when I did have, I was confident it would go into the world unperused by anyone but a publisher.

Wilbur was as puzzled by my non-collaborative nature as I was by his – what is the word? – collectivism perhaps. I pictured him sitting in circles of the faithful, a bit like Alcoholics Anonymous, sharing setbacks and excitements, discussing plotlines and paragraphing. Soon it would be called Creative Writing and everyone would be doing it.

'We're not in America,' I said. 'I don't do show and tell.'

'Why not?'

'Because it embarrasses me.'

This reminded us both of another argument we'd been having ever since we met. An argument over explicitness. 'Don't spell it out,' I was always saying. 'Let meaning leak.'

He was the most persistent questioner. What did I mean, *leak*?

How did I know what I meant? Just as I thought meaning should leak, I thought understanding should permeate.

Wilbur took me more seriously than I deserved to be taken. He was the son of an internationally known missionary, author of countless books on the Christian life. I was the son of a children's magician. I think he saw me as some sort of unspoilt, untutored prodigy. This both flattered and abashed me. A time came when I needed to come up for air from this equivocal overvaluation, and before I was able to explain the reasons for this sabbatical (to me as well as to him), he had died in a walking accident in France. A question I go on asking myself is why I hadn't been able to accept his strange companionableness at face value. Was it because I didn't believe I deserved to be its object? Did I value myself at too low a price to trust anyone who enjoyed my company and praised my intelligence? Or was there an insult to me buried deep in his offered admiration? Did he marvel at me as we marvel at a dog able to walk on its hind legs?

The sad thing is that I'd vowed to repair whatever the damage was. I had started to imagine a scene in which I pulled him to me and nuzzled his beard, held the back of his head, shook his shoulders, and told him I loved him maybe, told him I knew no one like him, told him I was known by no one like him, and known in a way no one else knew me, told him he had done more for me professionally than anyone, told him it was a singular honour to enjoy any place in his affections, told him his friendship was far, far more than I merited or ever would merit, and in that way, make it all right, heal whatever needed healing, leap across the extraordinary cultural difference that he'd leapt to be my friend and supporter, and then, then I didn't know what, just say it, do it, be it . . . Which didn't happen because he fell in the snow (I might be insolently inventing snow) just like Gerald Crich in Lawrence's *Women in Love*, a novel we both loved and discussed endlessly together, where (again as I have no warrant to imagine) 'something broke in his soul, and immediately he went to sleep'.

20

HOW TO LIVE

We are in a supermarket in Lichfield, where Dr Johnson was born on this very day in 1709. Because Dr Johnson's birthday just happens to be one of those dates I have in my head, I'd suggested a drive out from Wolverhampton to commemorate it. There's also an important cathedral here. I've known the whereabouts of all the important English cathedrals since my Gothic outings with my auntie Joyce. I thought the twin seductions of a cathedral and Dr Johnson's birthday would be hard for an Australian to say no to.

We've been discussing literature in the car. Her favourite play is *Medea*. But she's also keen on *Agamemnon* and *The Bacchae*. She seems to have a liking for classical plays in which a woman kills at least one man. I tell her about *Shakespeare's Magnanimity* which is with a publisher. She is pleased one of the plays I have written about is *Antony and Cleopatra*, another of her great works. 'Even though Cleopatra doesn't kill Antony?' I query. She throws me a sideways, am-I-joking-or-am-I-in-earnest look. She will do this again often in the ensuing years.

We are buying Heinz tomato ketchup. She wants to buy

two bottles. I want to make do with just one. I am poorer than I want her to know, so every little saving counts.

My nerves are frayed. There has already been a small scene in the butcher's. She wants to buy fillet steak. I tell her this isn't Australia and that no one has afforded fillet steak in England since the War. We eat sirloin, when we eat steak at all. Rather than buy sirloin, which no Australian can eat without throwing up, we leave the butcher's empty-handed. A similar scene has played out in the wine shop. In the bread shop. And in the cheese shop. Do we really need a whole wheel of brie?

The ketchup, therefore, is the last straw for us both.

'I'm buying them, whatever you say,' she says.

'As you choose. But you don't know how to live here.'

'Here?'

'Here, there, anywhere.'

The bottles slip from her hand. Has she dropped them by accident or deliberately? They lie like the decapitated corpses of small creatures – the children we will never have? – spilling blood.

'Let's go,' she says.

'I should pay for these,' I say.

'You do what you want to do,' she says. 'You're the one who knows how to live.'

It's a phrase that will haunt our marriage. *You don't know how to live.*

Back in the car she asks if my book on Shakespeare is as preposterous as my behaviour has been? Do I submit Antony and Cleopatra to my how to live test? And is that their tragedy in my view – that Antony thinks Cleopatra shops irresponsibly?

We haven't been together very long. Scenes like this apart, we are in the throes of passion. We are not like anyone either of us has ever known. I can't speak for her but I'm harbouring long-term ambitions for us. *Us!* See.

Might it not be possible, therefore, that these explosions of rage are, on both our parts, expressions of fear that we're moving too fast?

She was Geoff's big surprise. 'Ros is here,' he says the minute I arrive. It is as though he's ordered her in for me.

Geoff is over on sabbatical. Suddy is back in Australia after hers. Though we talked of getting back together, we know we won't and slide imperceptibly apart. So I am on my own.

'Ros who?'

Geoff's wife, the Jen-Jen – the name suggests a mythic creature possessed of mocking wit, and that's how I think of her – laughs unbelievingly. 'Ros *who!*' As though there's been no one on my mind but Ros since I met her. That's if I've ever met her.

But I had. That night at the Women's Literature conference in Lorne. It was Ros who had tried to get me thrown out.

'Oh, that Ros. Does she know I'm here? She might not be too pleased.'

Whereupon she enters, golden and sardonic, wearing an army surplus flak jacket with a poppy in the buttonhole, jeans that hug her thighs, and I at once feel what I'd felt at Lorne. 'Now her . . .'

He had nothing to do, and she had hardly anybody to love . . .

That, put cruelly and succinctly, as only Jane Austen knew how to put it, was the state of things between us. We were both available. I had finished my half of the Shakespeare book, and she was over on that Grand Tour indispensable to the education of all Australians. Not that it took any accounting for on my side. Ros answered to an ideal of infuriated warrior womanhood I'd always hankered after. Don't ask me why. Something to do with proving I could conquer such a being in hand-to-hand combat, maybe. Unless it wasn't victory I was in the market for but defeat. I won't have been the first to long for death in love.

Kill me with your kiss.

And she looked as though she could.

Hard to explain, but I felt I was embarking on a literary adventure as much as a love affair. I mean more than that we talked books together from the moment we met: I mean that she seemed to be someone with the scorching intelligence and energy to jeer me out of my staid Cambridge cavillings; someone with a touch of the bohemian about her, who read contemporary literature and would have no time for my wanting to write like an Edwardian; someone who would make me a novelist because she wanted a novelist for a companion; maybe even someone who would turn out to be the subject I had so far been lacking – a woman who threw bottles of tomato ketchup in supermarkets and men like me out of literature conferences. From the start she felt entwined with my ambitions, someone to whom I was already, in my head, dedicating the novels I hadn't written.

Halfway through Geoff's feast she rose, looked me challengingly in the eye, and said, 'Take me for a drink.'

That I would never be the most impulsive of lovers must have been plain to her at that moment. Instead of leaping to my feet, I made some bumbling speech to the effect that it wasn't considered good form in this country for a guest to leave the table in the middle of a meal and go to the pub. But that I would be far too pliable a lover was plain to everyone else the moment later when I rose to follow her.

When we returned from the pub, I was wearing her flak

jacket. This was the beginning of her trying to make me look like someone else. The tooled cowboy boots with Cuban heels would come later.

The following day, or it may have been the day after, I drove her to Wolverhampton. Cruelty number one.

What I need, she told me on the drive up, is a rock. I wondered if she was talking a diamond ring already. But what she meant was someone she could lean on. I didn't say in that case you've got the wrong man. Cruelty number two.

I half expected her to turn on her heel the minute she saw where I was living. But she rose to the challenge and sent me out to buy rubber gloves, bottles of Dettol and as much soap and detergent as I could carry. She took back the little chequered scarf she'd given me at the pub and made a turban of it – in style a bit like the one Gracie Fields wore to entertain the troops, but in effect more like the one Lana Turner wore in *The Postman Always Rings Twice* – then set about scrubbing every surface, singing as she went. If I transpose time I can hear her singing Wagner – Brunnhilde entering the flames – but it was later in our marriage that she discovered a kinship with Brunnhilde (and immolation) and by that time the flames were enveloping me. The flat – to return to that – was unrecognisable by the time she'd finished. She even threw away the green carpet in the bathroom and left a note on the door listing instructions as to communal hygiene, such as empty the bath when you get out, or better still don't get in. For a whole week I entertained the fantasy of our living happily together here forever.

One day, despite that optimism, she caught me sitting on the edge of the sofa in the suit she was determined should go the way of the carpet.

'Where are you off to?' she asked.

I told her nowhere.

'Then why are you sitting like that? And why are you dressed like that?'

She wanted to know if I always wore a suit for lounging around at home in. The answer was yes; ever since I grew out of my old leather jacket.

And did I never sit back in a chair?

'No, never.'

'In fact you don't live here at all,' she observed. 'You're just parked, waiting to take off.'

I reminded her that I was Jewish. Which made her laugh. I reminded her that I'd been brought up to expect the worst and be ready to make a run for it at a minute's notice.

'You think there are Nazis in Northampton?'

'There are Nazis everywhere.'

'In Northampton?'

'Stop calling this Northampton.'

'Why? Where are we?'

'*Wolv*erhampton.'

I waited for her to say Wolverhampton Shmolverhampton, but she didn't. 'I've seen no Nazis on the streets,' she said.

'You haven't been on the streets.'

'You won't let me.'

'That's because I'm saving you from the Nazis.'

'The Nazis won't come after me. I look like one of them.'

And it was true, she did. High shoulders. Square jutting jaw. Fierce blue eyes. I could picture her in uniform.

'It's not just the Nazis,' I said. 'There's also the Cossacks.'

'Cossacks Shmossacks,' she replied, as quick as a whip. She was full of surprises. 'Leave the Cossacks to me,' she went on. I wanted her to enthral me with stories of what she'd do to them. I didn't give them a chance, but I wanted to hear how they'd die.

'Tell me. Tell me.'

But she knew a diversion tactic when she saw one. 'How much of this is serious?' she asked, changing her tone.

'Are you asking me if I really believe someone's coming for me?'

'Yes.'

'I don't know if I really *believe* anything. It's mainly a joke.'

'Mainly? Why would you joke at all about something as serious as this? Nazis aren't funny.'

'Jews make them funny. It's the way we cope with things.'

'What things?'

'Being chased by Nazis.'

By which time she'd had enough. 'If you expect me to live with you in this shitheap,' she said decisively, 'you've at least got to pretend you live here yourself. Take your jacket off and undo your fucking tie.'

And this was how a Euripides-and-Wagner-loving Catholic girl from Perth ended up living happily ever after with a fraught and unfulfilled Jew in the West Midlands of the United Kingdom.

She'll have her version.

My version is that we had a good few weeks doing what lovers who are new to each other do. I'd see her lying next to me in the morning and I'd be amazed. How had I done' this? Was it real or were we making each other up?

'So this novel of yours . . .' she'd begin, as though we'd finished the project of getting to know each other and were now ready to start work in earnest.

'It's still up here,' I said, tapping my head.

'Well, it's no good up there.'

I knew that.

'Write it down,' she'd tell me if I said something she liked. But just as often she got me to write down something *she* said that she liked. Years later the issue of collaboration split us up. What neither of us realised until it was too late was that we were in the same boat. She too had a book lodged inside her. If she could help me get out mine, why couldn't I help her get out hers?

Some weekends we drove out to Shropshire which she enjoyed, or to Manchester which she didn't. She decided pretty quickly that my parents didn't like her and that she would therefore not like them. I'd bought her an antique, figure-hugging, scarlet velvet dress in a Shropshire curio shop. 'This feels like a Jamesian purchase,' I'd said. I the Prince, she someone else's wife. She shook her head over me. Fucking Henry James! She wore it nonetheless – at my instigation, she maintained – the first time she met my parents. In the towering heels, which I'd also bought her, she looked, I thought, magnificently Amazonian, taller than both of them combined, taller than they'd have been had one of them stood on the shoulders of the other. But I refused to accept it was my intention that she should scare the living daylights out of them.

'You wanted to show me off to them as your shiksa whore,' she said.

'Even supposing I did see you that way, which I don't, why would I want to show you off to them?'

She threw her head back and laughed. 'Every Jewish son has to bring home a whore.'

I remembered she'd done Psychology 1 at Melbourne University. Maybe she'd done Theology 1 as well. I told her I hadn't encountered any such injunction in Leviticus or any such analysis in Freud.

'Please yourself,' she said. 'It's not for me to penetrate your religion's sickness.'

Not that she would ever stop trying.

She had what amounted in my eyes to a Jewish backstory.

She had grown up a convent girl in Perth in Western Australia, the daughter of a suburban bank manager father and a piano teacher – more than that, a concert pianist – mother. Theirs had been a paradisal life, boating, fishing, making music. Then, into their garden of earthly delights, slunk the Devil and his family – four city-wise Viennese Jews – fur-stoled mother, flirty father, delectable daughter, smouldering son. They moved in next door, smelling of schnitzel and singing Richard Tauber. Austro-Hungarian decadence danced in their eyes. What happened next is entirely my reading of what happened next. Ros's mother – a striking, musically gifted but socially naive country woman – showed signs of falling a little bit in love with the father; Ros, aged fourteen or so, showed signs of falling a little bit in love with the son; the father and son showed signs of reciprocating, in the way that only Viennese Jews can – sultrily; the Viennese wife showed signs of being jealous, and pretty soon Ros's West Australian father showed signs of wanting to get his endangered family away. Hence, by my reasoning, their abrupt move to Melbourne, which thereafter would always seem, to Ros and her mother, to be an expulsion from the Garden. Ros had little time for this theory even its embryo form, and no time at all for it as a convoluted Jamesian tale of seduction, adultery and deceit, in which the devils of the Old World ran erotic rings round the innocents of the New. 'Bullshit,' she said. 'Are you suggesting that this is why I'm with you? Do you honestly think I'm genetically in thrall to Jews?'

I shrugged. 'Isn't everybody?'

Call me Hymie.

Ros did. Sometimes sweetly, sometimes savagely, often mischievously, but never maliciously. The nuns who'd taught her in Perth had singled out the Jews as uniquely deserving of prayer on account of their being destined for hell. Ros saw it as her mission to save me. Not from perdition and not from Jewishness itself, which would have been the nuns' preference, but from the equivocations in which I clothed my version of it. 'Get it out there, Hymie,' she said. The first time I visited Israel was in Ros's company and she was far more overwhelmed by the experience for me than I was for myself. She clutched my arm as the plane touched down. She wanted me to kiss the tarmac when we disembarked. 'Hymie, you're home,' she said.

It's often said that the best wives for keeping a Jewish man Jewish are Gentile. Barbara's mother Mary was a case in point. It was she who made Shabbes dinner and remembered to put Yom Kippur in the diary. Ros was a good Jewish wife in another way: once I began to write polemical pieces about matters Jewish she saw a new career path for me. Not quite as Messiah but as a sort of secular Moses who taught his people to keep the faith without all the rules and rituals. How to be a Jew without the skullcaps and the fringes. How to be a Jew who read Henry Miller and went dancing on a Friday Night. How to be a Jew who wasn't afraid of life. British Jews, especially, she thought were desperate to be liberated in this way and would follow me if I led. Sometimes I was crazy enough to believe her.

Although she promulgated this view of me on all occasions, she also believed the opposite. The Jew who most needed liberating from a mouldering faith was me. She enjoyed enumerating the failings ascribable to my being Jewish. My social reserve, for example, which she characterised as marked by a deficiency in any sense of entitlement, as witness my hesitancy at the door of an expensive restaurant or hotel. My all-round lack of boldness which spilled over into my literary tastes, stopping me from reading the scabrous, counter-culture books she liked – the Ken Keseys and Hunter S. Thompsons and Nabokovs – and would no doubt stop me writing them. In my mother she saw the embodiment of this Jewish timidity and censoriousness and fought her influence over me ferociously. Over the years, people who noted my inclination to negativity put it down to the influence of Leavis. Ros begged to differ. It was my mother. 'You're sounding just like *her*,' she would say whenever it was her intention to land the lowest blow in her armoury. This was meant to comprehend the way I looked at the world, the way I expressed disapproval: of a book, a pop song, a person; my penchant for character assassination (as often as not, Ros's); my rancid running commentaries on any film or television programme we happened to be watching – in sum, my sour disposition.

Was it because I didn't feel up to the job of companioning her that I brought down a curtain of disparagement over everything? She'd lived a wild and often reckless life. She'd hung around with some powerful men in Australia, and with some dangerous ones too. She'd been a swimmer, a sailor, a singer, a pianist, a cellist. There was an immensity about her. Short of making a joke, she seemed capable of doing anything and engrossing the attention of anyone. I was small potatoes. A lecturer at a poly. How much smaller could a potato get? Could it be that my censoriousness was no more than a cover for my limitations and fears?

So when it came to my negativity it was hardly necessary to invoke the influence of my mother. In the matter of my judgementalism, however – from casual disapproval, to heart-crushing rejections, all the way up to full-blown misanthropy – I recognised truth in the charge. There were times when I was young when I saw myself as my mother's representative and champion, her little Lancelot, riding out with his armour ringing, tirra-lirra by the river – not to right the world's wrongs on her behalf exactly, but to castigate it for its abominable taste in not admiring what she admired. I say 'when I was young' but in truth I am still doing it. I have only to turn on the television and accidentally catch Little Mix or One Direction and I am aware of my lip curling just as my mother's does. The truth is, she was the stern critic in my life long before F. R. Leavis, no matter that her *Great Tradition* would have included A. J. Cronin, Nevil Shute and Somerset Maugham.

Compared to my mother, yes, Ros was a roaring girl. 'Stop saying no to everything, Hymie,' she would shout. 'Try saying yes to life for a change.'

And that meant a yes to more daring literature too. As well as *Medea* she was reading a Henry Miller novel when I met her. I forget which. *Tropic of Something*. And Norman Mailer. And Philip Roth's *Portnoy's Complaint*. I, of course, found that stuff indecorous. 'Tight-arsed,' Ros called me. If I was ever going to write this effing novel I'd need to embrace some of that indecency. It was how people wrote now. I wanted to say I didn't care how people wrote now, but I knew what her response to that would be.

Whichever of them was to blame for my saying no to everything – FRL or my mother – I went on weaving a sticky web of deprecation around Ros until at last the mirror cracked, she made three paces thro' the room, and look'd down to towered Camelot.

Boscastle actually, but that was near enough.

Ros swapped Wolverhampton for Boscastle in her head the minute she saw it. We'd been in Cornwall helping Wilbur decorate a cottage he'd bought in St Teath, had driven across to Boscastle for a cream tea, and that was that. She took one look at the whitewashed, never-never elfin cottages leaning against each other for support, the millpond medieval harbour protected by the gracefully curved arm of the harbour wall, the high, secret-enfolding cliffs, felt the dizzying conviction as you enter the village from the top road that once you have descended you will never emerge again, and decided never to emerge again. Three days later I was driving back to Wolverhampton on my own, charged with getting the bank to give us an overdraft so Ros could buy *objets d'art* with which to stock a shop she'd negotiated to rent from hippies who were throwing pots in an old watermill they claimed was haunted. In fact, everything in Boscastle was haunted. It was to Boscastle that Thomas Hardy had returned as an old man, haunted by the memory of the woman he'd met there in his youth, married and subsequently treated abominably. Ros and I separately knew and loved the poems of remorse Hardy wrote on his return to north Cornwall and she saw them as an added inducement to stay.

I took this to be a passing enthusiasm, but she would run this shop and much else in the village besides for the next twelve years. For the first six I would commute from Wolverhampton, thereafter I would live here with her, walking the cliffs Hardy walked, my head filled with his old man's sadness, sometimes in the irised rain, sometimes blinded by the opal and the sapphire of that wandering western sea, imagining my second novel. But I remained a stranger to the place. Because she was on her own for most of every week, Ros took possession. The gossip and politics were hers. The topography marked by *her* wanderings and discoveries also hers, and so hers to introduce me to whenever I came down. 'Hymie, I've got something to show you. Look.' Look, Hymie, look. Well, her enthusiasm to share beat her reluctance at other times to let me anywhere near. But I wasn't always a graceful recipient of that enthusiasm. Every invitation to look carried an implication of ownership on her part and exclusion on mine.

I didn't feel right stretched out flat on precipitous rock

peering into those blowholes Ros wanted me to be overwhelmed by, or clambering over her beetling cliffs, dressed
like Barney Fugleman in that second novel *Peeping Tom* – in *a
long sleek-piled fur coat and Bally slip-on snakeskin shoes decorated
with a delicate gold chain and having the added advantage of slightly
built-up heels*. I wasn't quite the alien presence Fugleman was,
thanks to Ros who had kitted me out in an anorak and walking boots, but it's possible I looked even more risible as a hiker
than he did as a Jewish accountant from Finchley. Boots or no
boots, I felt myself a trouble to the place. Had the average
Cornishman ever met a Jew? And did it matter? Only one
person ever made an overtly off-colour remark to me in Boscastle and he wasn't Cornish. He came from Sevenoaks, was
reputedly a golf champion, sported a bounder's moustache,
and owned a B&B in the harbour. We happened to be talking
when a Jag sped through the village. 'Don't often see a Jew's
canoe here,' he mused. I told him he shouldn't say anything
like that to anyone but definitely not to me. He couldn't
believe he'd caused offence, apologised and doffed his hat to
me whenever we met thereafter. He made it his practice to
leave his wife and run off with one of his guests at the end of
every season and then return with her as his new manager at
the beginning of the next. One year he went out of his way to
introduce me to his latest. 'This is Sarah,' he said, before clos-
ing one eye and adding, confidentially, 'Sarah Kaufman.'

Over the years, I kept expecting him to start the new season
by driving into the village in a Jag, but business was never
good enough.

Business was never quite good enough for anyone in Boscastle. Ros made no money in her shop and in some hippy part
of herself would have liked to make less. It was more a craft
gallery than a shop, which meant she sold beautiful things

which no holidaymaker on the Bude to Tintagel trail could afford to buy. I offered to water the exclusiveness down with swag from Manchester but Ros wouldn't hear of it. I was to leave her to it. She had fixed up my Wolverhampton life for me, thrown out the bathmat, taught me how to sit in a chair as though I wasn't on the point of leaving it, got me into jeans and Cuban heels. The way I could do the equivalent for her was to let her make her own decisions.

She cut a dash in the village from the start. People stared out of their windows as she passed. It wasn't that no one of her imposing presence had ever been seen in the village before, but they weren't expected to be there in the morning. That there was as much suspicion as admiration in this attention goes without saying. She hadn't been in the village more than a month before she was accused of stealing someone's dog from the Wellington Hotel, in order, it was supposed, to perform black magic with it, on it, or to it. A bag of giblets was thrown at the craft-shop door from a passing car, and offal in various states of suppuration was posted through the letter box, to show Ros that she didn't have the monopoly on sorcery in the village. The scandal died down when the dog suddenly turned up safe and well in the village, though the fondness with which he greeted Ros whenever he saw her, leaping into her arms and licking her face, kept mistrust alive.

But at least the suspicion with which she was viewed lent her the glamour of the uncanny. I was excluded in more mundane ways. I just looked out of place, had a thunderous expression, and dragged Ros away from a good singsong. How much of the exclusion of which I speak was real or imaginary I have no idea, but I felt it especially acutely on those Friday nights when I drove down from Wolverhampton at breakneck speed in order to get there before the pubs closed. Ros was never hard to find. Often I was able to hear her singing 'Once I had a bunch of thyme / I thought it never would decay' from as far away as the Devon/Cornwall border. The look on the faces of the fishermen when I turned up – using 'fishermen' as a collective noun for those who lived here permanently, 'here' being the pub – wasn't hard to read. 'Uh-oh, here's the husband,' their expression said, no matter that I wasn't the husband yet.

I saw some of them exchange covert glances with Ros. 'Want us to get rid of him for 'ee, lass?'

Over the side of a fishing boat, under a tractor on old Charlie's farm, into the blowhole where I'd be found three days later with my mouth still stuffed with pasties, fudge and mackerel? Countless were the ways of removing unwelcome visitors from this wild and lonely coast. They'd been doing it for centuries.

Occasionally they'd ask me for a song in order that I shouldn't feel left out. I sang them 'The Foggy, Foggy Dew'.

What eventually happened was bound to happen.

21

THE HARD MAN

I believe my father wanted me to be a hard man.

Wasn't he hard enough for both of us? Capable of tearing a Manchester telephone book in half with his bare hands, bending a six-inch nail into the shape of a horseshoe and lifting a dining chair one-handed with my friend John Heilpern in it, what need had he of James Cagney for a son?

Well, none except in the area where he didn't see himself as a tough guy – namely intimate relations with a woman. He was not remotely henpecked but entertained the fancy that he was. 'Right,' he'd say, slapping the side of his head with an open palm, the minute my mother proposed an alternative strategy to his own on any subject under the sun. 'Right! It doesn't matter what I think. You have it your way. You're the boss in this house.'

I'm not saying he wanted me to push my mother around for him. Or any other woman come to that. But it was as though he saw a grotesque version of himself when I went at the knees over a girl. An amiable young woman with a twisted smile (I loved twisted smiles), who sold cheese on Oswestry market, offered me a taste of Caerphilly on a toothpick and winked at me, whereupon I lost my heart. I was fourteen. 'Come on, Charlie, chop-chop,' my father shouted down from his van. 'There's a lady over there wants a candlewick bed-spread and you're dreaming of the cheese woman. Or are you just dreaming of the cheese?' The punters' derision still roars in my ears.

The following week the van broke down on the way to Oswestry and we didn't get there. The week after that the cheese woman ignored me. I am ashamed to say I cried all the way back in the van. For most of the journey my father said nothing, just concentrated on the driving and shook his head. Within half an hour of Manchester, however, he gave way to his fury. 'I don't want a son of mine crying over a girl he hardly knows,' he said.

'It's my business,' I said.

'Not if you make a fool of me it isn't.'

'How have I made a fool of you?'

'By being a *kunilemelly*.'

Ah, him again.

'Can't I fall in love without you having an opinion?'

'Love! You've known her five minutes.'

'I fall in love quickly.'

'That's what I'm afraid of.'

I mooned about for days and then claimed to be too ill to travel when Oswestry rolled around.

'You're coming,' he said and dragged me out of the bed.

When we got there the cheese woman had gone. Had my father pulled a few strings? Was she lying at the bottom of Wookey Hole?

As the years of my adolescence ticked by, I saw that he drew an important distinction between getting along with girls, even taking advantage of girls, and falling in love with them. Falling in love was somehow letting *them* take advantage of *me*. My father was a chaste, courteous man. He never swore. He never spoke slightingly or lewdly of women. But he wanted me to be able to look after myself around them. He wanted me to have defences. A soppy boy would end up on the canvas.

And he was right about that.

But isn't the canvas where a writer belongs?

There were to be other scenes like this one – non-events in the life of a well-adjusted scamp, but moments of anguish in mine – and my father oversaw them all with the same withering disdain.

'The world's full of girls,' he would say, 'what's so special about this one?'

'I like her.'

He'd slap the side of his head. *I liked a girl.* It was as though I'd told him I wanted to take ballet lessons.

Something happened in my seventeenth or eighteenth year that briefly changed his opinion of me. I think he'd heard me on the phone breaking it off with a girl, which is hard to believe, but even a *kunilemelly* can turn. Thereafter, I became for him a model of masculine intransigence. 'Our Howard wouldn't put up with that,' I'd hear him saying to my mother, as though to inform her he'd learned a lesson from me and could no longer be relied on to capitulate to her every whim. I found the idea of my father using me as an example of how a man should behave with a woman so exciting that I'd sit at the top of the stairs when he was on the phone in the hope of catching some other compliment to my strength of character. Did he talk to his taxi-driver friends about me like this? I wondered. Was I a byword, in the 'town', for manly resolution?

That this admiration for my 'hardness' would not extend to my leaving Barbara goes without saying. He ceded the reprimanding to my mother on that score – I think he was too angry to trust himself to words – but he set his mouth, made a fist, made two fists, and wouldn't look at me. Where had they gone wrong must have been a question he and my mother asked themselves. I wouldn't have been surprised had he blamed her for scrubbing my knees in a bowl of soapy water all those years before.

If my father's view of me had changed – and not always for the better – with the advent of Ros it changed back again, this time entirely for the worse. He didn't like her, she didn't like him. More than that, he didn't like what he took to be my ready accession to her every demand.

You are free to imagine, then, the emotions that shook his powerful frame when I turned up without warning, aged thirty-five or thereabouts, wearing the same lachrymose expression I'd worn in Oswestry twenty years before. I fended off questions from him and my mother with the assurance that I was fine, nothing the matter, a bit fed up, needed a change from Boscastle and Wolverhampton, that was all, needed a lie-down in my old bed, don't ask me why. My record player had long ago been thrown away so I couldn't play Caruso at full heartbreak throttle. But I knew every sob by heart anyway. *Ridi, Pagliaccio, e ognun applaudirà.* Well, I wasn't laughing and my father wasn't applauding. I heard him, pacing the landing outside my bedroom and half expected him to burst in and unbuckle his belt. When I surfaced, late the next day, I met his eyes and saw the fury of God the Father whose gift of life I'd squandered on – well, let's continue with no words.

What had happened was this. I had turned up late at the Cobweb one Friday night, tired after the drive from Wolverhampton, and knew at once, from Ros's air of operatic distraction and from the atmosphere of low mirth at the bar, that the Saucy Cornish Fiddler who steals away your bonnie bunch of thyme had stolen mine. Around Ros a chorus of fishermen and farmers formed a menacing circle of fire. To get to her I'd have to get through them.

I didn't wait to find out more, but drove straight to Manchester without stopping, arriving in the early hours of the morning and going to sleep in the car. Why Manchester? It was as though I'd forgotten I had ever lived anywhere else.

'I am sorry to see this again,' my father said.

'Sorry to see what again?'

'You in this state. I thought you'd got over all this.'

'You make it sound like the recurrence of a chronic illness.'

'That's what it is.'

'Then I can't do anything about it.'

'You can pull yourself together. You're a grown man. You've got a child.'

'What's that got to do with anything?'

'You don't behave like a child when you've got a child.'

'Oh, no?' What about you, Dad? Bleh, bleh, bleh. *Taugetzmeowgetz*. Your garages full of kids' toys. How grown up a life have you lived, making rabbits disappear from top hats, twisting party balloons into giraffes?

But I didn't say a word. Just let him go on. Without doubt, I needed him to go on.

'I'm ashamed of you,' he said. 'At your age.'

Good. That was what I wanted him to say.

'You have let yourself down. You have let me down. You have let your mother down. Where's your self-respect?'

More, more.

If he'd brought his hammer fist down on my head I'd have thanked him for it. How wonderful to feel a pain somewhere else.

He didn't talk to me for another couple of days, then, quite out of the blue, he said, 'Anyway, I thought you had a novel to write.'

216

I could have said, that's a non sequitur, Dad, and re-established a bit of authority over him as a man with more than a dozen words, some of them in a foreign language. But it wasn't a non sequitur as it happened. It was a perfect sequitur. I wasn't supposed to be happy, I had claimed unhappiness as my birthright and my testament, so what was I doing crying over a woman? I should have been grateful. Treachery is the stuff of art and I had art to make. Jealousy is the crowning theme of nearly all great novels and I had a novel to write. Misery made its home in art, did it not? If I had to blubber, blubber on the page.

Being manly was all very well if one's sole ambition was to be a man. My ambition comprised being both more and less than that.

I shook my father's hand, kissed my mother and, like the hero of all the novels I hadn't yet written, drove out into the humming future.

Which just happened to be in Oxford where, before I'd met Ros, I'd done the odd bit of language teaching – a euphemism for taking foreign students on pub crawls on the Banbury Road and dancing with them until the early hours.

How Ros knew I was in Oxford, unless I'd dropped her an abject note, I don't recall, but it was while I was there that I received a postcard from her. She had been unwell and was recuperating on a friend's farm above Boscastle. If I felt I could 'go quietly around her', she was prepared to try having me back. Meaning, whatever had or hadn't happened – and if there had indeed been a saucy fiddler there was no mention of him now – had been my fault.

Many another man would have tossed that letter in the bin. But I was who I was. I 'dreaded a future without affection'. That description from *Middlemarch* of Lydgate's capitulation to

Rosamond (another Ros!) is withering. George Eliot no doubt had reason to scorn gifted men who threw their careers away on calculating, lightweight women, but Ros was no flibbertigibbet and I had no career. But I did have a lonely nature and needed to receive affection. And if that meant 'going quietly', or 'eating shit' as George Eliot didn't quite put it, very well, I'd give it a try.

But I didn't go back to the Land of Saucy Fiddlers immediately. Oho, no! Not me. First I fiddled saucily myself, completing my time at the Oxford Summer School, dancing to 10cc's smoky 'I'm Not in Love', that song whose chorus, I like to think, was composed in the living room of my parents' house in Prestwich – *Big boys don't cry*.

Then – *then* – I went back.

22

MAKE SOMETHING HAPPEN, HYMIE

Three things of note fell out in 1978. *Shakespeare's Magnanimity* was published. Ros and I married. And Woody Allen's film *Annie Hall* was released. Neither of the first two made the planet judder on its axis, but all three were, in their own way, a spur to my finally starting a novel.

I'd seen a few of Woody Allen's earlier films and not particularly cared for them. Screwball was not a genre I enjoyed. But *Annie Hall* was another order of achievement and of especial interest to me because of its undisguised contemporary Jewish content, its high Jewish-anxiety count, and that now famous scene in which Alvy Singer, the Allen alter ego, accepts an invitation to an Easter Dinner with Annie Hall's uber-Gentile relatives in the course of which, as discomfort mounts, he sees himself as he imagines they see him – a Hasidic Jew in full Orthodox regalia. Whether Ros found Allen's Hasid as funny as I did, I can't remember. It's possible she berated me, out of the best of motives, for identifying quite so closely with the paranoia. 'Do you really think Gentiles see you like that?'

'Not *think*, know. There were medievalists at Cambridge who backed themselves against a wall and sprinkled holy water around their room when I turned up for a supervision. That, my dear, is what your people have done to us over the centuries. You've read Kafka's *Metamorphosis*. Who do you think the giant cockroach is? How do you think it got onto the ceiling?'

I was growing Jew-lonely. There were one or two Jews teaching at Wolverhampton poly but I didn't know them well and, as for Cornwall, I guessed it must have been a hundred years or more since anyone had been buried in the Jewish cemetery in Penryn. I'd heard mention of a scattering of Jews living around Truro, but I had Boscastle to myself. Beyond those twin centres of my alienation the story was the same – I had no Jews to talk to. My old Jewish friends were scattered. I had fallen out with Gabriel. John was in New York. Malcolm was in Sweden. Stuart was I had no idea where. Harry I occasionally saw, but he was a socialist, which meant I had to tread carefully. One way or another I had no one of the faith to discuss *Annie Hall* with. And yet, however these things happen, I found myself part of a wide and not always well-tempered conversation. On the one side were Jews who laughed as I'd laughed and knew exactly the freak you were made to feel by Gentiles who'd never met a Jew before. For them, Woody Allen had performed a service. He'd aired a madness. Healed a trauma even. On the other side were Jews who thought it was time to get over the pathology of self-disgust. It wasn't the Gentiles who turned us into light-fearing shtetl dwellers. We had done that to ourselves for centuries and, with Woody Allen's connivance, were doing it still. Time we accepted that we had a place in the modern world. There was nothing funny about going on regarding ourselves as medieval meshuggeners and mujiks. Allen seemed to think that the very entity, JEW, indeed the word JEW itself, was endlessly amusing. It wasn't.

And I – where was I in this?

On the side of those meshuggeners who thought the word JEW was endlessly amusing.

After the initial excitement of *Shakespeare's Magnanimity*'s publication I began to wake to that sensation of acrid emptiness known to all first-time writers when they realise that nothing in the whole wide world is going to change as a consequence of their words. In low moments Ros had been wont to say, 'Make something happen, Hymie.' On the morning the book came out, I gave her a fulsomely signed copy. 'For you,' I wrote, or some such words, 'the thing you always hoped for from me.'

She was very nice about it. Kissed me warmly. Took the book to her bosom. It was no small thing for me, she knew. And therefore no small thing for her. A critic for a husband. She almost made it sound Jewish. *A critic for a husband, noch!* But in our hearts we both accepted I hadn't really made a big something happen.

I say she was nice about it, but not for long. 'You mean your two essays,' she would say later when I cited the work as evidence of my literary progress.

Did she mean to be cruel? I think she meant to be frolicsome. Ros frolicsome was not always to be distinguished from Ros annihilative. She often said that her father had never taught her how to do anything lightly. As a consequence, whenever she tried to play, she played rough. Her dance of choice, in our early days together, had been the bump. I went along with this, letting her bump me regardless of the tempo of the music. When the urge to bump was on her, she could bump to Schubert. I can't say I enjoyed it, but how could I ask her to play more and then refuse her the bump? Yes, I looked ridiculous, being buffeted on the dance floor in the Cuban heels she'd persuaded me to wear in order to add another inch or two to my height. But at least the sight of me – bowlegged and staggering like Dustin Hoffman's 'Ratso' Rizzo in *Midnight Cowboy* – made her laugh. We needed a laugh.

Eventually the time would come when we would add up the pros and cons of our life together and agree that neither of us had known how to be gentle. Ah yes, the bump, I said. But Ros meant intellectually. In her view I'd chipped away at her confidence every day since the sauce bottle episode in Lichfield. The withering sarcasm of 'You mean your two essays' was something she'd learned from me.

Though *Shakespeare's Magnanimity* could hardly be blamed for this, I felt that Ros wasn't her old self. She was less uproarious. Friday night came around and she wouldn't feel like going to the Cobweb. A quiet fell on Boscastle.

One evening, while I was back in Wolverhampton preparing a lecture on 'The Ancient Mariner' – *And a thousand thousand slimy things / Lived on; and so did I* – she rang to ask if there was any way I could get down to Boscastle sooner than planned. She held the phone out so I could hear Camelford Brass Band playing the 'Furry Dance' outside the shop. This she did only when she was feeling loving towards me. She hadn't wooed me with the 'Furry Dance' for a long time. I was worried. Ros not on a war footing was not Ros. I rushed my lecture, killed the Albatross and drove to Boscastle early the next morning. The shop was closed when I arrived and Ros was in bed.

Considering that we'd only recently mended our fences you'd have thought I'd have made her a hot lemon drink with brandy, turned up the heating, and otherwise ministered to her needs, leaving the shop closed for as long as it took her to recover. But some demon drove me to ask if she'd like me to look after things for a while. To my surprise, she agreed.

And thus, at last, was I given the chance to make her shop a bit more like a market stall.

When a rep came in selling fabric witches on broomsticks to hang from the ceiling, I ordered a gross. Boscastle was a witchy village. All right, these witches weren't locally produced. They came from north Lancashire where they had their own witch culture. But who'd know? A witch was a witch was a witch. The next rep who came by had a nice line in highly polished clocks that resembled feral amoebas made from the giant redwoods of Missouri. True, Missouri wasn't Cornwall, but they were handmade! From reclaimed timber! And then two thousand paperweights from China. Two thousand sounded a lot, but it was only by buying that many that we could get them cheap and thus undercut the beautiful hand-blown ones from Liskeard Ros found hard to sell.

The resigned way she took all this worried me. I was so accustomed to her opposing me, as I opposed her, with every weapon in the armoury of couples-war, that her capitulation to my interference filled me with remorse. My God, had I broken her spirit? I apologised profusely, offered to send the tat back or take it to a dump, and made a solemn promise not to impose my bad taste on her enterprises ever again. She shrugged.

This wasn't the reason we got married. Ros's Australian passport was coming up for renewal and the simplest way for her to get British citizenship was to become Ros Jacobson. But I did hope, and maybe she hoped too, that my remorse would be a grace note to our nuptials.

A muted affair at the Wolverhampton Registry Office was followed by a honeymoon in Paris that I'm sure Ros would agree was the worst honeymoon had by anyone anywhere. A friend from the Oxford language school, who happened to be working in Paris, booked us a dreamy room with a balcony at the cruelly named Hotel Paradis in the Quartier Pigalle, from which we could see all the sights that make lovers rejoice in each other's company unless one of them has told the other that she doesn't know how to live. Ros had not, after all, given in to me. And I had not, after all, become a different, less dogmatic person. In many ways I was harder to be with than ever on account of the failure of my first book to change anything. Publication can be a terrible thing. Is this, you ask, what you have been waiting half your life to happen? It began to cross my mind that I'd lead a happier life if I gave up all idea of being a writer.

Ros and I carried into the streets every bitter moment we'd ever experienced together. We knew what we were doing – we were even sorry for each other – but we couldn't stop. Being in the most romantic city on earth was too savage an irony. On our last day we agreed to salvage something. A fine Parisian meal and a good bottle of wine should do it.

We started out from our hotel early to find the restaurant we would talk about lovingly as our salvation in years to come. We walked and walked, deciding against this one because it was too pretentious, that one because it was too plain, a third because it was too expensive, a fourth because it was too empty, a fifth because it was too full, there and back across the Seine, out of one suburb famous for its choucroute into another famous for its bouillabaise, until we arrived in Montmartre after midnight and fell into the only restaurant still open – a hugely expensive honeytrap for gullible American tourists, complete with Toulouse-Lautrec prints on every wall, violinist, accordionist, and sellers of red roses. What looked like exquisite cuts of fillet – the fillet Ros had been after since her plane landed in England – were delivered to our table. The wine had the name Rothschild on the label. We ate without speaking. At the best of times, Ros carried her own ecosystem around with her. In some moods she could melt the polar ice caps with her wild gaiety; in others she could freeze the Sahara with her ire. Tonight, though it had been a warm autumnal day in Paris, she sent a mistral through the restaurant, rattling the shutters, blowing out the candles on our table and extinguishing the flames on the flambéed crêpe Suzette at the other end of the room. The rose seller came over with a basket on her arm. I chose the loveliest bloom and slapped it down beside Ros's plate. I half expected her to eat it. The violinist came over to ask if we had a favourite romantic tune. 'Do you know the "Dead March"?' Ros asked.

I have no memory of how we got back to Wolverhampton, whether we exchanged a word or even noticed the other's presence. But I thought I saw people staring at us in fear. It's possible we looked like the undead, or one-time lovers wandering through the lowest of Dante's circles of hell, unable to recall what had ever brought us together but knowing we could never separate.

Ros showed immigration her new passport. I guessed what was going through her head. *Please don't let me in.* There is only one word for what I felt for her: grief.

I went to bed not expecting her to be there in the morning. 'Let her go,' I said to myself. 'Don't even open your eyes. For her sake, let her slip out of your life. You have done her nothing but harm.'

I, of course, had slept on the couch in the living room. When I crept into the bedroom to get my clothes – crept, just in case she was still there – I saw her, rolled so tightly into the duvet, like a polar bear trapped in the ice, that I had to lean over to be certain she was breathing, just as I had with my

225

brother all those years before. A mad hope that she would throw off the duvet, cry 'Oh, Hymie', and open her arms to me, died in the imagining.

The relation of cause to effect might take some fathoming, but the following day I moved a card table to the remotest corner of the flat, shuffled papers, sharpened a dozen pencils, set up a rudimentary office, turned my face to the wall, and began a novel.

When I say *began* ... but let's leave it there momentarily.

23

UNDER THE WATERFALL

In 1951 a primary school teacher wrote my mother a letter on a small blue sheet of notepaper. It described an essay I'd written on the uses of newspapers. 'I have every confidence,' it concluded, 'that Howard will be a great writer one day.' It was signed Esther Herman.

After my mother won the television the letter enjoyed pride of place on it.

Who can estimate the influence a good word from a teacher can have on a person's life? It's my belief that I was born possessed of that discontent of which novelists are made. Why I don't hear my mother saying 'Rubbish', I can't explain. Could it be that she agrees with me? *He was always a difficult child, pale, dyspeptic and complaining. Only later did we discover that he had a novel lodged inside his hippocampus.* Which isn't to detract from Esther Herman's gift. It's one thing to believe in your destiny, it's another to have it confirmed. And it's hardly her fault that throughout my teenage years, my twenties and most of my thirties, the bile of failed promise would force me onto a regimen of Andrews Liver Salts, Rennie, milk of magnesia, Mylanta,

Gaviscon, Nexium, charcoal tablets – anything, in short, that tasted like chalk, and none of which worked. Can you die of not writing a novel? I thought I might.

Can you die of others thinking you're a fantasist? I thought I might.

My fault, of course, for ever telling people I was working on a novel when I wasn't. It's possible that the words 'How much longer do we have to wait for that novel of yours?' were kindly meant, but I heard a jeering reproach in them. Was that because, along with the ambition, went my own jeering disbelief in myself? Why don't you just shut up about it, Howard? Do it or don't do it. Give us a break. Give yourself a break.

It didn't help, either, that I was called Howard. Can you write a novel when you don't have a novelist's name? *Howard Jacobson?* I didn't think so. Scott Fitzgerald, now. Virginia Woolf. Evelyn Waugh. With those names you had a fighting chance. Even my father's name had a writer's ring. *Max Jacobson* – I could have been a writer of tough-guy Chicagoan prose had I been a Max.

I didn't look right to be a novelist, either. I didn't look mad enough or sane enough. On top of which I was running out of time. For many years I'd kept a mental calendar of how old the great writers were when they published their first novels. Charles Dickens and Tolstoy, twenty-four. Dostoevsky, twenty-five. E. M. Forster, twenty-six. Emily Brontë, twenty-nine. Charlotte Brontë, thirty-one. Those buses had left without me. I was thirty-six when I returned from that wreckage of a honeymoon in Paris, twenty-seven years after Miss Herman's letter. Thirty-six was Jane Austen's age when she published *Sense and Sensibility*. Joseph Conrad was thirty-seven. George Eliot was forty. After that, the deluge.

Deluge, madness, wreckage – my vocabulary had turned cataclysmic. In so far as inspiration could be said to have put in an appearance at last, it came with a bad complexion and acid reflux, beckoning derisively, not with the elegantly shaped arms of the classical muses, reaching out through gold-edged clouds, but with the gnarled, crooked fingers – as though from some disreputable alley – of low, self-disgusted mirth. It's atmosphere I'm talking about, not subject. I didn't come back from Paris believing I finally had a specific tale to tell. The story of a sour marriage told from the husband's point of view was the last thing I wanted to write. No, I came back from Paris of a mind, of a temper, maybe the word is humour in the medieval physiological sense – of a *humour* that wanted words to express its choleric depressiveness.

Ros, too, had hit rock bottom. I couldn't feel sorry for myself without feeling still more sorry for her. What had we done? Neither of us was cut out for marrying at all, least of all for marrying each other. It seemed to me that we deserved medals for having tried. She had told me at the outset that she wanted a rock. I hadn't told her what I wanted because I didn't know, but it certainly wasn't someone who needed me to be a rock. We were both frustrated, unproductive, blocked, of artistic temperament but without the art that might have made such temperaments bearable. We were not in the slightest bit alike and yet in this we were identical. We offered each other no respite, whether from ourselves or from our incapacity to make our way in the world. At the beginning she believed in something she had seen in me, I in something I had seen in her. If those things were illusory it would be hard now to admit it without our hearts turning to ash. One of us, at least, had to make good on the fantasy. Never mind Esther Herman's 'great writer'. Just this minute I'd settle for a lot less. Drop the 'great'. Drop the life-affirming. One novel. One measly little novel. If I could write just that – *one measly sour savage rancid little novel that Leavis would never read but if he did*

229

would think of as doing dirt on life – I'd be proving to Ros that she had not been entirely mistaken in me. What she thought she'd seen was in there. And my productivity would rub off on her. Ours would be a novel-making marriage.

After several months of not speaking, we drove to Cornwall for Christmas and, because the weather was benign, took long walks in the Valency Valley, a romantic place consecrated to the young Thomas Hardy's love affair with Emma Gifford. 'When I'm dead and you're eighty,' Ros used to say, 'you'll come and walk here and remember me, just as he remembered his wife, and wish you'd been a better husband.' After Emma Gifford died, Hardy found a book she'd written about him in the attic bedroom to which she had been consigned or had consigned herself. It was entitled *What I Think of My Husband*. To the chagrin of Hardy scholars, and to his own shame as a man, Hardy burned it. 'I plan to write a book with that title myself,' Ros said.

'I can't wait to read it,' I said.

'I suppose you'll burn it,' she said.

I reminded her that a Jew didn't hold with burning books.

Above the babbling of the Valency River I heard a brief intake of breath. 'Here comes the Holocaust,' Ros was thinking.

She quickly changed the subject. 'I do love it here,' she said.

'Me too,' I said.

It was a lovely, maudlin walk. Ros led, I followed. Careful not to touch, we squelched along. Forded streams. Climbed stiles. Ran from cattle. Sometimes we read from the poems, sometimes from *The Wormwood Cup*, the story of the Hardys' romance written by Kenneth Phelps who lived locally and whom we stocked in the shop. He called in every day, with extra copies in a canvas bag, in case we'd sold any. I prayed to God I would never be reduced to hawking a novel from shop to shop. Though being reduced to never writing one was worse.

Ros must have read my thoughts. 'So how's it progressing?' she began, pretend absent-mindedly. I knew how much the question must have cost her.

We were looking into the pool in which, on an early picnic with Emma, Hardy had rinsed a glass when 'it slipped, and it sank, and was past recall'. The event is commemorated in 'Under the Waterfall', a poem in which the intense sadness of love mislaid finds expression in the loss of a small, domestic object.

> *By night, by day, when it shines or lours*
> *There lies intact that chalice of ours*

It was a fancy of *ours*, romantics that we were, that if we looked hard enough into the water we would find that chalice, and in the finding . . . well, make everything between us good again.

How was my novel progressing? I tapped my forehead to suggest it hadn't yet escaped onto the page, but was busy, whirring away . . .

After a long pause, she surprised me by saying, 'I wish you'd write more criticism.'

'What? You've always laughed at *my two Shakespearean essays*.'

'I have not. I think you're a good critic. You notice more in a book than you do in life.'

'That isn't what I want to hear, Ros.'

'I'm sorry. It's just what I think. So do you have a title?'

'No.'

'Do you have a plot?'

'Plot? God no. I don't do plots.'

'A subject then. Do you know what it's about?'

231

I wanted to say life but she'd just told me I was no good on life. 'Failure,' I said. 'Disappointment, degradation, frustration, animosity, envy, futility ...'

I could see her trying hard not to laugh. She let the cold water of Thomas Hardy's pool play over her fingers. 'Sounds a hoot,' she said. 'Should fly off the shelves.'

I let the poetic associations of the place temper my annoyance. I could no more blame her for her sarcasm than her doubts. It's hard to give your all to a project that the projector blows hot and cold on himself. And let this be said on her behalf in advance: when there was something tangible to believe in she would believe in it wholeheartedly. She wept when the novel I did finally get around not only to writing but to finishing was accepted for publication, opened her arms wide, embraced me, and shed warm tears. But that was sometime in the future; there were a lot of words to make it out onto the page, and a lot of pages to be screwed up and thrown away, before that happened.

In the meantime – 'A hoot.'

24

WRECKERS

I need now to concertina time.

If this narrative seems to be shuffling there and back, between Wolverhampton and Boscastle, that is because it is following the aimless trajectory of my unwriterly – and yet burgeoningly writerly – life at the time.

We were in Boscastle for twelve years, allowing for one or both of us being in Wolverhampton for some of that period, and then in London once what I'd written about Wolverhampton necessitated my leaving it, but I don't recall those years sequentially. Boscastle was a scoop out of our lives, not to be measured in earth years.

Did we enjoy it? Ros loved Boscastle when she didn't hate it. I hated it a little when I didn't hate it a lot but hated it less than Wolverhampton which I hated absolutely. In between times, a succession of small scandals, some sad, some ridiculous, helped persuade us we were having fun. 'You should be writing about this,' Ros had been saying from the off, and she was right. But it takes time to learn to write about what's in front of your eyes when you go about with your eyes closed.

Take the case of Molly Meneger, a scowling matron who wore her hair in an Edwardian bun and tutted about visitors, traffic, noise litter and depravity, spotted hiding in the passenger footwell of a teenage apprentice mechanic's Toyota as he pulled out of a lay-by on the Bude road. Her story was that her own car had broken down, he'd offered her a lift and she'd slipped off the seat. She might have been given the benefit of the doubt had she not slipped into exactly the same position coming out of exactly the same lay-by a week later.

Morwenna, whom Ros employed to iron and otherwise refresh the Indian clothes she sold in a little boutique above the craft shop, turned the air blue with her denunciation of Molly Meneger's behaviour. As though it wasn't bad enough that teenagers ran wild in the village, now the middle-aged were behaving like prostitutes too. Morwenna Trevaskis – pretty, permed and short-sighted – drove the six miles every morning from Delabole where they mined slate and spoke of Boscastle as the Devil's playground – a reputation Boscastle worked hard to maintain. A village with a fine history of luring ships onto the rocks and then claiming wrecking rights, it had been reduced, in modern times, to doing something similar to visitors. Fascinators of both sexes worked the village pubs like teams of moral pickpockets, beguiling wives from Nuneaton with roguish shanties and whispering the words 'me 'andsome' into the ears of husbands who heard the tide rolling out over shingles and had no choice but to walk out into the sea and drown. Though Morwenna Trevaskis didn't have the excuse of being new to the area – her family had lived in north Cornwall for generations – she too soon succumbed to the Boscastle sickness, losing her heart to the owner of a garage on the Bude road in whose Mercedes convertible she spent whole nights parked in the very lay-by, rumour had it, where Molly Meneger twice lost her balance.

'What is it about that lay-by,' people were asking.

'We're in love,' she couldn't wait to tell Ros when she rolled up late to work and explained her hands were shaking too much to iron.

'Still?'

'More than ever so. Last night he said, "I could die for you, maid," and I said, "I could die for you, Gryffin," but in the morning we wanted to live again.'

Though Ros never set her face against sincere passion, she warned Morwenna of its hazards. 'Can't do nothing 'bout it,' Morwenna said. 'I'm in its grip.'

Sooner or later Morwenna's husband was bound to turn up and blame her ruination on the village, us, and the job he'd never wanted her to take. I happened to be in the shop, trying on a cheesecloth, unisex pirate shirt, when he did. 'This place is a cesspit,' he shouted.

'Do you think you could settle this at home?' I suggested.

'Home? I have no home thanks to you lot.'

'Who do you think he was referring to as *you lot*?' I asked Ros later.

'I can't say for sure but definitely not the Jewish people,' Ros said.

Killjoy.

But the true killjoy was me. The poet Dryden said of Chaucer that he 'must have been a man of a most wonderful comprehensive nature ... he has taken into the compass of his *Canterbury Tales* the various manners and humours of the whole English nation in his time'. Boscastle might not have been the 'whole English nation' but it was a pretty good sample. So why wasn't I scribbling like fury?

The answer, as always, lay on that battlefield where my parents fought for control of my spirit. If my father was the generously sprawling Chaucer, my mother was the ever watchful, wise and waspish Jane Austen, and for the moment my mother's influence was in the ascendancy.

Having expanded from one shop to two, Ros's ambitions for the Old Mill knew no limits. Next, after some tough negotiation with the landlord, she set about transforming the entire top floor into a craft centre. All I had to do was put the odd-job skills I'd acquired in Melbourne to good use, paint the floorboards, erect chipboard space dividers, and rub my back like an itchy bear into wet plaster. The only shame was that we couldn't find any craftspeople to fill the craft centre with, or at least none prepared to fulfil the basic expectation of a craft centre which is to let the public watch them craft. With nothing to do in Boscastle except walk the cliffs, eat crab sandwiches and visit the Witch's Museum, tourists were desperate for something to look at. They would gather to watch open-mouthed as I parcelled up a piece of precious pottery on the little drystone wall outside the shop. 'What's he doing now?' I'd hear children whisper to their parents. 'Shush – he's wrapping.' On more than one occasion, after an especially elaborate wrap, I was applauded.

But for exciting interest, nothing beat the sight of me working in the waterwheel at the side of the building. It was an old, rotten wheel, but with a bit of attention to the wooden blades it could be made to turn again. When there were no other calls on my time and I wasn't in the mood to return to my novel – *Chapter One* – I would climb into the wheel with an assortment of hammers and saws and chisels and do some maintenance. So long as the leat was dry and the wheel immobile, this was a pleasant enough way to forget life's cares. But one day, on account of the leat having mysteriously filled, the wheel began to turn while I was inside it. In order not to be spun round at an increasing and possibly fatal speed I had to walk against the direction of the wheel's circuit, exactly like a gerbil in a tread-mill, only a gerbil simply has the wheel to contend with, whereas I had to dodge the hammers and the saws which, by the opposite law to centrifugal gravity, the wheel would carry upwards to the height of its revolution before dropping them down on me, sharp edges first. At least thirty holidaymakers watched this with increasing fascination and even whoops until one of them realised I was in trouble and organised help to get me out.

I mention this only to give some idea of the hunger for amusement we thought a craft centre might go some of the way to satisfying. But we had difficulty overcoming the reluctance of local craftspeople to appear in public. The best we could come up with was a wood-turner who wouldn't turn while anyone was watching him, a slate etcher whose speciality was hunchbacked garden birds, and Sylvania, a maker of hand-blown glass toffees who got rolling drunk by noon and took her blouse off. On a couple of occasions Sylvania burned herself badly falling into her kiln. The day the paramedics came to tend her and talk her back into her blouse was the craft centre's busiest day ever. Had I been trapped in the water-wheel at the same time we'd have emptied Cornwall of its tourists.

But waiting for a fatality is no way to run a business. 'This we can't have,' Ros said, announcing her intention to close the craft centre and turn it into a restaurant. She was not, let it be said, entirely without experience. She had run a tea garden in the village for a while, and after that a cafe that served

237

home-made cakes, crab sandwiches and steak, so long as you wanted the latter rare. I was helping out on the cafe's opening night. The first customer sent his steak back three times because it wasn't well-done enough.

'Tell him I don't do well-done,' Ros hissed at me in the kitchen.

'I have.'

'Tell him this is Australian cooking.'

'I have.'

'Tell him to get fucked.'

'I have.'

'Offer him a crab sandwich instead.'

'I can't do that. We have no crab.'

'Offer him a cheese sandwich.'

'I can't do that either. We have no bread.'

'Then *you* get fucked.'

Which I did, throwing off my apron in what Ros, in future descriptions of the event, described as a 'flounce'. I later learned that she came out of the kitchen and addressed the remaining diners, telling them that I thought of myself as a writer rather than a waiter on the strength of a couple of essays on Shakespeare (signed copies of which, by the way, were on sale in the craft shop below), and that if they wanted to go on eating *chez elle* they'd have to assist her at the stove and serve themselves, which they willingly did. They had such a good time they kept coming back, helping Ros serve rare steak *à l'Australienne* every night for the duration of their holiday, booing whenever they saw me in the village, and on one occasion coming into the shop to find *Shakespeare's Magnanimity*, reading random samples of my prose aloud to one another, and chortling.

Here is not the place to trace the history of the Old Mill Restaurant. Suffice it to say that Ros bestrid the open kitchen

238

like an empress, cooking cabbage soup, lasagne, cassoulet, meatballs, boeuf bourgignon and other classics of 1960s Australian bistro in full view of the hungry populace, some of whom she didn't hesitate to throw out if they grew impatient at the time it took for them to get their food or expressed dissatisfaction with it when it came. I washed up when we had staff and waited on tables when they forgot to turn up. Often we fought and I'd be thrown out. An academic couple from Milton Keynes, who had purchased *Shakespeare's Magnanimity* from the shop below and brought it to the table for discussion, felt they had some sinister tripartite thing going with me and would eat only if I served and then sat between them. One night, discovering I'd been barred, they refused either to order or to leave unless I was reinstated. Ros sent out a waitress to find me. 'This time,' she warned me as I was putting on my apron, 'try not to blow in her ear when you're telling her the specials.'

'Sure, but then don't expect them to come back,' I said. Which got me thrown out again.

In keeping with Ros's Melbourne cuisine, we ran an Australian-style BYO system which kept our margins down but improved staff-customer relations. Diners who bring their own wine drink more and stay longer. It was not uncommon for them to invite us to their table at the end of the evening to share whatever was left in their bottles.

'Hope you're writing about this, Hymie,' Ros would say as we staggered home to bed, flushed with conviviality.

I wasn't. Life, when it was too vivid, wrote itself. A writer of the sort I aspired to be didn't simply put down what was already there. The novelist's task was to invent, not record. Henry James famously advised a would-be writer to be one 'upon whom nothing is lost'. My advice – at this stage only to myself – was to be one to whom nothing happened.

And if there was no avoiding event? Then wait for quiet. Art was commotion recollected in tranquillity.

When I wasn't being a waiter, I would drive across Bodmin Moor to a butcher's in Liskeard to collect pasties useful to have in the freezers in case we ran out of Ros's lasagne. I kept my blank manuscript open on the passenger seat in case the big idea I'd been waiting for suddenly hit me. Sometimes, when the smell of fresh pasty coming from the boot of the car was more than I could resist, I would pull off the road onto the moor, wind down the window, wait for the salivating ponies to approach and share a pasty or two with them. Once, a vegan pony more interested in paper than meat put his head all the way into the car and tried to eat the manuscript. It would, I thought, have been a fitting end to a career that, to this point, delivered so much less than it had promised.

It was round about this time, too, that I drove sometimes hundreds of miles a day in pursuit of potters whose work I'd seen in other shops and galleries and thought would look good in Ros's. This was part apology for the Chinese paper-weights and part escape into my thoughts. It turned out that I had an eye for pots, or at least an eye for potters whose prin-cipled seclusion intrigued me. It's possible I was imagining my future life as a writer in exactly such dilapidated cottages as theirs, with their kilns forever burning in a shed at the bottom of the garden and their wives talking to themselves – unless they were the potter and the husband was talking to himself – in the kitchen. On I drove, splashing through fords, rattling over stubbled meadows, often getting bogged down in fields of dung and potter's clay, only to encounter, when I at last arrived, a level of surly introversion found in no other profes-sion on earth, not even that of writer. What the connection is between the lovely undulations of that unravished bride of porcelain quietness, of no use for anything but looking beautiful on a sideboard, and the determination of its maker to hate anyone who wants to buy it, I have yet to discover. But I felt I had something to learn from the potter's example. Deep in the dark of dank nature they found the tranquillity to make art that wasn't damp or dark; so why shouldn't I do the reverse and find in a tranquillity that was far from the ugly farce of polytechnic politics the spleen necessary to finish a damp, dark book?

If it sounds from the above that I was never at the polytechnic, that was how it seemed to me when the world of Boscastle held me in its faerie thrall. But no sooner was I back there than I couldn't believe I had ever been anywhere else. I'd drive back from Cornwall in the early hours of a Monday or a Tuesday morning and arrive so tired I feared I would fall asleep during my own lectures. And once I did. Whether my students noticed or simply took down my snores in hieroglyphic form, of no more interest or clarity to them than any other sound I made, I have no idea. But they never commented on my psychic absence. A great demoralisation had seized the institution. Things were brewing in the worlds of educational politics and ideas that put both on a collision course. On the one hand there was pressure on us to demonstrate the usefulness of what we were teaching, and to locate the things we taught to the students' own experience – so what about the iconography of the football scarf as a module, or the contents of each student's waste-paper bin, for was not the very concept of 'waste' worth examining? – on the other, the theoreticians were importing a language inimical to English with the result that Wordsworth's idea of the poet as 'a man talking to men' sounded suddenly imbecilic and sexist, for the poet wasn't necessarily a man and certainly wasn't talking to anyone. As though to worse confound this confusion the polytechnic decided to house us – us being humanities, who else? – in Molineux, Wolverhampton Wanderers' football stadium, accommodation that happened to be going cheap on account of the club having spent money on a grandiose refurbishment after the team had a good season whereupon it had a seemingly unending series of bad ones.

'Try to see the benefits of this,' the Dean of Arts told us. 'You'll be able to look up from your desks and watch the match.'

I can't say this came as a shock. It had been building for some time. Hence my willingness, in those cruel days after the fiasco of our honeymoon when I made a writing desk of the card table and turned my face to the wall, to go in whichever direction the gnarled, crooked finger of inspiration pointed. Low, self-disgusted, mirth? Very well – low, self-disgusted mirth it would be. I shared a rancid bathroom in a flat with no hot water in the middle of one of the ugliest towns in the country and would soon be teaching in a football stadium. Who knew more about low, self-disgusted mirth than I did?

But that still left open the possibility of doing something in the vein of Rabelais or Lord Rochester or the Marquis de Sade or Alexander Pope or Flaubert. D. H. Lawrence had written about the East Midlands: why shouldn't I write about the West Midlands, throwing in a bit more comedy? And who was to say that low, self-disgusted mirth absolutely precluded Jamesian elegance? If I had set myself an impossible task, if these were modes that could never be reconciled, that might explain why I drove thousands of miles across Cornish moors and down Cornish lanes with the manuscript open and forever empty on the passenger seat of my Renault.

So you could say that finally moving to Molineux, where we could teach A. E. Housman while watching Wolves play Burnley, was a godsend. My reading of the genre was limited – as my reading of anything post 1930 was limited – but was there not already a form ideally suited to the situation in which my fastidious colleagues and I found ourselves? Kingsley Amis, Malcolm Bradbury, David Lodge, Tom Sharpe (though I would surely never descend that far into farce) – had they not carved out a groove, a furrow, a rut, in modern English letters?

My epiphany. Write a campus novel.

My second epiphany: write a campus novel not about a university, as was the wont, but a polytechnic.

And then my third: I was already without a plot, a plan, an intention or a hero. Why not a campus novel without a campus?

25

READER, I WROTE IT

Why *had* I wanted to write like Henry James? More, say, than Dickens whose tumultuousness I loved, or D. H. Lawrence whose voice had been a trouble and a stimulus to me since adolescence and a copy of one or other of whose novels I used to carry around with me as a sixth-former when I wanted to attract a girl? Ask my brother. Ask why one of the paintings he most admires is Piero di Cosimo's exquisite *A Satyr Mourning Over a Nymph*. I suspect both questions will get the same answer. Forget subject matter. We sought the formal orderliness of extreme quietude or, put another way, the extreme quietude of formal orderliness.

We never discussed this. We certainly never swapped artistic credos in our formative years. But our formative years must explain it. If we seek a melancholy stillness in composition – if we make art precisely in order to inhabit such stillness – it can only be because in life we grew up in anarchy. For a while, after my father gave up the markets, our house looked like everybody else's. You could walk from one room to another without stumbling over boxes of faux-brass candlesticks or

Rexine pouffes imported from Hong Kong. But that turned out to be but a brief interregnum of domestic unclutteredness and serenity. With his new passion for magic came new obstacles. Coloured scarves flew out of cutlery drawers. Mechanical toys walked across your path if you happened to clap your hands. Invisible wires garrotted visitors. Help yourself to fruit from the fruit bowl and you found yourself biting into a ball of magic sponge. And all the while I sat with my head in my hands doing my homework while my brother crouched on the kitchen floor spinning screws until his fingers bled. That we have both sought in art the illusion of tranquillity is hardly a surprise.

It's time I owned up to a lie. While it's true that I tried to write *The Wings of the Dove* and *The Golden Bowl* at an age when other boys with literary ambitions were having a go at *A Farewell to Arms* or *The Great Gatsby*, it's false that I wrote the following in my fourteenth year:

> All things considered, for Hugh St John Vereker* the day had gone swimmingly – though he was himself no swimmer, not a man of water, truth to say, of any sort – well. He contemplated, in their all too subtle efflorescence, the gardens which the night before – was it only one night? – had borne mute witness to the first and so far only indiscretion of his young, and still all too beautifully untouched life.

I composed that fragment much later as a pastiche of a pastiche, a joke at the expense of the earlier me, though the years spent trying to write sentences I had no business trying to write, about matters of which I knew nothing, in flat refusal to confront matters of which I knew at least a little more, now

* 'Vereker', by the by, is a highfalutin, cod Jamesian moniker that Thurber beat me to.

strike me as too wasteful to be a joking matter. When you start running out of years you find yourself wishing you had put the squandered ones to better use.

Literary is a word writers run from. Literary Editor describes the job you hope you never have to take; Literary Novelist is an insult; Literary Fiction is atrocious marketing. Writers are meant to have read a lot but not to let the reading show. If too many cooks spoil the broth, too many Roths spoil the book. Which is itself an example of the sort of jokes writers make when their heads are too cluttered with literature. In my case it wasn't a matter of not seeing the wood for the trees; it was that the wood I saw was sacred. And yes, such reverence does sometimes lead to morbid reticence. Or, if you are somehow able to overcome that, to a profound disappointment in yourself. You write down words you think are as much your own as words ever can be, only to realise that it's the Great Tradition, with the addition of Tolstoy and Turgenev, talking through you. This time, though – as a published writer with two essays to his name – I believed I could o'erleap the lot of them. Not better them – they were unbetterable – but literally o'erleap them in the sense of jumping the logjam of genius in my brain for which they were responsible.

When I pictured myself doing it I saw Evel Knievel.

And a Campus Novel Without a Campus was what I ended up with.

Over a period of more years than I willingly remember, I wrote one hundred and ninety pages – take what follows as an approximation: ninety of them in my Wolverhampton flat, thirty of them on Bodmin Moor, five of them in the Membury Services on the M4, ten of them in the garden of a pub in Bishop's Lydeard in Somerset, five of them in my head while trapped inside the Old Mill waterwheel, and however many that leaves on side roads and bridle paths in the course of my searching out pasties and potters in Devon and Cornwall. These I handed to Ros to read during a rare peaceful weekend in Wolverhampton together.

I put three bottles of Australian Shiraz on the table for her. 'You think three will do it?' she said.

I told her I could always nip out and get more. I didn't want to be there while she was reading, anyway.

When Wilbur showed me one hundred and ninety pages of his first novel I went aloof and prissy on him. We weren't a kindergarten writers' collective, I said. Just write the thing, Wil, then I'll read it as any reader would. I'd say the same today, but that just means I'm still the unsympathetic prig I was. So how to explain my showing one hundred and ninety pages to my wife? Desperation is the best explanation I can offer. I was getting too old to disappear down the rabbit hole of delusion. I needed my long-bottled-up words to be looked at, and if no good, told they were no good.

Which is what Wilbur must have felt . . .

Barbara and I had named Conrad after Joseph Conrad, whom we had both read and loved. Barbara's mother Mary was against it, saying people would call him Conks. That sounded far-fetched to me. Who called anyone Conks? As though to prove me wrong, Mary crooned 'Who's my little Conky?' the moment she saw him.

In *A Personal Record*, Joseph Conrad tells a deeply affecting story of showing the unfinished manuscript of his first novel to a fellow passenger named Jacques travelling for his health aboard 'the good ship *Torrens*'.

'Well, what do you say?' Conrad asks, when Jacques returns the manuscript to him. 'Is it worth finishing?'

The man's reply, 'in his sedate veiled voice', is succinct. 'Distinctly.'

Needing to hear more, Conrad asks if he was 'interested' in what he read.

'Very much.'

Jacques dies not long afterwards.

I wished no such fate on Ros but I hoped for a similarly encouraging response. I didn't leave the flat but paced up and down as she sat with her knees drawn up in an armchair, her hair falling into her face, dropping each page to the floor as she finished with it. It was a composition I liked. Egon Schiele would have liked it too.

'Has anyone ever told you,' I said, 'that you look ravishing when you're reading.'

'Get fucked,' she said . . . in her sedate veiled voice.

I quit the living room and paced the bedroom. It was in her bedroom, propped up against soft pillows, that I found my mother laughing hysterically over Thurber. OK, Ros – do thou likewise . . .

After an infinity of silence, I returned. 'I don't hear you laughing,' I said.

'Not everything has to be funny.'

'No, not everything, but I hoped that maybe some of this was . . .'

'Well, it's not.'

'What is it then?'

'Sad.'

'Sad as in pathetic?'

'Sad as in upsetting.'

'I can't tell if that means you like it or you don't.'

Say '*Very much*', Ros. Say '*Distinctly*'.

But she didn't. 'Neither can I,' was what she said instead.

'That's not very helpful.'

'Shush,' she said, 'let me finish.'

She went on reading while I went on pacing then suddenly she called me to her. 'Here,' she said, pointing to page one hundred and eighty-nine.

'Here what?'

'It starts here.'

'Here? Page one hundred and eighty-nine? There's only one page left. It's not starting, it's finishing.'

'To me it's just starting.'

'Why here? What happens here?'

'It comes alive.'

'In what sense?'

'In the sense that I'm interested.'

'And you weren't before?''

'Not much, no.'

'So what changes on page one hundred and eighty-nine?'

'You're the writer,' she said. 'You work it out.'

26

'BEING JEWISH . . .'

I was lucky to have in Ros not just a champion of Jews and novels but an excellent reader. Her musical training had given her a good ear. Strike a bum note and she heard it. She had no taste for trivia. Her favourite dramatists were Aeschylus and Euripides. Her favourite composer was Wagner. She couldn't do small talk herself and was impatient of it in the conversation or writing of others. She was incapable of falsity as well. The minute she heard it, or thought she heard it, in a friend, she dropped the friend. Often brutally, much as she had dropped the one hundred and eighty-eight pages of my novel. That she didn't drop the one hundred and eighty-ninth page, in that case – no matter that she wouldn't, or couldn't, tell me what she found there that she hadn't found earlier – amounted to a massive vote of confidence. I was ready to start for no other reason than that she – the first reader of my fiction – said I was.

What being ready to start there and not a page earlier meant was that I could think of what I'd done so far not as a waste but as a sort of apprenticeship to myself. The pupil, so to speak, could now take over from the master. That still left open the question of what exactly Ros had seen that marked a change. *Neshome*, I decided. Soul. Right at the very end of what I'd given her to read, the novel had found its *neshome*. Laugh at the plight of the hero all you like, he was in pain. The indignity of his position, reduced to teaching literature in a football stand in a West Midlands town was ludicrous all right, but it cut deeper than he, and maybe even I, had realised. *Shande*, the Yiddish word for shame, doesn't stop at personal humiliation. It carries a suggestion of societal disgrace. Scandal. Something that should never have been allowed to happen. This, I decided, was what Ros – who, I repeat, had no taste for lightness – had seen on page one hundred and eighty-nine without fully realising she was seeing it – which was hardly surprising given that I hadn't realised I was writing it. Whether he knew it or not, my hero had failed the sacred function for which he had been *chosen*. My hero, to my surprise, consternation and (I don't now mind admitting) disappointment, was *Jewish*.

The discriminating reader – to disinter a phrase from 1960s Cambridge – will more than once have wondered whether there wasn't some obstruction to my taking so long to write a page of fiction other than those I have so far given. *Wouldn't it be true to say, Hymie, that in your canon of greats and deadweights there is no writer with a Jewish name . . . ?*

In my defence, I ask the jury to identify the great, the good, or even just the goodish Jewish novelists writing in English between the birth of Jane Austen and the death of Henry James. All right, Disraeli. And who after that? As for that flowering of Jewish literary culture in America that coincided with my Leavis discipleship, it didn't fall within my purview. No, Ros, I don't want to read about a Jew who fucks the family dinner, I'd said. Put plainly, it never crossed my mind to wonder whether there might be Jewish writers out there from

whom I might pick up something – I still don't know what
the word for it would be – *exemplary*? Pick up something not
in the sense of learning how to part company with the non-
Jewish greats, but how to coexist with them in full and cheerful
knowledge of one's difference.

And why was that?

The quickest answer is that when it came to words, sentences, paragraphs, I didn't feel different. Or, more accurately,
didn't know I felt different.

How about: didn't *want* to feel different?

I didn't swap Manchester for Cambridge in order to ditch
the Jew in me, but if it fell away of its own accord, well, I
wasn't going to make a song and dance of hanging on to it.
But who *was* the Jew in me? And how much of it was left,
anyway, by the time Leavis claimed me?

A question for my mother:

Dear Ma,

Do you remember that time I went with you to some
crumby auction in Chorlton? 'The bid is with you, Mrs
Jackson,' the auctioneer said after you'd raised your arm.
Mrs Jackson!!! And do you remember what you said after
I'd accused you of being ashamed to let on you were Jewish? You said, 'It's not that. It's just to avoid confusion. People
don't know how to spell Jacobson.'

Well, pull the other one, Ma. I know why you called
yourself Jackson. It was because to your ear 'Jacobson' was a
barbarism.

So guess what? It was to mine too.

Some Jews deal with the barbarism of their names by changing them. The odd auction in the middle of nowhere aside, we
didn't do that. But we didn't go around waving flags with our

252

names on them, either. So it was with my writerly ambitions. I didn't aspire to be a Jewish writer because I didn't know what one was. For the same reason I didn't aspire *not* to be one either. But without putting it to myself in so many words, I believed that if I was ever going to make some contribution to the English literature I loved it wouldn't be as the doubly-ghetto'd Jew, strapped into his musty tefillin and tied to an uncouth industrial tongue. And so I remained Hugh St John Vereker on the page until, with masterly intuition, Ros pointed to the exact place where Hugh St John Vereker would have to speak his last if ever I were to speak as myself, or find a self to speak as at all.

She hadn't thought the pages I'd given her funny. I hadn't wholly expected her to. She never denied that her humour was defective, what with her monotonic, vowel-chewing, sailor father – a man I very much liked but never joked with – her lovely, funny, but depressive, forever-exiled mother, the nuns who taught her to pray for the souls of the Jews, and the all-round slowness of the West Australian mumblers and rumi-nators she'd grown up with on the Swan River. But I trusted her nonetheless. Like the ailing Mrs Gradgrind in Dickens's *Hard Times*, who wasn't exactly in pain herself but knew there was a pain somewhere in the room, Ros knew when there was a joke somewhere on the page even if she didn't get it. This time, though, she knew to a certainty there *wasn't*.

As I ran what I'd written over in my head I no longer found it funny either. The comedy was too – dare I say goyish? There it all was, the polytechnic on open day, desperate for students; my friend who kept his jacket permanently on the back of his chair to suggest he had briefly popped out of his room, but in reality had been selling refectory tables in antique fairs in Shropshire; my Oxbridge-educated colleagues, readers of Georgian poetry and Walter Pater, men and women of letters who burned with a hard gemlike flame, now lumped together as Humanities for Business and housed in a football stadium; the dismal town with its ring road that ran right through the middle of it; and a ludicrous figure not entirely unlike my dismal self – funny enough when I described it conversationally, but somehow on the page not funny at all.

Something was missing from the comedy. The smell of blood and metaphysics. Some crowning humiliation that explained why my hero felt as preposterously suicidal as he did and, more than that, lifted him out of the dimension of mere self-sorrowing ego. I can't now remember what name I'd given him. Something provisional, I suspect. Bill maybe. Alf. Every name I'd tried embarrassed me. I'd wanted to keep it unassociated. Nothing Jamesian or Conradian. Nothing that sounded like Raskolnikov or Julien Sorel. A name with no literary baggage. But you can't have an entirely baggageless hero. With only a provisional name he could barely speak for the particular let alone the general. Then it came to me – the person washed up in a hell less cosmopolitan even than Manchester, more out of the swim of things than I'd been in Cambridge, more disregarded than I had always been in Boscastle, the person born for better, greater things, just don't ask him what, the splenetic, self-lacerating failure whose miseries I couldn't adequately render until I'd plumbed the dankest depths of absurdism, had to be called Sefton Goldberg.

Sefton Goldberg. Not Sefton Hugh St John Goldberg, but simple Sefton Goldberg – to my ear, the perfect nebbish name.

And he was born in a verbal afterbirth of the most disconsolate simplicity. 'Being Jewish,' the phrase that bore him went, 'Sefton Goldberg ...'

Thereafter I would repeat the faux-naive phrase again and again throughout the novel. 'Being Jewish, Sefton Goldberg ...'

254

'I think we've got the point by now that Sefton Goldberg is Jewish,' I remember some grudging, tone-deaf reviewer writing. But the person who needed to get the point was Sefton Goldberg. And behind him, me. Despite myself, I was writing a Jewish novel. And it was only because it was a Jewish novel that I was finally writing it at all. There it was – the perfect chain of causation. No Jew – no novel.

The idea that I'd put Jewish Manchester behind me was a fantasy. Cambridge hadn't ironed out the moral convolutions, the dark self-denigrations, the bloody provocations, the messianic ambitions alternating with the cringing fears, that I'd carried around with me since – well, since the beginning. Trying to express myself some other way – letting English sunlight into my prose – had proved impossible. Being Jewish, I had contradictions to resolve that necessitated my sending a far more fraught language – at once feckless and reverential – on a far more overwrought mission. And the unlikely captain of my tremulous craft, if only for this maiden voyage, was an unhappy, unsuccessful, thin-skinned (and yes, all right, over-eroticised) teacher of English literature called Sefton Goldberg, whose existence so astonished me I couldn't stop writing his name.

The Yiddish-speaking critic and scholar Ba'al Makshoves famously castigated the shtetl Jews of Mendele Mocher Sforim's Yiddish novels for the obscure lives of repetitive ritual they consented to lead while all along believing themselves to be the Chosen. He could have been describing Sefton Goldberg – a self-appointed Parnassian Jew, destined by his birthright to achieve remarkable things, reduced to explicating diabolically serpentine prose to reluctant students of Business in a polytechnic in the centre of a soulless West Midlands town that processed dog licences. The polytechnic was his shtetl.

Ask by what sane reasoning Sefton Goldberg could consider himself as Chosen, in these, or indeed in any circumstances, and it will take me another of Tet's 'two thousand years of Jewish suffering' to find the answer, which is that there is no answer.

But the one thing Sefton didn't mean was that as a Jew he enjoyed any sort of aristocratic or sacerdotal exemption. Quite the opposite. Chosen, for Goldberg, meant appointed to perform a task. As a schoolboy is chosen to be the team goalkeeper, with the purpose of keeping out the ball, so, by his understanding, was a Jew – every Jew – chosen to keep up an idea. Specifically *what* idea didn't matter. In the vagueness lay the duty to find a purpose beyond vagueness. Chosen means enjoined to make life purposeful, not to squander it on vanity or selfishness or triviality. Not to let it vanish like a dream. To feel called to devote it to high purpose. For some that equates to making the world a better place. For others a still higher cause, for which they have been chosen, is to honour the magnificent conception of God's creation. And you don't have to believe in God to believe in that.

Teaching English literature in a football stadium in Wolverhampton was not, to Sefton Goldberg, to honour God's magnificent conception, whether for humanity or just for him. It could have been. Had he been a different kind of Jew he might have seen his calling in it, shedding light where there was darkness, taking knowledge to a place where knowledge was in short supply. But he was the Jew he was. The comedy in the novel I came to entitle *Coming From Behind* – which doesn't sound Jewish in the slightest – is the gauge that marks how far from high purpose Sefton thinks he's strayed. But it is also the gauge that marks the preposterousness of his belief that it was for high purpose he'd been called.

You can see why, even in its unformed state, Ros found the novel sad.

There, anyway, was the tale I had to tell. 'Being Jewish, Sefton Goldberg ...' And on the wave of that deceptively innocent refrain, the novel crashed at last onto the rugged shore of a conclusion.

The End.

It had been a long time coming, and I was not alone in having for many years believed it never would come. That it had, I considered nothing short of miraculous.

I am too superstitious to celebrate anything wildly. Punch the sky and the sky will fall down. I see myself sitting back in my chair – though whether in Boscastle or Wolverhampton I have no memory – breathing deeply, not with jubilation but relief. *Got tsu danken.* An old phrase of my father's. A thank you to God, for anything from the news that a desperately sick relative had pulled through to rain stopping on Oswestry market.

Had I been someone else's son I might have said phew! But relief, if and when it came, had a metaphysical dimension for both sides of our family. My grandmother resigned herself to the will of an inscrutable Almighty. My father, who couldn't wait, made it more personal and direct. *Got tsu danken.* Either way, we didn't get out of trouble without His help.

I have tried to explain why it had been so important to me, from my earliest years, to write. But the history and nature of any obsession is hard to convey. It wasn't that I felt I had something I desperately had to say. It was more that I felt I had to be saying but was yet to find *what* it was I had to say. Not any old thing, but not me – not my story, Heaven help us! – either. If you like, it was form that beckoned, long before I had any interest in content. It was the idea of making something up,

257

being Lord and Creator of a world that had never before existed – not a fanciful world but our actual, sublunary world refashioned – employing words in a way they were not familiarly employed, engrossing myself in the telling, the doing, the manufacture, as though in order to vanish from the dull distractions of the ready-made, hand-me-down here and now, though where to re-emerge I had no idea. And if never to re-emerge – well, there was glamour in that.

In so far as this could be called an ambition, its ultimate aim wasn't fame, prizes, riches, desirable as they were. Am I saying there was nothing, outside of the activity itself, that I'd ever wanted?

Yes no. Yes – there was something. The last line of Kafka's *The Trial* reads, 'It was as if he meant the shame of it to outlive him.' That was it. I wanted *the shame of it to outlive me* . . .

But I no sooner catch myself saying, 'Yes, yes, that was it,' than I think, 'No, no, it wasn't.' It was more that I wanted to outlive my shame.

And what shame was that? Jew shame.

27

'OUR BEGINNINGS NEVER KNOW OUR ENDS'

So much for getting *Coming From Behind* written. Now all I had to do was get it published.

Assuming they had first refusal, having published *Shakespeare's Magnanimity*, I'd sent the manuscript to Chatto & Windus, who hummed and hawed. I fell at once into a trough of dejected defeatism. Not far to fall for me, but a fall is still a fall. Ros hauled me out. 'Go and see them,' she said. Now it was my turn to hum and haw. Maybe I'd write a letter addressing some of their concerns. 'Just go and see them,' Ros repeated. 'Face-to-face is always better.' I said I'd go in a couple of weeks. She said, 'Go now.' She even drove me to Bodmin Road Station, kissed me goodbye, urged me to be strong, wished me luck, and kissed me goodbye again. The occasion reminded me of my first journey to Cambridge when my father sat me down opposite a corpse. This time everyone, at least at my table, and with the possible exception of me, was alive. Ros stood on the platform and waved me off with a fist of determination. She has every right to feel she was instrumental to getting my career as a novelist off the ground.

Under her steam, then, I went to London, stayed at the Strand Palace Hotel just round the corner from Chatto & Windus, ate a hearty breakfast, superstitiously avoiding bacon – if ever there was a time to have God on my side, this was it – and marched in with Ros's injunctions to take no shit, Hymie, ringing in my ears. Jeremy Lewis and Dennis Enright, whom I'd met before over the publication of *Shakespeare's Magnanimity*, greeted me. They reminded me of the sinisterly courteous emissaries who knife K. through the heart in that bleakly funny novel Kafka wrote as a gift to men like me. They had that same air of bemused culpability, of not fully understanding why they were doing whatever it was they were doing. Jeremy Lewis was jovial and bear-like. Enright narrow-eyed and ironic. Good cop, bad cop. 'The real question is, will it make it as a paperback?' Dennis Enright mused aloud. He seemed to look at me through the side of his face. 'Could you put in more jokes about Sefton Goldberg disliking sport and have him sweat more?' Jeremy Lewis wondered. 'Sweaty' was an adjective dear to his heart and I would later have to beg him to delete it from the blurb. Neither mentioned Jewishness. Was it possible they hadn't noticed? *Being Jewish, Sefton Goldberg* . . . Hadn't I made him Jewish enough? The question of an agent arose. They felt I should have one. I wondered where an agent was to be found. 'Upstairs,' Jeremy said. I asked if there was anything to stop me going up there with the manuscript right this minute. Ros would have been proud of my celerity. 'Absolutely nothing.' Except the stairs themselves which could have dated from Dr Johnson's time. Up I went, left the manuscript with a secretary, and descended. Two weeks later up I went again. Mark Hamilton shook my hand. 'Does that mean I have an agent?' I asked. It did. Dennis and Jeremy were waiting for me at the bottom of the stairs as though to catch me if I fell. 'Well?' they asked. 'He liked it.' 'Wonderful,' Jeremy exclaimed. Dennis Enright looked at me through the other side of his face. They shook my hand. 'Does that mean I have a publisher?' I asked. They nodded.

Easy.

Or would have been easy had Chatto & Windus stayed the way it was. Not an extravagant expectation since it looked as though it had stayed the way it was for three hundred years. But enter, several months after I did, Carmen Callil, famed for founding the feminist publishing house Virago, and now new managing director of Chatto. Incoming publishers, eager to make a splash with writers of their choice, don't as a rule like the books they inherit. Carmen hated mine. *Coming From Behind* had already been copy-edited but that didn't stand in the way of her copy-editing it a second time. Nothing if not conscientious, she fell upon my manuscript with her pencil, putting a blue line through every mention of a woman's body parts. *Every* mention? *Every* body part? Armpits, shoulders, knees and elbows? Fingers and toes? Well, it's a long time ago. Was she having fun with me or warning me to keep my invasive masculinist prose off women's bodies altogether? I asked Jeremy what he thought. 'Oh, Lord, just ignore it,' he said.'

He became a tremendous friend over the coming years, though he never again enjoyed anything I wrote as much as he'd enjoyed *Coming From Behind*. He was old-fashioned on principle, unabashedly Wodehousian, a 'Grub Street irregular' in his own words, and feared success was turning me into a modernist. He and his wife Petra were lavish entertainers and Ros and I, once we came to live in London, were lavish entertainees. They gave Ros what she described as her best ever times in England. I'm not sure I saw her happier than at the Lewis table, eating Petra's English food and roaring with laughter at

Jeremy's English jokes. Here, at last, was what she'd quit Australia to find so many years before. Jeremy's death in 2017 left another crater in my life, and, I am sure, in Ros's, though by that time we were living oceans apart and not speaking.

A month or so before publication Carmen rang me. I was in Cornwall. 'No one knows who you are,' she said, without any other preliminaries. 'When are you next in London? You need to have an affair with someone famous.'

I didn't have speakerphone turned on. I doubt I had a speakerphone. But Ros was sitting near and Carmen had a loud voice.

'She means her,' Ros said.

I doubted I was Carmen's type. And besides, I said, I didn't see what kind of an affair we could have if I had to stay away from elbows.

'You can have an affair without reference to a woman's elbow,' Ros said.

I felt a joke coming on. 'What about . . . ?'

'Don't,' Ros said.

'You're just no fun,' I said.

'By the sound of her, I'm more fun than she is.'

She was right about that, but then they were both Australian and this was the ideological 1980s when the fun was beginning to go out of everything.

My next conversation with Carmen was at a launch party she threw for a number of Chatto authors whose books were being released simultaneously under a PR slogan that went something like 'Announcing the End of the Demise of Literary Fiction'. Catchy or what? We stood in a line like new recruits waiting to be inspected. She showered compliments on this one and promised wild success to another. When she came to me she said, 'Well, I don't know what I'm supposed to do about you, Mr Jacobson. If you ran naked down Bond Street I couldn't sell this book.'

Am I making that up? Exaggerating? Embellishing just a little?

No.

A sad event occurred shortly after the novel appeared. I received a letter from the sister of Esther Herman, the primary school teacher who'd written to my mother a thousand years before to say she thought I'd be a great writer one day. Well, she didn't live to see me be a writer of any kind. She missed it by a whisker, having died only the month before. She would have been so proud, her sister wrote.

Time's Laughingstocks indeed. Thomas Hardy couldn't have engineered crueller timing.

It was all my own doing. I'd taken too long. I wasn't only too late for Mrs Herman, I was too late for myself. I would always feel on the back foot, trying to catch up.

You need luck to be a successful writer and a measure of that equanimity writers rarely possess. To the unpublished, publication is the Promised Land you glimpse while you are still wandering in the wilderness. But the moment you are published, futurity is off the table. Yes, you have a book out, but where the hell is it? In the darkest moods, when they have blamed everybody else for the anticlimax of publication, writers will blame their publishers. Are they disseminating your work or secreting it? Well, Carmen had laid my options on the table. Forgo my modesty or endure modest sales. I'd gone for modest sales.

My stroke of luck came in the person of an energetic, non-censorious publisher with a sense of humour called Patrick Janson-Smith who brought out *Coming From Behind* with lashings of publicity in Black Swan paperback, a bold new imprint to which Sefton Goldberg's hapless scabrousness was perfectly suited. It was published with an enticing jacket drawn by the cartoonist Charlie Griffiths who made Sefton Goldberg look a little too like me – for the writer must never be taken for his protagonist – but even that didn't get in the way of its going into many editions.

Twenty-seven years later I would win the Booker Prize with a novel whose hero wasn't Jewish but wanted to be.

By that time Ros and I were long divorced and not speaking. So whether she thought I had made good on the promise she'd so assiduously nurtured I am unable to say. Our break-up had been anguished and prolonged. 'Make something happen, Hymie,' had always been her refrain but I seemed unable ever to make something happen for her. The truth of it is that she'd been the one who'd made something happen for me.

28

ECCE IUDEAUM

It turned out to be a two-way street. If the words 'Being Jewish' got me writing, writing them got me being Jewish.

I don't only mean that I found myself cast at once into the role of professional Jew. That was bound to happen. There was a shortage of us. Rabbis and chroniclers of the Holocaust we had in plenty, but Jewish writers, especially Jewish novelists, were harder to come by. Why more Jewish writers turn to the theatre than the novel I can't explain. It might be that a playwright enjoys more distance. He's hidden behind the curtains. Whereas in a novel you hear the Jew as you never quite do in a play. And not all Jews – not all English Jews at any rate – want the Jew in them to be heard. But from now on I had no choice in the matter. Having come out to the degree I had with Sefton Goldberg, there was no possibility of my going back in.

At the simplest level that meant I could no longer shrink from the Jewish world I knew. It would be a while before I found the courage to go the whole way and write a novel entirely about Jewish Manchester, the gaffes, swag, shmondries, aunties and a shy Jewish boy's dream to be the greatest table-tennis player in the world, but I had taken the first baby steps. The greater challenge, anyway, would be to explore just what 'being Jewish' entailed, and that had to be a lot more than Sefton Goldberg's mock-heroic persecution complex and a vague sense of being destined for better things. I don't say I became a scholar of Judaism overnight, but instead of reading *Women in Love* for the tenth time and *Great Expectations* for the fifteenth I put myself to school with the likes of Moses Maimonides and Gershom Scholem and Martin Buber and eventually the countless rabbis whose ongoing controversies comprised the Babylonian Talmud, all eighteen volumes of which were available on the open shelves of the British Library Reading Room.

A Talmudist I was not, but I loved the labyrinthine reasoning – for which the Hebrew word is *pilpul* – the extravagant leaps of logic, finding harmony in dissonance; that subtilising which Germans call *Spitzfindigkeit*; the idea of an inexhaustible text; the sense that conversation could never be concluded or controversy resolved; that once a ball of thought was in the air it fell to successive generations of Talmudists to keep it there. Reading the Talmud I felt I was being drawn back to my old Leavis seminars at Cambridge. It was Leavis's contention that interpretation of a work of literature passed from reader to reader, with one saying 'Isn't this so?' and the other replying 'Yes, but', the demurral being the great promise made by disinterested curiosity that the flame of criticism would never go out. It was wonderful to me to think that I had gone to Downing College to put the narrowness of my upbringing behind me, to shake off whatever suggestion of cultural backwardness and blight clung to me as a Northern fugitive from the Pale of Settlement, and all I'd done was return to the same source. No, not God. But a rooted conviction that truth was ongoing and that argument was the breath of life.

Whatever Leavis would have thought of *Coming From Behind*, it never seemed to me that writing it was anything other than putting all he'd taught me into action. To be funny required the same vigour of expression, the same eye for absurdity, the same attentiveness to small differences, the same near-religious conviction that there was a fight to be fought and that to lose it was to lose everything. Toss the Talmud into this mix and it became clear that I had written myself back not only to Downing College circa 1960, but Babylon circa two thousand five hundred years before that.

Beyond all this, a further aspect of novel writing, as I experienced it, bound me to my Jewish forebears. Be patient with me if I give it the fancy name of spiritual calling. The more I wrote, the more I felt an allegiance to the language I wrote in — yes, English not Hebrew, but words do feel sacred once you wrestle with them, demand a fealty from you, and remind you that you are risking everything by climbing into the ring with them at all. The Second Commandment, forbidding the making of graven images, is often taken (rightly in my view) to be an injunction against the making of art at all. It is a blasphemy to create an alternative universe to God's. This commandment has not put a stop to Jewish art; indeed the very idea of the blasphemous is empowering. For art must be disruptive indeed to put all heaven in a rage. And in the sense that the artist rivals a hyper-jealous God, art too is a religion.

Sefton Goldberg's larky Jewishness surprised me in another way. I couldn't leave 'being Jewish' where he'd left it. The issue was too serious. The anti-Semitism he and I had played for laughs had a deadly history and, as Holocaust deniers went on shape-changing and anti-Zionists decanted old poisons into new bottles, a no less deadly future. I soon found myself taking issue with those who declared open season on all things Israeli as a way of declaring open season on all things Jewish without having to feel guilty about it. Anti-Zionism, I argued – and would still argue – was anti-Semitism's get-out-of-jail-free card. Thus, in no time, had a comic novel turned me into a polemicist. People who knew me found the change unsettling. Jewish jokes were one thing; but since when had I become *politically* Jewish?

Even my dying father summoned the strength to express concern. As I sat holding his magician's hand for the last time, he blurted out the words, 'I just hope you're not planning to be a rabbi.' He was sufficiently alert, somewhere in his brain, to see the irony of that. After all those family rows about marrying out, he now dared to worry that I was, as it were, marrying in. Not that when his Jew-madness was at its height he had wanted me, or any of us, to go into the ministry. A flickering flame was all it had ever been about. We had to keep something burning – a prompting that had been passed down, along the blood, from generation to generation, and queerly ended up in his. But the one thing he had never intended was for me, or any of us, to go overboard with it. He was a true sceptic underneath and didn't really like religion at all. Still, had he not been dying I'd have told him he had a nerve.

He left the rabbi subject as soon as he began it, giving my hand a squeeze and saying, '*Kuk*.' Look. What he wanted me to look at was the line of men desperate to try their luck in the toilets at the end of the ward, the cardboard pots which they would probably never again piss in clutched to their chests. He smiled, not at them but for humanity. His lovely, incorrigible smile which had got him out of trouble a thousand times but wouldn't get him out of this.

He told me he'd had a good life, repeated he was ready for his sleep, but wouldn't have said no to just five more years.

A quarter of a century on I still hear him saying it. *Just five more years.*

I have recently completed those five more years on his behalf. And haven't become a rabbi – though Chief Rabbi Sir Jonathan Sacks did once suggest we change roles. 'That's just because you want to be a novelist,' I told him.

In 2005 I married the television director Jenny De Yong with whom I'd worked on a number of documentaries, including *Into the Land of Oz*, *Roots Schmoots* and *Seriously Funny*. Lord Sacks officiated at the wedding. Our friends looked on open-mouthed, alarmed that in our love for each other Jenny and I had lost our minds and turned Orthodox. They needn't have worried. We just happened to believe that, when it came to the exchange of vows, only the language of high religion would suffice. To us this was a solemn as well as a joyous event. Jenny had never married before, which meant her mother had never seen her daughter veiled. And as for me, I knew I would never marry again. We were neither of us young. We weren't testing the water. This was it. The real thing. Comprising love, unbreakable promises, *naches* for our mothers, and a pinch of God, no matter that we knew He was unlikely to attend. What atheists sometimes fail to grasp is that religion for some occupies a territory between true and false that is accessible only to metaphor and the imagination. Inviting God to our wedding didn't mean we believed in His existence.

The Chief Rabbi, anyway, knew what we were about. He had studied philosophy at Cambridge and understood the negotiations the rational mind must sometimes make with the irrational.

Fifteen years later he died, at exactly the same age my father had. They looked a little alike, which might be why, when I think fondly of the one, I find myself thinking fondly of the other. Father/rabbi – what's the difference?

It was no coincidence that Jenny and I valued high seriousness in matters of religion even though we weren't religious: our

Jenny and I under the *chuppah*

ancestors hailed from a world that disdained lightness, hers from
the part of Poland that abutted Lithuania, mine from the part of
Lithuania that abutted Poland. But we had other stringencies in
common as well. She had been taught by William Empson at
Sheffield University, which was second only to being taught by
Leavis at Cambridge for inculcating a passion for close textual
analysis. I don't say we corrected each other's usage over breakfast, but we liked getting things right, and that meant knowing
when it was all right to get them wrong. I am not happy letting
anything I write leave the house without Jenny reading or
hearing it first. She has a keener ear for English idiom than I
have, and a better sense, thanks to her experience as a radio pro-
ducer and television director, of when enough's enough. I hit a
fertile, arrogant patch in the years immediately following our
wedding, writing novels that even Jenny, with her Empsonian
background, thought at times unnecessarily challenging. Of *The
Finkler Question*, I recall her finally saying, after much editing, 'I
think you've done all you can to fix it now, but I still wonder

whether anyone's going to get it.' We exchanged astonished glances when it appeared the Booker Prize judges did.

My mother was equally sceptical and rang me every morning after it was shortlisted to caution against optimism. (As if.) 'It's too Jewish,' she said. I didn't ask her what she meant because I agreed with her. *Too Jewish* – is there such a genre? Maybe. Don't ask me to explain what defines it. I doubt it has anything to do with our killing Christ, though in a literary culture that has strong Christian antecedents you never know. But too expostulatory might go some of the way. I have been accused of being a noisy writer. On the surface 'noisy' is a culturally neutral disparagement, but it denotes a parvenu outlandishness. At the time of *Coming From Behind*'s publication the highest word of praise on the jacket of any successful 'literary' novel was 'spare'. Spare, not as in a spare wheel, but as in pared down. Thin. Thus 'noisy' is a euphemism for all that isn't spare – the foreign, the showy, the exegetical, the overexcitable, the persistent, the gaudy, the exaggerated. I have a mental picture of those custodians of literary decorum whose nerves are shredded by flamboyance. I see them as so many lookalikes of Bitzer, the eyelashless, rote-taught villain of Dickens's *Hard Times* who defines a horse as 'Quadruped. Graminivorous. Forty teeth, namely twenty-four grinders, four eye-teeth, and twelve incisive', and whose own 'skin was so unwholesomely deficient in the natural tinge, that he looked as though, if he were cut, he would bleed white'. When Dickens invented Bitzer he might have been thinking of the bloodless mandarins of high Victorianism, who were as much offended by his flashy waistcoats as the vitality of his imagination. Which just goes to show that you don't have to be an actual Jew to unsettle English sensibilities. So maybe – though I am reluctant to let go of the suspicion that disrelish for hyperbole is a species of anti-Semitism – it has always been as much a class thing as anything else. Dickens came from nowhere and so do Jews. He was not sedate, and nor are Jews. He was nouveau riche . . . but why go on?

I must quickly add that no Jew has ever accused me of exaggerating.

Philip Roth once described the wonderful feeling American, especially New York, Jews enjoyed after Vietnam 'that one was entitled to no less than anyone else, that one could do anything and could be excluded from nothing'. Far from their natural vigorousness marking them out as different, it seemed to place them 'at the heart of the city's abrasive, hypercritical, potentially explosive cultural atmosphere'.

I'm not sure what, as an English Jewish writer, I most miss – belonging for belonging's sake, or an explosive cultural atmosphere to belong to.

Finkler, anyway, was surely far too Jewish to win the Booker.

29

KVELLING

There was another way in which writing the words 'being Jewish' gradually changed the way I felt about myself. Without turning me into a *balebatisheh yiden* exactly – a respectable, suburban, synagogue-going head of an extended Jewish family whose wife remembered to light the Shabbes candles – it did make it easier for me to enjoy some of the more humdrum pleasures of unquestioning tribalism. I kissed my mother more. I sent my sister boxes of smoked salmon on her birthday. I bought my wife a menorah. I went to the occasional bar mitvah in Boreham Wood.

The Yiddish verb to *kvell* – from the German verb *quellen*, 'to gush' – means to take excessive pride in the appearance, achievements or just plain existential fact of your children, grandchildren or – *kayn aynhoreh* – great-grandchildren.

That it hasn't so far cropped up in this memoir needs, alas, no explanation. You go to Cambridge, you don't kvell. You leave your family to make great art, you lose the right to kvell. It's probable that very few Jewish writers do kvell, unless it's over their own sentences, and in the Land of Kvell they don't strictly count. Thanks to Sefton Goldberg, however, I am now free, like any old Jew, to kvell over his son. And thanks to Conrad and his wife Kate I am now free to kvell over their daughter, my granddaughter Ziva.

Whether, over time, Conrad had been able to attend to my unhappy confessions with any degree of sympathy – how I had never left him in my heart but left a country, a marriage, a self; how I'd been out of my mind with dismay and dissatisfaction, not just fed up but deranged with unfulfilled ambition and thwarted expectation; how I'd suffered headaches and depressions; how a pool of acid, as black as the River Styx, had sloshed around in my stomach; how I had been a lost soul spiritually and a basket case psychologically and a waste of space familially – whether or not he believed a word, or cared, or just wanted me to shut the hell up, because this was all just about me again – Howard the Unhappy – he listened quietly, over those weeks and months and years we got to know each other again, and never proffered a remonstrance. No, I do not feel judged by him but I do read his unflagging devotion to Ziva as a reproach to me whether he intends it that way or not. *This is how you do it, Dad.*

As for Ziva herself, well, I kvell over her musical, literary and artistic gifts. Below is a portrait she did of me when she was six. I am inordinately fond of it. Out of the rich, dappled mix of her genealogy – one Jewish parent, one not; two Jewish grandparents, two not; three and a half Jewish great-grandparents, four and a half not – I fancy that she found the wherewithal to see in me what others who had tried to capture my likeness had not – Sigmund Freud watching Benny Hill.

274

'My grandfather' – a portrait by Ziva Jacobson

EPILOGUE

In a saturnine mood my mother once asked me if I'd had a happy life.

'But for the odd bad day, wildly happy,' I told her.

I could see she wasn't sure I was telling the truth. 'Believe me, I've had, and am still having, a wonderful time,' I went on. And thanked her.

'Why are you thanking me?'

'Well –'

'I read somewhere,' she interrupted, 'that you said you found being a Jew a tremendous adventure. I didn't know you felt that way.'

'I haven't always, but I do now.'

'You really mean that?'

'I most certainly do,' I said. 'I wouldn't have been anything else. I'm only sorry for those who miss out on it.'

She adjusted her glasses with difficulty, her poor arthritic hands of little use to her. 'I can't tell you how pleased I am to hear you say that,' she said.

'You sound surprised.'

'More relieved,' she said.

A week after my mother dies my sister sends me a couple of padded envelopes which I know, before I open them, must contain my mother's diaries. Sometimes you can smell treasure.

The contents aren't preserved as though they have any particular value, which somehow makes them the more valuable – just a few dusty cellophane bags containing some postcards, letters and three very small pocket diaries, dating from 1939 to 1941, of the sort that have a pencil holster on the side. One is a Jewsbury and Brown's Sports & Games Records Pocket Diary and Notebook, though I can't imagine my mother having cared much by what score the England men's hockey team beat Ireland the year before, or who was amateur rackets champion. The others are just ordinary diaries but extraordinary to me by virtue of their being here, in my possession.

They are infinitely precious. More than a record of the past, they are the living witness to her, as incandescent as Holy Scripture, but fleshly too, her words eager to escape the confines of these tiny books the minute I turn the pages. When they arrived I feared I would have to treat them like ancient artefacts that would fall apart if I so much as breathed on them. Not so. In truth it's only me who's in danger of falling apart.

She is a natural and vivacious writer. She is eighteen, give or take, when most of these entries are made. Having left school at fourteen, she works as a seamer at a milliner's and goes from door to door collecting for the Jewish Hospital. Her family is poor. And the world is dangerous. 'WAR!!' she writes on 3 September 1939. 'At 11 o'clock England declared war on Germany. We are all worried about Joyce.' Not William Joyce, the Nazi propagandist, but my auntie Joyce who has been evacuated to Lancaster. In a later diary my mother reports that there has been a pogrom in Romania. She is concerned there might be a rise in anti-Semitism in this country. Her mother thinks there won't be.

18 January 1940 – 'Everyone is depressed and I am trying to cheer my friends up. There are many deaths.'

When she isn't writing about war, air-raid sirens and her fears for the safety of friends, she paints a vivid picture of a clever eighteen-year-old's social life, buying material for dresses, dancing, taking long walks, talking late into the night, going to the cinema ('*Wuthering Heights* was marvellous but I don't believe such love exists'), the theatre and the library. She reads a lot. She has many boyfriends. There's a guy called Motty. There's a guy called Eddie. There's a guy called George. An airman. ('He is so nice, I wish he was Jewish.') One of them declares his passion in words snitched from T. E. Lawrence. 'Dearest Anita, As time went on my need for you increased to an unquestioning possession, riding with spur and rein over my doubts ... Willy nilly it became a faith.' (Think of that – for some men, loving my mother amounted to a religion.) And there's a guy called Max, my father.

It takes Max a while to become the chief contender for her hand. He resorts to drink when she refuses him a kiss. 'He said I am being unfair. I think myself justified.' On 4 December 1940, she writes, 'I foresaw that Max would get drunk on Sunday because he told me he gets drunk to forget me ...' And then on 7 December she adds, 'Max told me again how much he loved me ... I have never seen anyone so drunk. I will never forget it. I cannot understand anyone drinking themselves into complete stupidity.' It would seem that he is easily roused to jealousy. 'Max doesn't like me if I do anything while he is in the house but look at him,' she notes in May 1941. Even the sight of her reading a book upsets him.

It's a pity I didn't know any of this when he was upbraiding me for mooning over women. What's this, Dad? Drinking to forget! At least I've never been jealous of a book!

There's no retrospective self-justification or vengeance in this. I'm sorry it pained him not to be the only thing in the whole wide world my mother looked at. I know what that's like.

But it's what my mother has to say about her hopes for herself that overwhelms me. In an entry extended over several days and marked AMBITION, capital letters and underlined, she looks into her future. 'I am beginning to think,' she writes, 'that I should have a fixed ambition in life. I have always wanted to have a cottage in the country, with nice plain furniture and a large writing bureau with a window overlooking the beautiful countryside and write books and lectures and anything that comes into my head. I wonder if that will ever happen? I don't suppose I will ever marry. Somehow, I don't see myself married. I should have to find the money for the cottage myself. Every morning I would go horse-riding and swimming, then I would breakfast and then I'd write ... I should roam around in trousers with a dog at my heels. I'm fond of my trousers because I'm broad and can carry them off well. Sometimes I can picture myself strolling round my cottage with a cigarette hanging from my mouth and my hands in my trouser pockets or sitting at my bureau and scribbling while the sun shines through the open window ...'

I could weep for her. For the innocent bohemianism of her fantasy life, for the ambition that never got beyond reverie, for the literary gift that was denied the opportunity to materialise, for the books that never got written, for the quiet, creative seriousness of her nature that marriage and motherhood engrossed.

With what sinking of spirits must she have looked on as

hope and promise threatened to slip from my fingers as they had slipped from hers. It's often said, unthinkingly, that we repeat our parents' errors and omissions. But that I was re-enacting her disappointments I didn't realise.

I write every day, but not at a bureau. I don't have a window that looks out over beautiful countryside. I don't stable a horse. And I don't have a cigarette hanging out of my mouth. Otherwise she is at last living the life she wanted to live.

Got tsu danken.